THE
ASTROLOGY
OF HUMAN
RELATIONSHIPS

Frances Sakoian
& Louis Acker

Harper & Row, Publishers, New York
Cambridge, Philadelphia, San Francisco, London
Mexico City, São Paulo, Singapore, Sydney

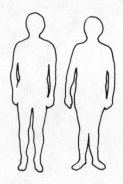

THE
ASTROLOGY
OF HUMAN
RELATIONSHIPS

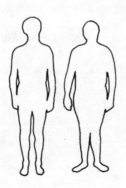

To
Frances Annanekian Simon
Wilma McIntyre
Fred Johnson
and husband "Sark"
who made this book possible

A hardcover edition of this book is published by Harper & Row, Publishers, Inc. This PERENNIAL LIBRARY edition was published in 1989. A reset PERENNIAL LIBRARY edition in a smaller format was published in 1987.

Chapters I and II appeared originally in slightly different form in *The Astrologer's Handbook*. Copyright © 1973 by Frances Sakoian. (Harper & Row)

Designed by Dorothy Schmiderer

Library of Congress Cataloging-in-Publication Data

Sakoian, Frances.
    The astrology of human relationships / Frances Sakoian and Louis Acker. — Perennial Library ed.
        p.   cm.
    Includes index.
    ISBN 0-06-091546-3 : $
    1. Astrology.   I. Acker, Louis S.   II. Title.
[BF1708.1.S244 1989]
133.5—dc19
                                                          88-24403
                                                          CIP

89 90 91 92 93   FG   10 9 8 7 6 5 4 3 2 1

Contents

PART III

COMPARATIVE INFLUENCES OF THE PLANETS

XIV. Uranus   285

XV. Neptune   313

XVI. Pluto   339

Preface

As evidenced by the turmoil in our world, relational problems of one form or another constitute the most widespread cause of human misery and depression. Whether these problems manifest themselves on an international scale as disagreements between national, political, or economic powers or they directly affect the affinity of two individuals, their importance must be recognized and understood.

In an effort to anticipate and ameliorate such differences and potential difficulties, one of the most valuable and important contributions made by astrology is in the field of horoscopic comparison, the astrological analysis of the relationship between two or more individuals. Unfortunately, many people exhibit such a superficial knowledge of astrology that they frequently draw erroneous conclusions in this area. This is especially true of judgments based simply upon the Sun signs of the natives involved. Often, one hears such remarks as "I'm a Taurus. I can't get along with you because you are a Leo, and you're square my Sun sign." Such statements reveal a fundamental misunderstanding related to the oversimplification of astrology.

Consideration of the general psychology and the level of consciousness of the individuals embraced by the relationship is mandatory. Even with many favorable comparative aspects and positive transposed house placements in a comparison, there can be a lack of rapport or a lapse in the ability of the natives to understand one another. This is particularly true if the individuals in question have differing levels of intelligence, education, experience, social background, and spiritual outlook.

The vast field of horoscopic comparison comprises two major fields of analysis. The first of these deals with the aspects or planetary positions of one horoscope in relation to another, while the second concerns itself with the placement of the natal planets of one individual's chart in the houses of the other's natal horoscope. However, it is only when all these factors are appraised, interpreted, and weighed as to their relative importance that an accurate understanding of the relationship can be reached. Comparative placements of the planets of two or more individuals' horoscopes reveal how the basic psychological drives of one individual affect the lives of the others.

Astrological horoscopic comparisons can be extraordinarily useful in marital, parent–child, employer–employee, professional, family, platonic, and business relationships, for they offer valuable insights into the future as well as the present or past of any relationship.

A great deal of the potential in any relationship depends directly upon the maturity of the natives involved. This potential may not be manifest until the attainment of astrological adulthood at age twenty-nine, marking the first full cycle of Saturn, an experiential milepost in the development of every individual.

A cardinal rule of astrological comparisons is that the importance of any planet's house or sign can be as great as the strength of that same factor in the natal horoscopes of the individuals involved. To a great extent, the relative importance of any given planet in a comparison of nativities will be determined by the nature of the relationship, for an individual can bring into a relationship only the qualities he has already developed within himself. Each planet and house will have a greater or lesser significance commensurate to the type of relationship involved, whether it be business, family, marriage, romantic, or social in nature. In a business relationship, Saturn and Mercury comparative aspects would be particularly important. In romantic relationships, Venus, Mars, the Sun, the Moon, and the Fifth House describe the interaction of the individual's feelings and energies.

Horoscopic comparisons use the same orbs as those of natal astrology (See *The Astrologer's Handbook,* Harper & Row). A 10° orb is permitted for major aspects involving the Sun or Moon and six degrees of orb are usually allowed for major aspects between planets.

The authors wish to remind the reader, at this point, of the first rule in astrology: Never try to change the other individual, for the only person we can really change is ourself. The comprehension of another's role in a relationship helps us to be realistic in our expectations and compassionate in our understanding of him or her. Only then can we grow side by side.

How to
Use This Book

This book is designed to equip the layman, the student, and the professional astrologer with the information necessary to understand and interpret comparative astrological charts. The process of comparing the horoscope of one individual with that of another is invaluable in determining the potentials of their relationship.

At the core of the technique is the absolute necessity of setting up accurate chart calculations. From the two charts done for the individuals whose relationship is under examination will be determined the aspects and house placements existing between the horoscopes.

The calculations are complex, and the effort that they require should not be minimized. Normally, about $75 worth of reference books, knowledge of the techniques of mathematical interpolation, and two or three hours of painstaking calculations are necessary for each pair of charts. If you are seriously interested in becoming a professional astrologer, you must master this science, and Chapter II gives a complete guide to calculating exact natal charts.

If, however, you are a beginning student of astrology or are unsure of your degree of interest, you might consider the computerized service developed by Astronomical Computations for Astrologers, Inc., for which you will find a number of convenient coupons in the back of this text.

ACA can provide you for your comparison study computerized readouts that will be mathematically exact and will include a list of all the aspects and planetary house placements existing between the two individuals' horoscopes. The information will be individually cross-referenced to the pages of this book.

ORDERING A COMPUTER CHART

To obtain the computer-cast readout, fill in completely one of the coupons at the back of this book—or list the name and address, town or city, and state; month, day, year, and local clock time (A.M. or P.M.) of the births of both individuals on a plain sheet of paper—and mail to ACA, Inc., Box 395, Weston, Massachusetts 02193. Enclose a check or money order for $9.50 for both horoscopes and their comparative readouts. (Important: Be sure that you have given your full information. Otherwise, the horoscopes cannot be accurately cast. If the time of birth of one or both individuals is not known, a solar chart will be cast.)

BASIC PROCEDURES

Once you have in hand the two horoscopes and their comparative interrelationships, charted either by computer or by your own calculations, you are ready to proceed with the comparative interpretation.

Prepare yourself for this undertaking by reading the four chapters that make up Part II of this book. These discuss basic principles in analyzing human relationships (Chapter III); the importance of signs in horoscopic comparison (Chapter IV); the importance of houses in horoscopic comparison (Chapter V); and the role of dispositors in the comparison of horoscopes (Chapter VI). At this point you should be ready to interpret individual comparative aspects.

When working with comparative aspects of any planet, determine first whether the aspect is a conjunction, sextile, square, trine, or opposition, as the aspects are organized in the book in this fashion.*

It is important to be aware of the possibility of hidden aspects in the comparison, when one planet is in the last degrees of a sign and the other

* These, and all other basic terms, are discussed and defined in detail in Chapter I, "For the Astrological Beginner."

is in the first degrees of another sign. Always consider the allowable orb of an aspect.

Determine the planets or points in the horoscopes involved and make a note of which comes first in the following lineup: Sun, Moon, Mercury, Venus, Mars, Jupiter, Saturn, Uranus, Neptune, Pluto, North Node (Moon), South Node (Moon), Ascendant, Midheaven, Descendant, and Nadir.

Then, finally, turn to the index listing of the aspect involved and look up the appropriate comparative aspect. For example: If A's Jupiter sextiles B's Saturn, look to "Jupiter sextile Saturn" under "Sextiles of Jupiter."

The methods of comparative astrological analysis and interpretation outlined in this book are those taught in the New England School of Astrology, Arlington, Massachusetts. Frances Sakoian is the school's director, and Louis Acker is one of its instructors.

ACA, Inc., Box 395, Weston, Massachusetts 02193

Please send me the comparative horoscopes offered in *The Astrology of Human Relationships*. I am enclosing $9.50 (check or money order—do not send cash).

Mail to

Name_____

Address_____

City_____State_____Zip code_____

Birth Information for subject A

Name_____

Date of birth: Month_____Day_____Year_____

Time of birth: (exact local time if known) _____A.M. ( )   P.M. ( )

Time of birth unknown ( ). Local noon will be used in this case.

Place of birth:
   City_____State_____Country_____

Birth Information for subject B

Name_____

Date of birth: Month_____Day_____Year_____

Time of birth: (exact local time if known) _____A.M. ( )   P.M. ( )

Time of birth unknown ( ). Local noon will be used in this case.

Place of birth:
   City_____State_____Country_____

IF YOU DO NOT WISH TO REMOVE THIS PAGE, INFORMATION MAY BE SUPPLIED ON A PLAIN SHEET OF PAPER. DO NOT FORGET TO PROVIDE ALL INFORMATION.

Note: The price of $9.50 for the two natal charts and comparison may change after publication. Readers may wish to confirm the price with ACA.

PART I

PART I

BASIC ASTROLOGY

Note: The two chapters in this section appeared
originally in slightly different form in our
earlier book *The Astrologer's Handbook*.

I
For the Astrological
Beginner

SUN SIGNS

A horoscope is a map of the position of the planets in the heavens at
the exact time and place of your birth. This map represents a circle of
360°, the path that the Sun appears to follow through the sky (actually
the plane of the Earth's orbit around the Sun), which astronomers call
the ecliptic. Astrologers divide this path into twelve 30° sectors. These
are the twelve "signs of the Zodiac," or "Sun signs." They indicate in
which sector the Sun was found at the time of your birth. For instance, if
you were born in the early part of October, then the Sun would have
been in the seventh sign, Libra. Your "Sun sign," therefore, would be
Libra.

The Zodiac most commonly used in Western astrology is determined
by the vernal equinox. This is the position of the Sun (about March 20
of each year) when the days and nights are of equal length. The vernal
equinox is defined in astronomy as that point in space where the plane of
the Earth's orbit around the Sun, the ecliptic, intersects the plane of the
Earth's equator extended into space. It occurs when the Sun moves from
a position south of the equator to a position north of the equator in its
apparent motion along the ecliptic as seen from the Earth (which we

CHART 1

The Cardinal Ingresses

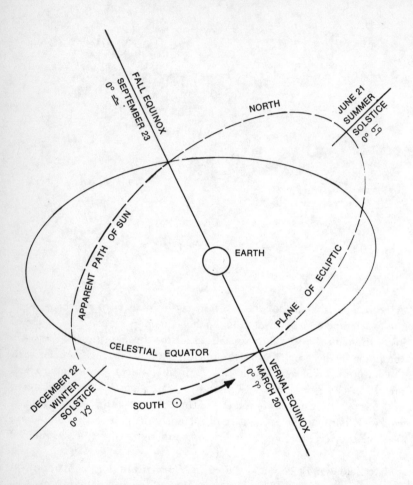

A cardinal ingress is the entry of the Sun into one of the signs of the cardinal grouping or quadruplicities. The signs are Aries, Cancer, Libra, Capricorn, indicating the beginning of the four seasons which are demarcated by the vernal equinox, the summer solstice, the fall equinox, and the winter solstice.

CHART 2
The Natural Zodiac

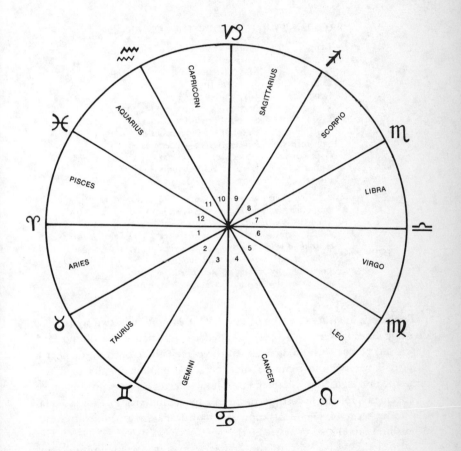

know is actually revolving around the Sun). In astrology, this moment is known as 0° of Aries. It marks the beginning of what is known as the "tropical Zodiac," the most commonly used Zodiac in Western astrology and the one on which this book is based.

In astrological terminology, a horoscope is called by many names: nativity, natal chart, natus, chart, map, wheel, etc. However, the signs of the Zodiac always follow an unchanging pattern: Aries, Taurus, Gemini, Cancer, Leo, Virgo, Libra, Scorpio, Sagittarius, Capricorn, Aquarius, and Pisces.

APPROXIMATE DATES OF THE SUN SIGNS*

Aries	March 21–April 19
Taurus	April 20–May 20
Gemini	May 21–June 21
Cancer	June 22–July 22
Leo	July 23–August 22
Virgo	August 23–September 22
Libra	September 23–October 22
Scorpio	October 23–November 21
Sagittarius	November 22–December 21
Capricorn	December 22–January 19
Aquarius	January 20–February 18
Pisces	February 19–March 20

* Note: Because of leap years, time zones, and other factors, the exact day and time when the Sun enters a particular sign of the Zodiac varies slightly from year to year. The exact time when the Sun enters a sign of the Zodiac for a given year and locale must be ascertained by means of an *Ephemeris*. (See section on the manual casting of the horoscope, on page 25.)

The Sun is in either one sign or another; it cannot be in two signs. The dividing line between two signs is called a cusp—hence the often-heard statement, "I was born on a cusp." In the case of those born on or near a cusp, it is necessary to compute the horoscope mathematically to determine the Sun sign. (See Chapter II on how to erect a horoscope, or make arrangements for the horoscope to be cast by computer.) For the calculation to be accurate, one must know the month, day, year, hour (minute, if possible), and location of the birth.

Each of the twelve signs of the Zodiac represents certain unique positive characteristics, as well as unique negative characteristics, of human behavior and development. Everyone has all twelve signs included in his horoscope. Their effect on the various departments of his life is determined by the position of the planets in these signs and the interaction between the signs of the Zodiac and the houses of the horoscope.

HOUSES

Like the signs of the Zodiac, the houses divide the horoscope into twelve segments. Each house is fundamentally related to one sign of the Zodiac. The houses, however, are defined by the Earth's 24-hour rotation on its axis, whereas the signs of the Zodiac are defined by the Earth's yearly revolution around the Sun. Like the Sun signs, the houses are also divided by lines called cusps. The First House cusp or Ascendant is found by determining that point in space where the eastern horizon at the time and place of birth intercepts the ecliptic. Thus any one of the twelve signs which lie along the ecliptic could be found on the eastern horizon. Time and location of one's birth, therefore, determine which of the twelve signs will be rising.

The rising sign is also known as the Ascendant. It indicates one's manner of self-expression, character, abilities, and appearance. It describes one's early environment.

Following the First House cusp are the Second through Twelfth houses, which represent different departments of practical affairs: money, marriage, profession, the domestic scene, friendship, etc.

The most important of these houses are called the Cardinal, or Angular, houses. They consist of the Ascendant (First House or rising sign), the Fourth House cusp (or Nadir, where the plane of the meridian passes underneath the Earth and intersects the ecliptic), the Seventh House cusp (or the Descendant, defined as the point where the western horizon intersects the ecliptic), and the Tenth House cusp (or Midheaven). The Midheaven, also written M.C., is defined as that point where the meridian—the line passing from north to south through a point directly overhead called the zenith—intersects the plane of the ecliptic. The other eight house cusps are spaced at approximately equal intervals between these four angular house cusps.

Each house cusp bears a sign of the Zodiac (see Chart 4). The sign will determine the way the department of life ruled by that house will be expressed in the life of the individual.

If your birthday is October 8 and you were born at 4:00 P.M., your Sun sign would be in the Eighth House. This puts Libra on the Eighth House, Scorpio on the Ninth, Sagittarius on the Tenth, Capricorn on the

CHART 3

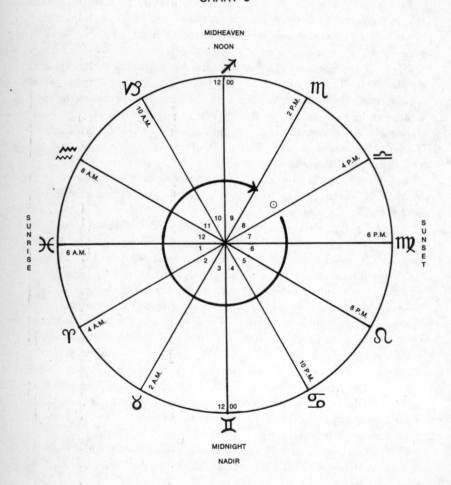

CHART 4

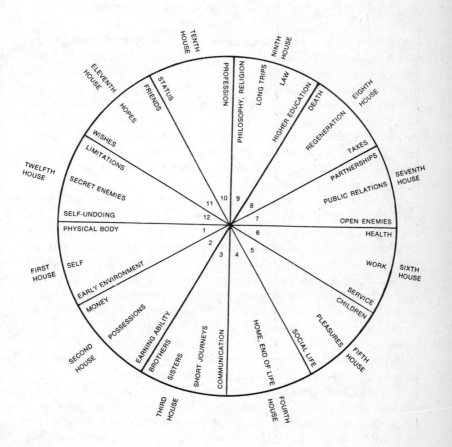

Eleventh, Aquarius on the Twelfth, Pisces on the First (commonly called the Ascendant), Aries on the Second, Taurus on the Third, Gemini on the Fourth, Cancer on the Fifth, Leo on the Sixth, and Virgo on the Seventh. This combination would give approximately Pisces rising. These calculations are not an accurate way of setting up the horoscope but a means of checking for errors in the original casting.

TRIPLICITIES AND QUADRUPLICITIES

The signs are also grouped into two more fundamental arrangements determined by the geometric layout of the Zodiac. These are triplicities, which deal with the tendencies of the temperament, and quadruplicities, which concern the basic modes of activity. There are four triplicities, one for each of the four elements Fire, Earth, Air, and Water, and each contains three signs. Conversely there are three quadruplicities, dividing into the areas of Cardinal, Fixed, and Mutable, and each of these contains four signs. Should a preponderance of planets be found in signs belonging to one of these groupings, it becomes an outstanding factor in the person's quality of expression in some phase of his life.

First, let us deal with the elements: Fire, Earth, Air, and Water. Aires, Leo, and Sagittarius belong to the Fire triplicity. The individuals born under them seek to display leadership in some way. In Aries, this desire manifests itself as a decisiveness in spearheading new efforts and endeavors. Leos possess the managerial capacity for acting as the central dramatic figure around which an organization or group of people gather. Sagittarians have the ability to act as spiritual, philosophic leaders in the areas of religion, philosophy, law, or higher education; they are concerned with the ideas around which human society is built.

Fire sign individuals are positive, aggressive, ardent, creative, and masculine in their expression. These qualities will manifest themselves in those houses or departments which have Fire signs on the cusp.

With the Earth signs, Taurus, Virgo, and Capricorn, comes the primary attribute of practicality. These signs indicate skill in using and managing the material and financial resources necessary to make other functions of human life possible. In whatever houses the Earth signs are found, one will manifest the quality of practicality.

Taurus's practical quality appears as the ability to accumulate and manage money and other material resources. In Virgo, practicality is evidenced as intelligence and skill in labor and constructing those mate-

CHART 5

Fire Triplicity (120° △ Trine Aspect)

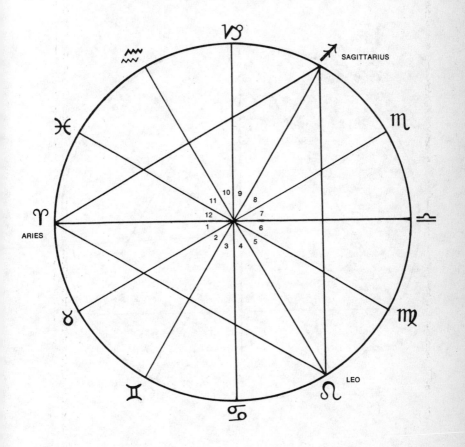

Always count 30° from one sign to the next sign.

CHART 6
Earth Triplicity (120° △ Trine Aspect)

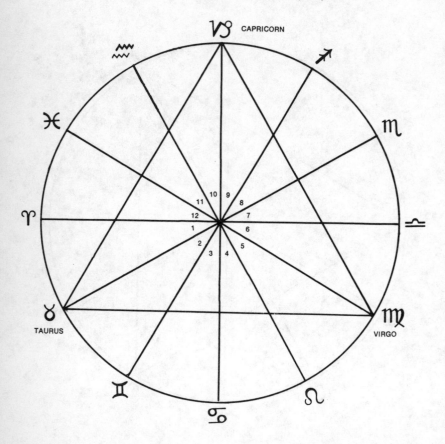

Always count 30° from one sign to the next sign.

CHART 7
Air Triplicity (120° △ Trine Aspect)

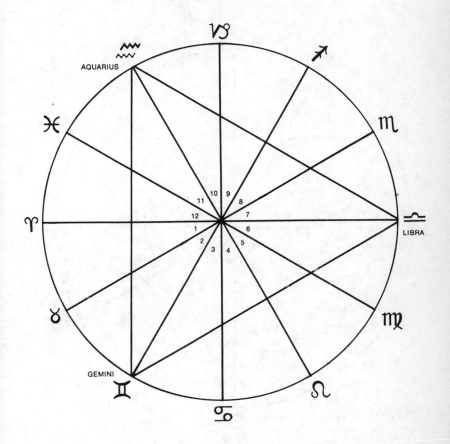

Always count 30° from one sign to the next sign.

CHART 8

Water Triplicity (120° △ Trine Aspect)

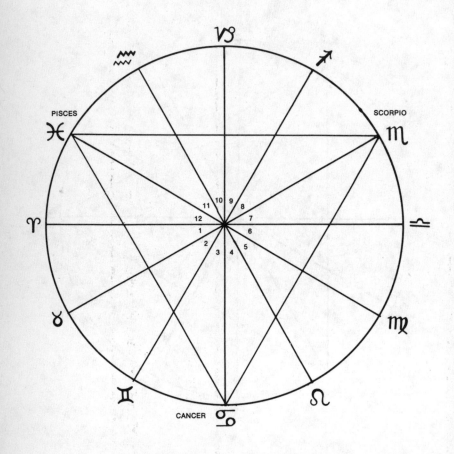

Always count 30° from one sign to the next sign.

rial objects essential to man. It is also concerned with properly maintaining our most valuable material possession, our physical bodies. With Capricorn, there is the practical ability to organize and manage vast business and governmental enterprises or, on a more mundane level, the ability to structure and organize ordinary business affairs.

The Air element, or Air triplicity, consists of the signs Gemini, Libra, and Aquarius. They deal with the intellectual capacity of man, which includes communication and social interrelationships. The air signs manifest strong mental abilities and intellectual attributes in one form or another. In whatever department of your horoscope the air signs are found you will evince social and intellectual qualities.

In Gemini, this intellectualism shows itself as the ability to acquire, utilize, and communicate factual information. A certain originality from repatterning of ideas is often present. In Libra, these qualities are manifested as the ability to weigh and balance, making just comparisons. There is also a strong social awareness which leads to natural ability in psychology and related disciplines. In Aquarius intellectuality is expressed as an intuitive grasp of universal principles, along with a concern for the universal well-being of humanity.

The Water signs, or Water triplicities, are Cancer, Scorpio, and Pisces. Concerned with the realm of emotion and feeling, they deal with sensitivity, intuition, and the deeper psychic aspects of life. In whatever houses the Water signs are found, one's deep emotions will be manifested.

This quality of emotion appears in Cancer as strong feelings about home and family. In Scorpio, it appears as strong feelings concerning death, joint resources, and the deeper occult mysteries of life. In Pisces, it is shown as a strong mystical feeling toward the Infinite and as unconscious telepathic communication with other people. (This includes a sympathetic awareness of the environment.) Such sensitivity leads to extreme impressionability, so that Pisces is strongly influenced by the unconscious.

The quadruplicities are groupings of four signs. They deal with modes of activity and with adaptability to circumstances and are known as the Cardinal, Fixed, and Mutable signs.

The Cardinal signs are Aries, Cancer, Libra, and Capricorn. People born under them possess the ability to act directly and decisively upon present circumstances. They have a realistic grasp of the immediate situation and its potentials for action. In whatever houses or departments of life the Cardinal signs are found, one likes activity and is capable of initiating and organizing new enterprises. Positively expressed, these

CHART 9

Cardinal Quadruplicity (90° □ Square Aspect)

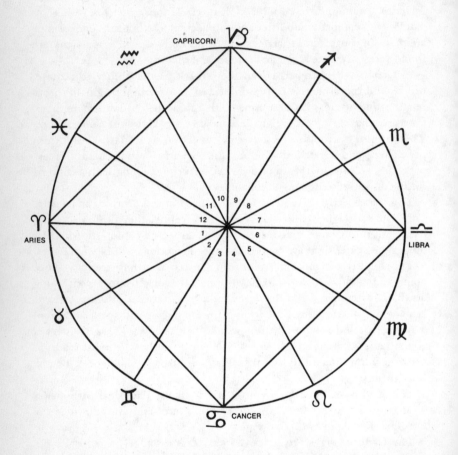

Always count 30° from one sign to the next sign.

CHART 10
Fixed Quadruplicity (90° □ Square Aspect)

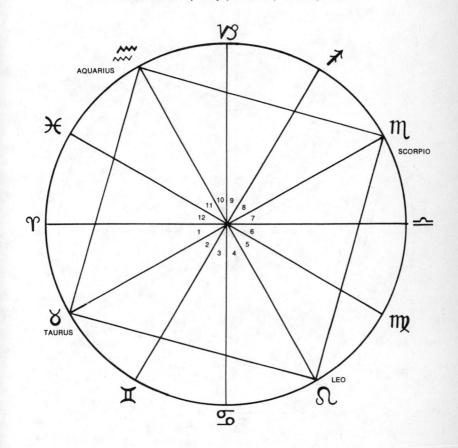

Always count 30° from one sign to the next sign.

CHART 11
Mutable Quadruplicity (90° □ Square Aspect)

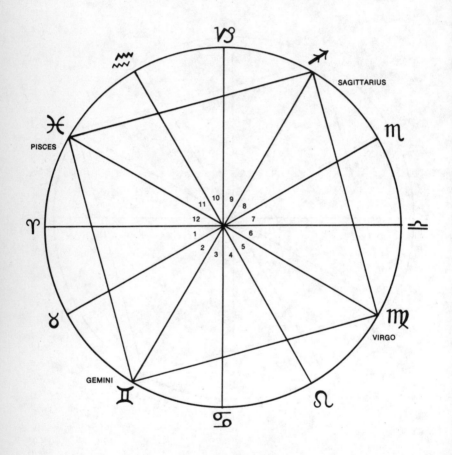

Always count 30° from one sign to the next sign.

signs manifest constructive initiative, but, on the negative side, there can be busybody tendencies and thoughtless actions.

The Fixed quadruplicity consists of Taurus, Leo, Scorpio, and Aquarius. Those born under these signs achieve results through persistence and determination; their success comes through unwavering perseverance over an extended period of time. They are goal oriented and in this sense concerned with the future. The positive attributes of fixity are constancy and reliability; the negative, stubbornness and rigidity. These people are not easily swayed once they have made up their minds about something. In whatever houses or departments these Fixed signs are found, one exerts sustained effort.

The Mutable quadruplicity is composed of Gemini, Virgo, Sagittarius, and Pisces. These signs indicate a richness of experiences in dealing with all varieties of circumstances, and an accompanying mental ability. Those born under them adapt themselves to the exigencies of life and like chameleons are able to meld into their circumstances and surroundings. They can be flexible and ingenious in emergencies. This ability comes from previous experience in similar circumstances. Mutable sign people tend to be concerned with the past rather than the present or the future. They should be careful not to get trapped in their memories.

Positively expressed, these qualities appear as resourcefulness; negatively, as worry, neurosis, nervousness, and the inability to live in the present. In whatever houses or departments of life the mutable signs are found, the person will express adaptability.

MASCULINE AND FEMININE GROUPINGS

The signs are also divided into masculine (or positive) signs and feminine (or negative) signs.

The masculine/positive signs are all the Fire and Air signs. They include the odd-numbered signs of the Zodiac (Aries, Gemini, Leo, Libra, Sagittarius, Aquarius) and correspond to the First, Third, Fifth, Seventh, Ninth, and Eleventh houses. Those born under positive/masculine signs are aggressive and self-initiating, taking action to achieve results rather than waiting for things to come to them. Wherever these signs are placed in your horoscope, in these areas you are likely to take initiative or go after what you want.

A strong preponderance of planets in masculine signs indicates a self-propelling person with positive aggressive tendencies. In a man's chart

CHART 12

Masculine Signs ♈ ♊ ♌ ♎ ♐ ♒

Negative Signs ♉ ♋ ♍ ♏ ♑ ♓

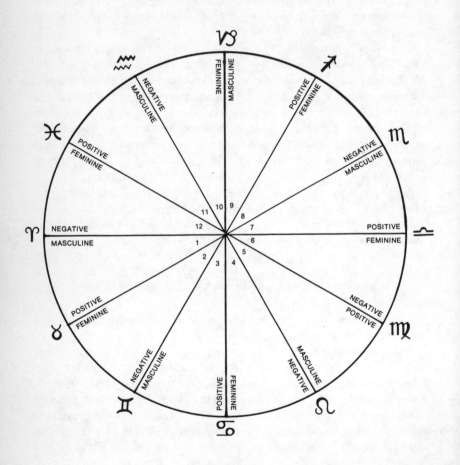

such a preponderance is favorable. However, in a woman's chart it can indicate an inclination to be more aggressive than is traditionally considered appropriate for her sex.

The negative or feminine signs include all the Earth and Water signs. They are the even-numbered signs of the Zodiac (Taurus, Cancer, Virgo, Scorpio, Capricorn, and Pisces) and correspond to the Second, Fourth Sixth, Eighth, Tenth, and Twelfth houses.

These negative/feminine signs indicate passivity. At times, however, persons born under them are capable of acting forcibly, although they usually wait for things to come to them before taking action. In this respect, they are passive and interact with what happens to come their way. They work by a principle of attracting what they desire rather than attempting to go out and conquer it.

If a strong preponderance of planets occurs in negative passive signs, the person probably will not manifest himself aggressively but can possess great strength in terms of passive endurance. A grouping of negative signs in a woman's horoscope makes her more feminine and is considered appropriate for her sex. In a man's chart it can encourage effeminacy and lack of aggressiveness.

ASPECTS

The eight planets we are concerned with in astrology, as seen from the Earth, all rotate at different speeds around the Sun in approximately the same plane in space. As a result of these planetary motions, various angles, measured in degrees, minutes, and seconds, are formed between the planets as seen from the Earth. An angle is defined as that fraction of a circle formed between two intersecting lines. The number of degrees between two imaginary lines connecting two planets with the Earth forms the angular relationship between those planets with respect to the Earth.

These angular relationships are called aspects. In geometry, an angle is that portion of a circle between two straight lines that intersect at the center of the circle. Imagine that two straight lines connecting any two planets to the Earth intersect at the birthplace. That portion between the two lines is the angular relationship between the two planets as seen from the Earth. Certain degrees of angularity are very important to astrology; 0°, 60°, 90°, 120°, 180°, for example, are the major aspects, known as conjunction, sextile, square, trine, and opposition respectively. (There are also several minor aspects.)

MAJOR ASPECTS

An aspect is the angle formed between two points in the horoscope and may be formed by two planets to each other or by a planet to some other point in the horoscope.

ASPECT	DEGREES APART	SYMBOL	INFLUENCE
Conjunction	0 (in the same degree)	☌	variable (expression, action)
Sextile	60	✶	good (opportunities, ideas)
Square	90	☐	adverse, inharmonious (goals and ambitions)
Trine	120	△	favorable, harmonious (creativity, expansion)
Opposition	180	☍	inharmonious (relationships)

The conjunction is the direct lineup of two planets as seen from the Earth. In an ideal conjunction 0° separates the two planets. However, an aspect has an orb, or orb of influence—the amount by which the two planets involved can deviate from the exact number of degrees of the aspect and still be considered to have an aspect influence.

In the case of the five major aspects, a deviation of plus or minus 6° from the exact number of degrees in the aspect is allowed. (This is known as an orb of 6°.) Should the Sun or Moon be involved in the aspect, an orb of 10° is allowed.

The conjunction is a very dynamic aspect, since it marks a strong focalized potential for expression along with a tendency for direct action and self-dramatization. The two planets in a conjunction indicate a specific psychological characteristic in the person.

The sextile aspect is 60° or one-sixth of a circle. The position of a planet in a sign is determined by degrees and minutes of degrees measured from the beginning of a sign. This distance can never be more than 30°0′ since there are never more than 30° in a sign. Planets in sextile aspect are placed two signs apart and occupy approximately the same number of degrees in these signs within an allowable difference of plus or minus 6°. However, if one of the planets is in the very beginning of a sign and another planet is in the last degrees of another sign, the two planets may still be within a 6° orb of being 60° apart, forming what is known as a hidden aspect. In this case, the signs occupied by the planets are adjoining, whereas in the case of most sextiles at least one sign intervenes between the two signs occupied by the two planets which form the sextile aspect. The sextile represents an easy flow of opportunities or ideas that, if acted upon, will help realize the individual's goals.

The square aspect is a 90° angle relationship. Planets in square aspect generally occupy the same number of degrees in signs which are three signs apart (or have two signs between the signs occupied by the planets). If there are one or three intervening signs, the aspect is called a hidden aspect. A square indicates the areas in the individual's life where adjustments must be made and where he must expend tremendous effort to realize gains.

The trine aspect is an angular relationship of 120°, or one-third of a circle, between two planets. Planets in trine aspect generally occupy the same number of degrees in signs which are four signs apart (or have three signs between them). In a hidden aspect there will be two or four intervening signs. The trine is an aspect of creativity and expansion; it is the most fortunate of all aspects.

The opposition aspect is an angular relationship of 180° between two planets. Planets in opposition generally occupy approximately the same number of degrees in two signs directly across the Zodiac from each other; they are automatically six signs apart with five signs separating them. If there is a hidden aspect, only four signs separate the signs occupied by the two planets. An opposition aspect indicates a situation in which one must cooperate with others or break with them.

It is important to remember that signs, not houses, are counted in this process of determining what aspects are present in a chart, since a house may contain considerably more or less degrees than a whole sign. In the commonly used Placidian system of houses, it is possible in extreme northern latitudes for one house to contain two whole signs or for a single sign to be present simultaneously on the cusps of three houses.

II
Basic Chart
Calculation

If the ancient wisdom disclosed in this book is the soul of astrology, then accurate chart calculations could be called the heart of astrology, for without accurate charts as a guide, one cannot utilize the ancient science at all.

Should you decide to attempt your own charts, rather than avail yourself of the computer readouts described in the introductory section "How to Use This Book," on page xiii, you will be provided here with all of the techniques of basic horoscope calculation.

INFORMATION NEEDED

The astrology chart is a precise picture of the heavens at the moment you were born. The planets must be located first with respect to the stars (the Zodiac), then with respect to the horizon (the houses). Thus it is necessary to have the exact birthtime (month, day, year, time) and birthplace (city, state, country). You should obtain this information as far in advance as possible to allow you adequate time to do an accurate calculation.

NECESSARY REFERENCES

Ephemeris

This is a set of tables that give the planets' location by sign at noon or midnight (Greenwich Mean Time—GMT) for each day of each year. We strongly suggest the *"Swiss" Zurich Ephemeris* and *Gollge's Ephemeris* for accuracy.

Longitude and Latitude

You must determine the longitude and latitude of the birthplace. There are several excellent books available for this purpose. Two books published by the National Astrological Library, *Longitudes and Latitudes in the U.S.* and *Longitudes and Latitudes Outside the U.S.,* are very good because they have the appropriate time correction factors. A much more complete reference is the *London World Atlas and Gazetteer,* but it is quite expensive.

Time Changes

A knowledge of time zones and daylight and wartime changes is needed to correct the birthtime to Standard Time. Doris Doane's *Time Changes in the U.S.A.* and *Time Changes Outside the U.S.A.* are the only good ones available and so must be used as a standard.

Table of Houses

This table gives the house cusps from a time calculation. *Dalton's Table of Houses* is the standard for work in the Placidian house cusp system used here. It is accurate, but the nonangular cusps are given only to a tenth of a degree accuracy. For really exact work you must go either to the equations given in *Dalton's* or to the computer.

Additional Calculation References

Several books on chart casting techniques are available. Alan Leo's *Casting the Horoscope* and Margaret Hone's *Modern Textbook of Astrology* are very good. The AFA (American Federation of Astrologers) puts out a series of math handbooks that are also excellent.

PROCEDURE

1. Assemble information and references. For this example I will use *Time Changes in the U.S.A.* (D. Doane) , *Longitudes and Latitudes in the U.S.* (AFA) , *"Swiss" Zurich Ephemeris,* and *Dalton's Table of Houses.* As an example I will use July 7, 1942; 9:30 A.M., Boston, Mass.

2. Look up location in *Time Changes in the U.S.A.* to check for Daylight Saving Time or Wartime. On page 78 note that July 7, 1942, falls during World War II, so one hour must be subtracted from the birthtime. Therefore, birthtime was 8:30 A.M. Eastern Standard Time.

3. Look up longitude and latitude in *Longitudes and Latitudes in the U.S.* to get location and time corrections. On page 46 note latitude *42N22,* LMT (Local Mean Time) variation from ST is *+15 min, 44 sec;* standard time must be increased by *5 hrs* (sum of two columns) to obtain GMT (Greenwich Mean Time) . The GMT is then 8:30 + 5 = *1:30* P.M. *July 7, 1942.* Also note GMT to LMT column of *4 hr, 44 min, 16 sec.*

4. Look up sidereal time at the *previous noon* in the *Ephemeris* (Swiss) column labeled "Stem-self." (Use previous midnight with any other ephemeris.) On page 317 note that since birth was before noon (local time) on July 7 the sidereal time at noon on July 6 must be used, which is *06 hr/55 min/21 sec.*

5. Perform calculation. Four items must be added. Make sure all four are present. They are:

a. The sidereal time at the previous noon (step 4) .

b. The elapsed time from the previous noon to the *local* birth time—in this case 12 hours from noon to midnight plus 8 hours, 45 minutes, and 44 seconds until birth.

c. Sidereal correction. The equivalent corrections are found in *Dalton's Table of Houses.* In Table A, "Mean to Sidereal Correction," on page v, look up the 20 hours, then the *45 minutes, then the 44 seconds* separately. Add the corrections.

d. The longitude sidereal correction term, calculated by using the value obtained in step 3 from the column labeled "To obtain GMT add to LMT." This value must be looked up again in *Dalton's* table on page v. The example in question is as follows:

	Hr	Min	Sec
a. Sidereal time at noon (step 4)	o6	55	21
b. Time from previous noon to birth (12 + 8:45:44) (step 3)	20	45	44
c. Sidereal correction of *b* from *Dalton's* Table A, page v		3	17
			7

c. 20 hr · 45 min · 44 sec } Item *b*

d. Longitude correction of GMT to LMT column using *Dalton's* tables, page v ... 39 / 7   4 hr · 44 min · 16 sec } GMT to LMT corr. (step 3)

	Hr	Min	Sec
Sum	26	103	135
Converting seconds to minutes		+2	−120
	26	105	15
Converting minutes to hours	+1	−60	
	27	45	15
Rounded off to 24 hours	−24		
	3	45	15

This is the final sidereal time accurate to one second.

6. Because the Earth is not a perfect sphere one more correction has to be made. The latitude must be changed slightly as given by Table B on page v in *Dalton's Table of Houses*. Note that since the correction for 42° is approximately *−12′* the latitude we check is 42°22′ minus 12 or *42°10′*.

7. The two parameters necessary to look up the house cusps in *Dalton's* tables are now at hand: the sidereal time of *3 hr 45 min 15 sec* (step 5) and the corrected latitude of *42°10′* (step 7). The house cusps are then obtained by two-dimensional interpolation. On page 12 of *Dalton's* the correct values are between the columns labeled 3/42/57 and 3/47/6 and are also between latitudes 42° and 43°.

Since the total time difference between the two columns is 249 seconds and the time difference from 3/42/57 and 3/45/15 is 138 seconds, to interpolate horizontally, find the difference in cusp values between the two columns and multiply by 138/249. Then, add this figure to the initial value. Interpolation must also be done vertically between the 42° and the 43° of latitude. Since a value of 42°10′ is desired, it is necessary to go 10/60 of the way between the two values. Therefore, calculate the difference in cusp values between the two rows (42° and 43°), multiply the difference

CUSPS	10TH	11TH	12TH	1ST	2ND	3RD
Initial value	28 ♉	3.1 ♎	5.5 ♌	3/15 ♍	26.3 ♍	24.5 ♎
(3/47/6) (42°)		(3/6)	(5/30)		(26/18)	(24/30)
Next horizontal value	29 ♉	4.1 ♎	6.3 ♌	4/3 ♍	27.2 ♍	25.6 ♎
(3/47/6) (42°)		(4/6)	(6/18)		(27/12)	(25/36)
Horizontal difference (min)	60	60	48	48	54	54
Hor. dif. × 138/249 (rounded off)	33	33	26	26	29	29
Next vertical value	28 ♉	3.4 ♎	5.8 ♌	3/30 ♍	26.3 ♍	24.4 ♎
(3/42/57) (43°)		(3/24)	(5/48)		(26/18)	(24/24)
Vertical difference (min)	0	18	18	15	0	−6
Ver. dif. × 10/60 (rounded off)	0	3	3	2	0	−1
Corrected cusps = initial value + hor. dif. × 136/249 + ver. dif. × 10/60	28/33 ♉ = 28 ♉ 33	3/42 ♎ = 3 ♎ 42	5/59 ♌ = 5 ♌ 59	3/43 ♍ = 3 ♍ 43	26/47 ♍ = 26 ♍ 47	24/58 ♎ = 24 ♎ 58

by 10/60, and then add to the initial value.

This procedure is followed for all cusp values in the table on page 28. The opposite cusp values are exactly 180° from these values.

8. A similar interpolation must be done to ascertain the exact planetary locations. On page 317 of the *"Swiss" Zurich Ephemeris* the planetary positions are given for noon Greenwich Mean Time. It has already been calculated that the subject was born at 1:30 P.M. July 7, 1942, GMT (step 3), so an interpolation is necessary to get the correct planetary locations. This is done by first calculating how far each planet moves during the 24 hours, then multiplying the result by the portion of the 24 hours passed until the birth (1.5/24 in this case). Since there are 1440 minutes in 24 hours and the subject was born 90 minutes after noon, the planetary daily motion is multipled by 90/1440.

This procedure is followed for all planet values in the table below.

	INITIAL VALUE (7/7/42)	NEXT DAY (7/8/42)	DIFFER-ENCE (MIN)	DIFF × 90 / 1440 (ROUNDED OFF)	FINAL VALUE
Sun	14/44 ♋	15/41 ♋	57	4	14/48 ♋
Moon	8/56 ♉	20/58 ♉	722	45	9/41 ♉
Mercury	23/34 ♊	24/37 ♊	63	4	23/38 ♊
Venus	11/16 ♊	12/27 ♊	71	4	11/20 ♊
Mars	14/28 ♌	15/06 ♌	38	2	14/30 ♌
Jupiter	6/10 ♋	6/24 ♋	14	1	6/11 ♋
Saturn	7/28 ♊	7/35 ♊	7	0	7/28 ♊
Uranus	2/57 ♊	2/59 ♊	2	0	2/57 ♊
Neptune	27/19	27/20 ♍	1	0	27/19 ♍
No. Node	6/55 ♍	6/55 ♍	0	0	6/55 ♍
Pluto	4/48 ♌	4/48 ♌	0	0	4/48 ♌

The final chart, then, in standard wheel form is:

CHART 13

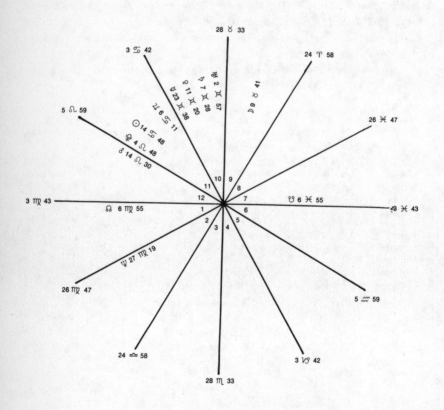

ASTROLOGY CHART

John Doe, born on July 7, 1942, at 8:30 A.M. at 42° Latitude
and 71° Longitude

POSITIONS OF PLANETS BY SIGN AND HOUSE

Sun	14°	Cancer	11th House
Moon	9°	Taurus	9th House
Mercury	23°	Gemini	10th House
Venus	11°	Gemini	10th House
Mars	14°	Leo	12th House
Jupiter	6°	Cancer	11th House
Saturn	7°	Gemini	10th House
Uranus	2°	Gemini	10th House
Neptune	27°	Virgo	2nd House
Pluto	4°	Leo	11th House
No. Node	6°	Virgo	1st House
So. Node	6°	Pisces	6th House

HOUSE CUSPS (OVERLAY PATTERN)

Virgo	is on your	1st House	Ascendant
Libra	is on your	2nd House	
Scorpio	is on your	3rd House	
Capricorn	is on your	4th House	Nadir
Aquarius	is on your	5th House	
Pisces	is on your	6th House	
Pisces	is on your	7th House	Descendant
Aries	is on your	8th House	
Taurus	is on your	9th House	
Cancer	is on your	10th House	Midheaven
Leo	is on your	11th House	
Virgo	is on your	12th House	

ASPECTS

Sun Aspects

Sun conjunct Jupiter	8° orb, separating
Sun sextile Moon	5° orb, applying, approaching

Moon Aspects

Moon square Mars	4° orb, applying, approaching
Moon sextile Jupiter	3° orb, separating, approaching
Moon square Pluto	4° orb, separating, approaching

Mercury Aspects

Mercury sextile Mars	9° orb, separating, approaching
Mercury square Neptune	3° orb, applying, approaching

Venus Aspects

Venus sextile Mars	3° orb, applying, approaching
Venus conjunct Saturn	3° orb, separating
Venus conjunct Uranus	8° orb, separating
Venus sextile Pluto	6° orb, separating, approaching

ASTROLOGY CHART (CONTINUED)
Mars Aspects

Mars sextile Saturn	7° orb, separate, departing
Mars conjunct Pluto	9° orb, separating

Jupiter Aspects

Jupiter square Neptune	1° orb, separate, approaching

Saturn Aspects

Saturn conjunct Uranus	4° orb, separating
Saturn sextile Pluto	2° orb, separate, approaching

Uranus Aspects

Uranus trine Neptune	5° orb, applying, approaching
Uranus sextile Pluto	1° orb, applying, approaching

Neptune Aspects

Neptune sextile Pluto	7° orb, applying, departing

QUADRUPLICITIES AND TRIPLICITIES

Chart has 2 Fire, 2 Earth, 4 Air, 2 Water signs and 2 Cardinal, 3 Fixed, 5 Mutable signs.

PART II

BASIC CONCEPTS IN HOROSCOPIC COMPARISON

III
Analyzing Human Relationships

Problems involving relationships are the most widespread cause of human misery and depression. Whether these problems manifest themselves on an international scale as conflicts between national, political, or economic powers, or on a personal scale as obstacles to better relations between individuals, their importance must be recognized and understood.

One of the most valuable and important contributions of astrology is in promoting better understanding between people through the field of horoscopic comparison. These comparisons can be extraordinarily useful in analyzing romantic, marital, parent–child, employer–employee, professional, family, platonic, and business relationships. They can offer important insights into the future, the present, and the past of any relationship.

Unfortunately, however, this area of astrology is all too frequently subject to careless and misleading interpretation when judgments are based solely on such superficial analysis as comparing only the Sun signs of the individuals involved. Remarks such as, "I'm a Taurus; I can't get along with you because you're a Leo, and you're square my Sun sign," indicate a fundamental misunderstanding and oversimplification. Make no mistake, this particular branch of astrology is one of the most complex and difficult. There are a great many factors to be considered that can make subtle yet significant changes in the final interpretation of the two charts. But the understanding we can gain through such comparisons can help us be more realistic in our expectations and compassionate in our dealings. With this knowledge, we can then grow side by side.

When we speak of the position of a planet in horoscopic comparisons, the following considerations are always implied:

1. The sign in which the planet falls
2. The house in which the planet falls
3. The sign the planet rules
4. The house the planet rules
5. All the aspects made to the planet by other planets

All these apply to the planet's position in both the natal horoscopes of the individuals in the relationship, in addition to its position in the horoscopic comparison.

There are two major areas that must be considered in comparing horoscopes. The first is concerned with what aspects the planets in one horoscope make to the planets of the other horoscope. For example, in one chart, Mercury may conjunct Saturn and oppose Jupiter, but in comparing this chart to another, Mercury may square the second person's Saturn and trine his Jupiter. The second area we must consider deals with *where* the planets in one horoscope fall in the houses of the other horoscope. In other words, Neptune may fall in the Fifth House of the first individual and in the Twelfth House of the second individual.

One essential consideration to bear in mind at all times is that the importance of any planet, house or sign is only as great as the strength of that planet, house or sign in the natal horoscopes of the individuals involved. The significance of each planet and house also depends on the type of relationship being considered. In a business relationship, for example, the comparative aspects of Saturn and Mercury would be particularly important, whereas in a romantic attachment, those of Venus, Mars, the Sun, the Moon, and the Fifth House would hold precedence. When determining the aspects in horoscopic comparisons, use the same orbs as those used in natal astrology: a 10° orb for major aspects involving the Sun or the Moon, and a 6° orb for major aspects between planets.

Basically, then, by comparing horoscopes one can learn how the psychological drives of one individual can affect the life of another individual. At the same time, it is important to consider the general psychological makeup and level of consciousness of the individuals whose relationship is being analyzed. Two individuals with many favorable comparative aspects and house placements can find themselves in difficulty if they differ greatly in intelligence, education, experience, social background, or spiritual outlook. Therefore, the authors wish to caution the reader that the first rule in astrology is: Never try to change another individual, the only person we can change is ourself.

FIVE RULES OF HOROSCOPIC COMPARISONS

1. Consider the nature and main purpose of the relationship.

Some relationships, such as those between teacher and student, have for their primary purpose the acquisition of knowledge. In such cases, the planets Mercury, Jupiter, and Saturn assume special importance in the relationship. Mercury deals with the basic communication of knowledge, and Jupiter with higher education and the conveying of a broad, philosophic understanding of the subject matter being studied. Saturn relates to the teacher's role as organizer of the subject matter, disciplinarian, and task master.

In romantic relationships, Venus, Mars, and the Sun will be of primary importance. The Sun, natural ruler of the Fifth House, strongly affects romantic attraction. Venus and Mars, because they rule the female and male sex principles respectively, are important in determining sexual attraction, especially if they relate to the Fifth House or the ruler of the Fifth House in the comparison. Comparative aspects between Venus and Mars, Venus and the Moon, Venus and the Sun, Venus and Uranus, and Venus and Pluto are especially important in determining the romantic potential of a relationship.

In a marriage situation, these factors are also important, but the Saturn influences in the comparison must be considered as well. Saturn is the exalted ruler of Libra and the Seventh House, the sign and house of the marriage institution. These Saturn influences indicate the natives' ability to accept the serious responsibilities of marriage and to exercise patience and discipline to build an enduring relationship.

In family relationships, including marriage, the house placements and aspects of the Moon are of major importance, since they show how the natives adjust to each other's emotional habit patterns, needs for security and creature comforts, and family background and conditioning. Jupiter and Neptune, which are exalted in Cancer, are also important in family relationships, since they indicate the natives' ingrained, subconscious, psychological tendencies and cultural, philosophic, and religious attitudes as these relate to home and family life. Comparative placements and aspects relating to the Fourth House and its ruler in either or both natal horoscopes are also of particular importance in family relationships.

In business and professional relationships, Mars, Saturn, Mercury, Venus, and the Moon are important. The compatibility of the natives' values where finances are concerned is indicated by Venus and the Moon, the Second House ruler, and the planets placed in the Second House in the natal horoscopes of both natives and in the comparison, with their accompanying aspects. How the natives will relate to each other concerning professional affairs, ambition, public recognition, and career goals, as well as the means used to attain such goals, are revealed by Mars and Saturn, the Tenth House and its rulers in the comparison, aspects to all these, and where Mars and Saturn are placed in the natal horoscopes. The know-how, educational training, special skills, experience, and intelligence that the individuals in a relationship can bring to bear, in cooperation, to accomplish business, professional, and general work are indicated by Mercury, the Sixth House, the ruler of the Sixth House in the natal horoscopes of the natives and in the comparison, and the aspects to all these.

2. Consider the natal horoscopes of the individuals in the relationship.

Regardless of how many comparative aspects a planet in one individual's horoscope makes to planets in the other native's horoscope, the influence of the first native on the second through the planet in question can only be as strong as the importance of that planet in the first native's horoscope. In short, a person can bring to a relationship only as much of a given quality as he himself has developed.

Suppose, for example, that Mars in A's horoscope makes a conjunction to B's Sun, a trine to B's Moon, an opposition to B's Jupiter, and a square to B's Saturn. One would expect that A would have a strong, arousing, energizing, initiating influence upon B. However, if Mars is weak by sign and house position and is unaspected in A's natal horoscope, then A will lack the basic Mars characteristics of energy and initiative. Therefore, A can have little energizing influence upon B, regardless of the comparative aspects of his Mars to B's planets. On the other hand, if A has a powerful Mars in his natal horoscope, indicating an abundance of energy and initiative in his own basic character, then even one or two comparative aspects of his Mars to B's planets may have a considerable energizing influence upon B. This principle applies to any other planets in a horoscope comparison.

3. Consider the relative ages of the natives in the relationship.

These considerations are particularly important in teacher–student and parent–child relationships. Saturn is the important planet here, as it deals with the discipline, maturity, experience, natural authority, and leadership ability that accompany age and experience. Naturally, Saturn in the horoscope of the older native will have a stronger effect upon a younger native than vice versa, although there are exceptions to this rule.

Occasionally, aspects made by the younger native's Saturn to the older native's planets indicate that the younger native will be a serious responsibility for the older. This rule also applies to a lesser degree to the Sun and Jupiter.

4. Consider the sexes of the natives.

This consideration is of particular importance in family, romantic, and marital relationships. The Moon and Venus rule women, at least in terms of woman's traditional role as wife, mother, and homemaker. Therefore, the positions of the Moon and Venus in a woman's natal horoscope and the aspects made to them, as well as the aspects made to them in the comparison, will indicate how she will relate to the other native (particularly a man) in terms of her feminine role.

Mars and the Sun rule men in their traditional role as father and provider. The placements of and aspects made to Mars and the Sun in a man's natal horoscope and in the comparison will indicate how he will relate to the other individual in terms of his masculine roles (particularly if the other individual is a woman).

In a woman's horoscope, the Sun and Mars indicate the type of man she would like to attract. Therefore, aspects to and placements of the Sun and Mars in a woman's horoscope in relation to planets in a man's horoscope indicate to what extent the man will conform to her expectations of him.

In a man's horoscope, Venus and the Moon indicate, by their sign and house positions and the aspects made to them, what kind of woman he would like to attract. Therefore, in a man–woman relationship, the aspects to and house placements of the man's Moon and Venus in relation to the woman's planets will indicate to what extent she will fulfill his expectations of what a woman should be.

5. *Consider the relative levels of overall, evolutionary development of the two natives.*

Obviously, a jungle primitive and an erudite college professor will have little basis for a relationship, regardless of how well their horoscopes compare. In most cases, for two individuals to relate closely and to find each other stimulating and worthwhile, they must be on a similar level of consciousness.

The overall evolutionary development of any native is determined by his ability to integrate the nature of each of the planets in his horoscope into the configuration of the aspects that link the planets together. The greater the degree of this synthesis, the higher the degree of evolution.

If Uranus, Neptune, and Pluto are found conjunct the angles, or have many exact aspects to natal planets, particularly to the Sun, the Moon, Mercury, and the ruler of the Ascendant, the native has reached a greater than usual degree of spiritual evolution.

For a relatively high degree of evolution to have taken place, Mercury, Saturn, and the Sun must be reasonably strong in the horoscopes. Saturn reveals the native's capacity for self-discipline, without which there is no real spiritual evolution. Mercury indicates the level of intelligence and communicative ability, without which there is no significant learning or practical mental organization of perceptions, intuition, and ideas. The Sun indicates the basic power and will needed for accomplishment. Without significant development of these faculties, a person is ineffectual, regardless of whatever else he may have in his favor, and cannot be considered highly evolved spiritually.

SIGNIFICANCE OF THE QUADRUPLICITIES

An emphasis on one of the three quadruplicities, Cardinal, Fixed, or Mutable, in horoscopic comparisons indicates the temperamental mode of interaction between the natives. A preponderance of Cardinal sign influences—Aries, Cancer, Libra, or Capricorn—in a horoscopic comparison will tend to indicate a very rapid-action-oriented interchange between the natives, concerned with the immediate situation and environment. In such cases, the natives' mutual concerns will be more with immediate circumstances than with the past or the future. Dominant

Angular (First, Fourth, Seventh, or Tenth) House influences will have a similar effect.

If Fixed signs—Taurus, Leo, Scorpio, or Aquarius—or Succedent Houses (Second, Fifth, Eighth, or Eleventh) are the predominant influence in the comparison of two horoscopes, the natives' mutual concerns will be with fixed, future-oriented goals and objectives. Problems could arise because of stubborn uncompromising attitudes on the part of one or both natives. On the positive side, the natives are apt to stick together and show a strong sense of loyalty and commitment to common goals.

If Mutable signs—Gemini, Virgo, Sagittarius, or Pisces—and/or Cadent Houses (Third, Sixth, Ninth, or Twelfth) are the dominant influence in a horoscopic comparison, the natives' relationship will tend to be based on past experience, mental communication, and adaptability. Difficulties may arise out of the natives' tendency to be preconditioned and prejudiced in their attitudes toward each other because of past experiences and subconscious psychological conditionings. The natives can become trapped in their memories and may be unable to relate constructively to the reality of present-time conditions. On the positive side, they can relate to each other with flexibility, intelligence, empathy, and understanding born of experience.

SIGNIFICANCE OF THE TRIPLICITIES OR ELEMENTS

If there is a predominance of Fire sign influences—Aries, Leo, or Sagittarius—in the comparison of horoscopes, the natives will react toward each other with a great deal of energy, ardor, and enthusiasm. They can initiate new activities and encourage each other to assume leadership roles. In romantic relationships, there can be a great deal of passion.

If there is a predominance of Earth sign influences—Taurus, Virgo, or Capricorn—in the comparison of two horoscopes, the major issues of a relationship will be determined by practical considerations. Financial and business affairs will play an important part in the natives' interaction. Matters of material status, comfort, and security will be of major concern.

If Air signs—Gemini, Libra, or Aquarius—are the predominating influence in a horoscopic comparison, intellectual stimulation and companionship will be of major significance in the relationship, and the natives' ability to communicate intelligently and relate to surrounding social influences and interpersonal activities will also be of paramount importance.

If Water signs—Cancer, Scorpio, or Pisces—are the predominating influence in the comparison of horoscopes, emotional issues, sympathetic emotional understanding, and empathy will be of major importance. Emotional issues can make or break the relationship. There can be an emotional type of psychic communication between the natives.

IV
The Roles
of the Signs

A strong emphasis on one or more signs of the Zodiac in a horoscope comparison can provide important keys to understanding the nature of the relationship under consideration. Comparative conjunctions in a sign or many comparative aspects made to a planet in a sign will give that sign considerable importance in the comparison. Sign emphases of this kind indicate attitudes, preferences, character traits, and modes of activity that will be prominent in the relationship, and the relationship will be colored by the particular type of role-playing characteristic of that sign.

ARIES

If Aries figures strongly in the comparison, impulsive actions and self-assertive modes of expression will figure strongly in the relationship. The natives are capable of carrying out decisive action together and getting things done, although there may not be sufficient sustained energy and follow-through unless other factors in the comparison supply it. The natives can be effective in initiating action together, breaking the ice, and getting things started. If one or both natives are too aggressive or impulsive, however, such actions can lead to resentment and discord. The natives should be careful to avoid a "me first" attitude. The relationship will have a high degree of ardor and enthusiasm. It can also be marked by a certain degree of competitiveness, which, in extreme cases, can lead to open disagreement and conflict. The natives are apt to be direct and straightforward with each other and will know where they stand in the relationship. They can bring out each other's self-confidence and positive leadership potential.

TAURUS

If Taurus figures prominently in a horoscopic comparison, creature comforts and financial security will be of major concern to the natives. The relationship is likely to be based upon a desire for material status or financial gain. In romantic relationships, there can be considerable sensuality and passion. The natives will have a strong and loyal affection for each other, but they are also capable of being jealous and possessive. If afflictions are involved in these Taurus influences, the association can be motivated by financial concerns and material status. Entrenched obstinate attitudes can interfere with the natives' compatibility. On the positive side, the natives will be very patient with each other and practical and realistic in their expectations about each other. They are likely to share an appreciation of nature, music, art, and all things of quality, beauty, and refinement.

GEMINI

If Gemini figures prominently in a horoscope comparison, the natives will share many intellectual interests. They can bring intelligence, ingenuity, mental resourcefulness, and adaptability to the solution of mutual problems. Their ability to communicate with each other intelligently enables them to handle and eliminate problems and differences. If negative aspects are present in these Gemini influences, the natives tend to be superficial, vacillating, or inconsistent toward each other. Important issues can be buried under a mountain of verbiage, or the natives may change their minds so often that they confuse each other. Gemini is not one of the ardent signs, but the natives can find many interests in common, and they are not likely to get bored with each other.

CANCER

If Cancer is predominant in the horoscope comparison, the natives' mutual concerns will be with home, family, emotional, and domestic issues, especially food and cooking. The emphasis on family affairs will make for intense emotional interactions in marital and family relationships. If favorable indications are present, this Cancer influence will help to cement a family or marital relationship. Under any conditions, however, there will be strong emotional ties between the natives, and the home will be a major concern.

If adverse influences are present, there could be emotional instability and frequent upsets.

If the natives' association is a business or professional one, they are apt to be concerned with home or domestic products and services.

LEO

If the sign Leo is a major factor in the comparison of two horoscopes, the pursuit of pleasure, romance, leadership, and dramatic self-expression will be of major consequence in the relationship. The natives will spark energy, self-confidence, and enthusiasm in each other. Romantic relationships with a strong Leo influence will be dramatic, passionate, and intense. If these Leo influences are associated with adverse aspects, there can be ego conflict in the relationship, and the natives may attempt to order each other around and thus arouse resentment. On the positive side, the natives will respond to each other with ardor and enthusiasm and will share an interest in art, music, drama, and social activities. They may also be interested in political affairs, sports, investments, and speculation, as well as children and their education.

VIRGO

If there is a strong Virgo influence in the comparison of two horoscopes, matters related to work, technology, health, medicine, and practical mental pursuits will be of major importance in the relationship. Styles of dress, personal hygiene, and dietary habits can be important factors in the natives' ability to get along. The work or service performed by the natives will also be an important factor in the relationship.

Performance of duty, attention to practical details, and practical accomplishment or, at worst, the lack of these things will be of major importance in determining whether the natives get along. There will usually be good logical communication between the natives and an ability to carry out practical planning effectively.

If adverse aspects are associated with these Virgo influences in the comparison, the natives may be critical toward each other and can influence each other to become wrapped up in nonessential details.

LIBRA

If Libra is an outstanding factor in a horoscopic comparison, marriage, partnership, human relationships, psychology, art, music, and social activities will be of major importance in the relationship. Libra is the sign dealing with human relationships per se; therefore, a strong Libra influence in a horoscope comparison is usually a positive factor, since both natives will have a basic desire to get along and to be on intimate terms. Often, they have a strong sense of loyalty to each other. The natives will usually share interest in psychology, sociology, human relationships, and their mutual friends. They will enjoy engaging in social activities together. There will be a strong mutual appreciation of all forms of beauty—whether art, music, nature, or people.

If adverse aspects are associated with this Libra influence in the comparison, the natives may become too dependent on each other or overly sensitive in their relationship. There can also be danger of divorce, lawsuits, or breakdowns of partnerships.

A strong Libra influence in a comparison can also be favorable for business partnerships related to art, music, or luxury items.

SCORPIO

A strong Scorpio influence in a horoscopic comparison makes for an intensely emotional relationship. Sexual compatibility and fidelity will be of major importance in romantic and marital relationships. These relationships will have tremendous intensity and passion. Scorpio is important in business relationships related to insurance, corporate finance, engineering, military affairs, taxes, inheritances, or mortuaries. When adverse aspects are associated with these Scorpio comparative influences, there can be intense, bitter disagreements or smoldering resentments over the handling of joint finances, inheritances, business affairs, alimony, and over any sexual aspects of the relationship. Jealousy is likely to be a problem. On the positive side, the natives can share an interest in occult subjects, life after death, spirituality, or the more profound aspects of science and technology. In such a positive comparison, there is an ability and willingness to confront the basic issues of survival and life's deeper meaning beyond the superficial veneer. The natives can bring out strength, courage, and resourcefulness in each other.

SAGITTARIUS

A strong Sagittarius influence in a horoscopic comparison indicates a mutual concern with and compatible ideas about religion, philosophy, higher education, foreign cultures, cultural trends, and travel. The natives usually make good traveling companions and will enjoy journeys together. A strong Sagittarius influence is often found in teacher–student and in guru–disciple relationships. In some cases, the natives share an interest in sports and outdoor activities. In general, they will increase each other's energy and enthusiasm, especially for some social or educational cause or religious ideal. There will be mutual involvement in philosophic discussions, educational and cultural pursuits, or religious activities.

If adverse aspects are associated with this Sagittarius influence, the natives may have major disagreements over religion or philosophy. On the positive side, they will reinforce optimistic attitudes in each other.

CAPRICORN

A strong Capricorn comparative influence indicates that the natives' interaction is based on professional concerns and a desire for material status and power. Financial security, fame, and prominence in the community will be a major motivational factor in the relationship. Capricorn influences are especially prevalent in business, professional, and political relationships. The natives will stimulate each other's ambition and desire to achieve status or prominence. The natives may tend to think in terms of how useful they are to each other; thus, the association is sometimes tinged with expediency. In real friendships with this combination, there can be great loyalty and sense of responsibility. In the case of adverse aspects, however, there can be mutual mistrust, competition, and a "me first" scramble to get to the top. The proverbial large corporate executive jungle is characteristic of such a negative Capricorn influence. On the positive side, the natives can strengthen each other's sense of duty and responsibility. A high degree of seriousness characterizes these relationships.

AQUARIUS

A strong Aquarius influence in a horoscopic comparison indicates an intellectual friendship between the natives. They will share interests in friends, group activities, exciting new experiences, or occult or astrological pursuits. They will encourage each other to try the new and different, bring out each other's tendencies toward original thinking, and stimulate each other's interest in scientific pursuits, inventions, or innovations. There will be a mutual concern with humanitarian, progressive causes, as well as with social and political reforms. The natives tend to bring sudden, unexpected, and unusual occurrences into each other's lives, and inspire intuitive, spiritual insights in each other.

If adverse aspects are associated with these comparative influences of Aquarius, the natives' friendship can be tinged with selfish, ulterior motives, or they may tend to encourage each other in impractical or unwise activities—perhaps, simply a dissipation of time in meaningless social activities.

PISCES

A strong Pisces influence in a horoscopic comparison indicates that the natives will have a strong subjective emotional and intuitive link. They will be intuitively aware of each other's moods and feelings. Memories of the past and subconscious factors will play an important part in these psychic interchanges. If adverse comparative aspects are associated with these Pisces comparative influences, the natives can tend to get embroiled in each other's emotional problems and psychological hangups to the point where it is hard for them to relate to present-time reality in a practical way. There is a danger of their pandering to each other's weaknesses, tendencies to self-pity, and self-destructive habits through misguided sympathy. On the positive side, there can be genuine mutual compassion, empathy, and mutual appreciation of esthetic and intuitive spiritual values. The natives can bring out each other's meditative qualities and stimulate each other's intuitive, creative imagination. There is likely to be a mutual interest in art, music, psychology, reincarnation, religion, spiritual philosophy, yoga, or the unfoldment of psychic or intuitive abilities.

V
The Influences of the Twelve Houses

The placement of planets in one individual's horoscope in the houses of the other native's horoscope indicates the ways in which the basic psychological drives and tendencies of the first native will influence the practical affairs of the second native. For example, if A's Mercury falls in B's Tenth House, then A's ideals, education, and know-how will influence B's career and professional affairs. These comparative house placements also indicate the ways in which the natives will influence the practical everyday affairs and circumstances of each other's lives. Whether this influence is constructive or destructive will depend on both the natal and the comparative aspects.

Comparative house placements of planets are also important in determining the nature of the relationship. Comparative placements involving the Eleventh House indicate friendships; comparative placements in the Fifth House indicate romantic or social relationships; Seventh House placements indicate marriage or partnerships; Tenth House comparative placements indicate professional relationships; Second House comparative placements indicate business relationships, and so on.

It is important to remember that interpretations of house influences in horoscopic comparisons are based on: (1) the placement of one person's planets in the other person's houses; (2) the comparative aspects made by the planets in one person's house to planets in the other person's horoscope; (3) the comparative aspects to the ruler of the house in either or both horoscopes being considered.

FIRST HOUSE

When planets in the horoscope of one native fall in the First House of the other native, the planet individual is likely to strongly influence the self-image and actions of the First House individual. In turn, the actions, the basic consciousness, and the mode of self-expression of the First House individual is likely to influence the planet individual through the affairs ruled by the planet in the comparative First House placement. In many cases, the natives will tend to identify with each other and acquire each other's traits and personal mannerisms. They will tend to influence each other's actions along the lines indicated by the planets involved. There is likely to be a very direct and personal interaction between the natives, which shows itself as a direct "here I am, and this is who and what I am" approach.

SECOND HOUSE

Comparative placements of planets in the Second House indicate that the natives are likely to be involved with each other through business, property, or financial affairs. They are likely to stimulate each other's taste for luxuries, fine and expensive items, art objects, and opulent surroundings. The desire for material gain and the status which accompanies it will be a significant factor in the relationship.

THIRD HOUSE

Comparative placements of one native's planets in the other native's Third House indicate major areas of intellectual exchange and communication of ideas and perceptions in the relationship. If one or more of A's planets are found in B's Third House, the affairs ruled by these planets in A's horoscope will provide topics for frequent mental exchange between the natives and may also occasion many short journeys. The planets in the Third House of B's natal horoscope and aspecting planets in A's horoscope will similarly become a basis for communication and travel. Whether or not the natives can communicate with each other harmoniously will depend on the nature of the comparative aspects involving the Third House, the ruler of the Third House, and the planet Mercury, which is the natural ruler of the Third House. With strong Third House comparative influences, the natives are likely to develop a mutual interest in such subjects as education, books, literature, planning, and decision-making, unless serious afflictions are involved in the Third House comparative aspects. The natives will encourage each other to be more alert and aware of their environment. Third House comparative aspects and placements should always be carefully studied before entering into contractual agreements.

FOURTH HOUSE

Fourth House comparative planetary placements and comparative aspects made to these planets or to the planets in either natal Fourth House indicate how the natives will react to each other in a domestic and family environment. These factors will give important information on how the natives will respond to and influence each other through deep-seated psychological habit patterns based on heredity, family upbringing, parental influences, early childhood experiences, and social background.

Whether the natives can get along harmoniously in these affairs will depend on the nature of the comparative aspects involving the Fourth House planets in both natal Fourth Houses, the rulers of both Fourth Houses, and the Moon, which is the natural ruler of the Fourth House. These comparative aspects and planetary placements will be an important factor in how the natives respond to each other's moods, feelings, and needs for creature comforts.

FIFTH HOUSE

The Fifth House in the comparison of horoscopes indicates how two people will relate to each other in romance, pleasurable pursuits, social activities, artistically creative endeavors, and in raising and educating children. The nature of these interactions will be indicated by comparative Fifth House placements of planets, comparative aspects made to natal Fifth House planets, and comparative house placements and aspects to the rulers of the natal Fifth Houses of both natives. Comparative influences involving the Fifth House are highly important in parent–child relationships, as well as in romantic, sexual relationships. These influences will determine whether the natives have compatible attitudes and interests in the pursuit of pleasure, the handling of financial speculations, social activities, and in artistic tastes.

SIXTH HOUSE

Sixth House comparative influences will indicate how the natives will interact with each other in a work situation, especially in carrying out practical duties and responsibilities. Sixth House comparative influences are also highly important in employer–employee relationships, co-worker relationships, and doctor–patient relationships. These Sixth House influences will also indicate whether the natives have compatible attitudes and habits with respect to dress, personal hygiene, diet, and the orderliness of their working or living environment. Comparative Sixth House placements of planets and comparative aspects made to the ruler of the natal Sixth House of both natives, or comparative aspects made to planets in the Sixth House of either natal horoscope or to Mercury, natural ruler of the Sixth House, can be important factors in determining the ability of the natives to work together.

SEVENTH HOUSE

If one native's planets fall in the Seventh House of the other native or make aspects to planets in the other native's Seventh House or to the ruler of his Seventh House, there is likely to be a personal attraction between the natives representative of the characteristics of the planets involved. If the planets are adversely aspected in the natal horoscopes and in the comparison, the association could lead to antipathy or dislike. In some cases, lawsuits or divorces occur. Seventh House comparative influences will indicate whether the natives will be suitable marriage partners and whether they can get along in a close friendship or a business partnership. These comparative influences will also show areas of mutual responsibility. When strong Seventh House comparative influences are present, the natives will share an interest in social activities, friends, art, music, and psychology.

EIGHTH HOUSE

Eighth House comparative influences indicate the likelihood of mutual involvement in joint finances, business ventures, insurance, tax matters, inheritances, or other forms of shared resources. If these influences are adverse, there can be conflict over such matters as corporate finances, insurance, taxes, inheritances, or alimony. If the natives are sufficiently spiritually aware, there can be a mutual interest in occult subjects, parapsychology, or science. With strong Eighth House comparative influences, the natives can help each other to fathom secrets and mysteries and bring out each other's resourceful qualities. If these Eighth House influences are favorable, the natives can cooperate effectively in business enterprises and scientific or engineering fields. These influences can also be an important factor in sexual attraction, in much the same way as Fifth House comparative influences.

NINTH HOUSE

If one native's planets fall in the Ninth House of the other native's horoscope or make aspects to planets in his Ninth House or his Ninth House ruler, religious, philosophical, and educational matters will be important in the relationship. The natives are apt to influence each other's religious and philosophic outlook on life. If these Ninth House comparative influences are adverse, there can be conflict and disagreement over these matters. Ninth House comparative influences indicate that the natives are likely to be traveling companions. There can be a telepathic spiritual link between them if these Ninth House influences involve Uranus, Neptune, or Pluto. The natives can have a mutual interest in exploring foreign cultures, religions, sociological trends, history, or other things relating to the social and philosophic climate of the larger culture.

TENTH HOUSE

Comparative influences involving the Tenth House will indicate the extent of the natives' professional involvement with each other. Where strong Tenth House comparative influences are present, one of the natives may be in a position of power and authority over the other, as in employer–employee or parent–child relationships. The older or more experienced of the two natives is likely to have a strong effect in shaping the career of the other. The natives are often mutually involved in some way in politics or publicity-seeking.

If the Tenth House comparative influences are adverse in nature, there can be competition for promotion, public recognition, or official favor, or the natives may disagree or be antagonistic about political opinions or methods of handling professional affairs. If the Tenth House comparative influences are favorable, the natives can help each other achieve prominence or career advancement.

ELEVENTH HOUSE

If planets of one native's horoscope fall in the Eleventh House of the other native or aspect planets in the other native's Eleventh House or the ruler of his Eleventh House, there will be friendship or mutual involvement in group or organizational activities, along with the possibility of working together on some serious social, humanitarian, scientific, or occult project. Because of the Saturnian co-rulership of Aquarius and the Eleventh House, these friends often work at and share tasks and responsibilities. Strong Eleventh House comparative influences indicate associations based on intellectual interests and exploration of new exciting aspects of life. The natives will tend to bring new and unusual circumstances into each other's lives. In marriage or romantic relationships, Eleventh House influences can provide an intellectual basis for shared interests and continuing friendship that goes beyond mere emotional and sexual attraction.

If the Eleventh House comparative influences are adverse, the friendship could be unreliable, false, superficial, or based on ulterior motives.

TWELFTH HOUSE

Twelfth House comparative influences indicate to what extent the subconscious minds of the natives and their psychic impressions will be a factor in their relationship. If the Twelfth House comparative influences are adverse, the natives can be deceptive or evasive toward each other. Neurotic tendencies or the tendency of one or both natives to live in a dream world can stand in the way of a constructive relationship. Strong

Twelfth House comparative influences can also indicate a karmic link between the natives based on past life associations. They can also indicate a psychic-telepathic or intuitive-empathetic link between the natives. There can be a mutual involvement in meditation, psychic investigation, mysticism, religion, occultism, or psychology. When favorable Twelfth House comparative influences are present, the natives can be attuned to each other's inspirational creative imagination and each can help the other to understand his subconscious psychological mechanisms.

VI
Dispositors of the
Planets

Dispositors and sign rulerships can be used in a number of ways to determine the compatibility of two people. If the Sun signs or rising signs of both natives, or the Sun sign of one native and the rising sign of the other native, are ruled by the same planet, there will be a natural understanding and similar approach to life. Individuals with natal signs which would ordinarily seem incompatible, like Gemini and Virgo, because of their square relationship, will get along to some extent because they are both ruled by Mercury and, therefore, share a similar rational, mental approach to life which enables them to reason out differences logically and impartially. Natives with signs such as Sagittarius and Pisces, Taurus and Libra, or Aries and Scorpio will also get along better than would otherwise be indicated by their square or inconjunct relationship because they respect the same values as a result of having the same planetary ruler.

If the ruler of one native's Sun or ascending sign falls in the other native's Sun or ascending sign, there will be a natural understanding between the natives and an ability to direct their energies in pursuit of the same goals. For example, if one native has the Sun in Gemini and Mercury in Taurus conjunct the other native's Ascendant, there would be a strong mutual interest in practical, material values. Or if one native has Aquarius rising with Uranus in Taurus, while the other native has the Sun in Taurus, there would be a mutual interest in employing new scientific or unusual ways of making money and achieving material security.

If one native has a planet which is heavily aspected and Angular, in its dignity or exaltation, ruler of the Ascendant, or a singleton in point focus, and the other native has a great many planets in signs ruled by this dignified, powerful planet in the first native's horoscope, there will be a strong common interest and mutual interaction through the things ruled by the planet thus powerfully dignified. For example, if one native has Mars in Capricorn in the Tenth House conjunct the Midheaven and a singleton in the Southern Hemisphere with strong trines to Saturn in the Second House and Uranus and Mercury in the Sixth House in opposition to Jupiter in the Fourth House, this Mars would obviously indicate an overriding professional ambition and would dominate the horoscope. If the other native has Sun, Mercury, and Venus in Aries with Jupiter, Saturn, and the Moon in Scorpio, the natives will react strongly toward each other in terms of action, ambition, competition, or drive to forcibly achieve some goal or desired objective. If they are in close proximity for a long period of time, these natives are bound to be consequential to each other in an action-oriented way.

When one native has a planet in the sign of its rulership or exaltation, and the other native has the same planet in the house of its accidental rulership or exaltation, they will have compatible or similar values with respect to the things ruled by that planet. For example, if one native has Venus in Pisces and the other native has Venus in the Twelfth House, these individuals would share sympathy, compassion, and an intuitive appreciation of beauty and refinement.

When both natives have several planets in two different signs ruled by the same planet, there will be mutual interest in the things ruled by that planet. For instance, if one native has Sun, Mercury, Venus, and Mars in Sagittarius, while the other native has Mercury, Venus, Mars, and Saturn in Pisces, they will share an interest in the affairs ruled by Jupiter and Neptune, such as religion and mysticism.

PART III

COMPARATIVE INFLUENCES OF THE PLANETS

VII
Sun

The influences of the Sun in horoscopic comparisons indicate the means by which the will power and creative self-expressions of the Sun individual affect the other party in the relationship.

Favorable and harmonious comparative influences of the Sun enable the Sun individual to spur the other to increased self-confidence and greater determination to further his major life goals.

With adverse or stress comparative influences of the Sun, the Sun person can assume an autocratic and egotistical air. Problems can arise from conflicting attitudes.

COMPARATIVE HOUSE PLACEMENTS

House placements of the Sun in a horoscopic comparison indicate the effects of the creative self-expressions and will power of the Sun individual on the practical affairs of the other. The individuals in the relationship direct their energies toward handling the affairs ruled by the house in which the Sun falls.

Favorably aspected comparative Sun placements inspire the individuals to a high degree of creativity in their endeavors, which shows itself in the affairs ruled by the house in which the Sun falls in the comparison.

Afflictions to the Sun's comparative position indicate strong differences in the individuals' attitudes toward how the matters ruled by the Sun should be handled, and these matters can become a source of ego conflict and confrontation in the relationship.

Because the Sun is the natural ruler of the Fifth House, concerns ruled by the comparative house placement of the Sun are often linked to artistic, romantic, pleasure-oriented, or child-related activities.

First House

As the Sun person's power potential and drive for creative self-expression tend to stimulate the First House native's self-awareness and desire for self-expression, their interaction can result either in competition or in effective, energetic cooperation in achieving some mutual creative goal. Since the Sun is accidentally exalted in the First House through its exaltation in Aries, the individuals tend to stimulate each other's will and drive for significance and to be alike in their basic consciousness and outlook on life. However, since both may try to play the same role, competition may take the place of cooperation. The individuals must put aside their egos to some extent if they are to cooperate effectively. Romantic and marital relationships with this combination are often founded upon a strong mutual attraction: the Sun's natural rulership of the Fifth House and the Ascendant's rulership of the physical body indicates the likelihood of physical attraction.

Second House

This comparative combination indicates cooperation on a financial or business basis. The Sun native's creativity and energy can stimulate the Second House native to improve his material circumstances. The Sun native may cultivate the Second House native to use his resources for some personal self-expression or creative endeavor. The Sun individual's creativity can influence the Second House person's esthetic and material values or vice versa. The Second House individual may provide the resources needed for the Sun individual's creative expression. In a romance, a marriage, or a friendship, however, resentments can arise from ulterior motives of personal material gain on the part of one or both individuals. Whether there is sufficient basis in other areas of the relationship to compensate for this danger depends on the rest of the comparison.

Third House

This comparative combination favors mutual mental stimulation. The Third House native's ideas can stimulate the Sun native's power drive and creative self-expression. The Sun person's energy can, in turn, spur the Third House individual to original, diversified thinking and greater willingness to communicate. This is a favorable combination for cooperation in writing and the exchange of ideas, especially in communications, science, and other work that requires mental insight. Teacher–pupil relationships that mentally vitalize the pupil and awaken his creative self-expression frequently have this combination in the comparison. The Sun individual encourages positive attitudes in the Third House individual's relationships with brothers or sisters and with friends and neighbors. The natives give each other ideas for pleasurable pursuits and for the education of children.

Fourth House

The Sun native's inner vitality and creative self-expression can have a dramatic effect on the Fourth House individual's home and domestic circumstances. This combination is particularly significant in family relationships and interactions with those who live under the same roof; often, it indicates intense interaction in a parent–child relationship. The creative self-expression and power potential of the Sun person have a powerful effect on the Fourth House native's basic consciousness. This effect is frequently felt on a subconscious emotional level and often produces a visceral response in the Fourth House native. If the relationship works out positively, the Fourth House native can provide the Sun person with a base of operations for his means of self-expression.

Fifth House

This comparative combination is a strong one for romantic and marital relationships. It confers great potential for emotional and romantic attraction. Whatever their relationship, these individuals enjoy each other's company. They are apt to share pleasure-oriented social activities—parties, games, sports, entertainment, the theater—and creative self-expression through the arts. Married couples with this comparative combination will want children and will take an interest in their educational growth and creative upbringing. This is a favorable comparative combination for parent–child and teacher–student relationships; it provides fun, education, and creative outlets for both parties. It also favors professional mutual interaction in art and entertainment. The relationship may indicate a mutual interest and involvement in speculative financial ventures or educational pursuits.

Sixth House

The Sun native's vitality and power potential can stimulate the Sixth House person to greater effort in areas related to job, career, health, and general self-improvement. This comparative combination is frequent in employer–employee relationships in business and the professions. It is a good combination for financial, business, and work cooperation, if the Sun native's authoritative tendencies do not create resentment in the Sixth House person. Each can inspire the other to greater effort toward practical accomplishments by stimulating each other's thinking about techniques and methods of getting the job done. Because the Sun native can have a vitalizing, regenerating effect on the Sixth House person's health, this is an effective combination for doctor–patient relationships. The natives' attitudes toward each other's personal mannerisms, dress, and hygiene can be a significant factor in their relationship.

Seventh House

This comparative combination is highly significant in terms of cooperation in all partnerships, be they personal or professional. The individuals act as mirrors of each other's personal deficiencies. Each helps the other to gain a wholesome perspective on the important issues of life. Ideally, this combination leads to a balanced give-and-take relationship. Should egos get in the way, however, there can be competition and either individual can resent the other's authoritarian attitudes. This comparative combination is common in marriage and close personal friendships. There is usually a strong mutual attraction, manifested in a sharing of pleasurable activities and the enjoyment of each other's company. The individuals are often sexually attracted, and the relationship can result in romance or marriage.

Eighth House

Individuals with this comparative combination often are involved in business partnerships or other corporate financial affairs. In some cases, this means merely that they have frequent occasion to do business with each other. Their contacts will often involve taxes, insurance, or inheritances. Occult or psychic matters are often of mutual interest. If other factors are favorable, there can be sexual attraction. The Sun person's energy and vitality can inspire the Eighth House native to greater efforts toward self-improvement and regeneration in various areas of his life. The natives may become involved in working together to improve environmental circumstances. In case of divorce, alimony settlements may cause conflicts, particularly if the Eighth House native's planets form difficult aspects to the Sun person's Sun, or if the Sun person's planets form difficult aspects to any of the Eighth House native's planets in that person's Eighth House or to the ruling planet of his Eighth House.

Ninth House

The Sun native stimulates the Ninth House native's interest in philosophy, higher education, religion, and other cultural pursuits. (Often they travel together.) The Ninth House individual's knowledge of these areas can stimulate the Sun native to new creativity. Their influence on each other's short- and long-term goals can bring about significant change, based on a new understanding of life. Teacher–student relationships involving spiritual, cultural, or philosophic subjects often have this combination in their comparisons. The Sun native tends to have authoritarian tendencies, and may arouse resentment by trying to convert the Ninth House person to the Sun native's own religious or philosophic beliefs. However, each can be a dynamic influence on the other's philosophic and spiritual outlook.

Tenth House

This comparative combination is significant in professional, business, and political relationships. The more powerful and established individual tends to influence the career and ambitions of the other. The Sun native can inspire the Tenth House person to greater effort in a career and creative work. The Sun person also is often in a position to improve the career circumstances of the Tenth House individual and lighten the burden of work responsibility by helping him overcome some fears and limitations.

The individuals' influence on each other's efforts to gain power, position, or status makes this an important comparative combination in political affairs. The combination is often found in employer–employee relationships. The individuals concerned can be rivals or allies in regard to their career ambitions and drive toward power and status; how this works depends on the overall comparison.

Eleventh House

Relationships with this comparative combination are often friendships, based on areas of mutual intellectual or scientific interest and humanitarian or cultural concerns. Common goals and objectives provide occasion for the individuals to work together in group and organizational activities designed to uplift and enlighten the cultural order. The Sun native may, through the ability to entertain and stimulate the Eleventh House person's friends and associates, become a social asset to the Eleventh House individual. The Sun person can also inspire the Eleventh House native to achieve goals and objectives. The natives can share many intellectual and spiritual interests which go beyond the physical and emotional levels of interaction. Often, they stimulate and inspire each other's creative and intuitive mental faculties.

Twelfth House

The Sun individual can help the Twelfth House native to be more outgoing and to realize potentials. In a positively oriented relationship, the Sun individual can help the Twelfth House person understand his or her subconscious mind. In a difficult relationship, however, there may be a psychologically disturbing effect on the Twelfth House individual, due to the stirring up of negative emotional reactions in his subconscious mind. The Twelfth House person's intuitive perceptions can give the Sun native insights into more effective means of self-expression. There could be a mutual interest in mystical or occult pursuits.

In some relationships, there is an intuitive telepathic communication. A karmic connection between the two individuals is a strong possibility, and they can act as catalysts, activating each other's karma. The relationship may involve secrecy or behind-the-scenes activities, or, in difficult relationships, some form of deception.

COMPARATIVE CONJUNCTIONS

When one person's Sun conjuncts planets in another person's horoscope, there is likely to be a dynamic interaction of wills. The Sun individual energizes the other in the affairs ruled by the planet the Sun is conjuncting. Much, however, depends on other aspects made to these conjunctions in the comparison and on other aspects made to the Sun and to the other planets in the comparative conjunction in the natives' individual horoscopes. If there are afflictions in either of the natal charts or in the comparative aspects affecting this conjunction, there can be a conflict of wills or a clash of egos. On the positive side, comparative conjunctions of the Sun can lead to dynamic, purposeful, and creative action and self-expression. The Sun individual can often help the other to be more self-confident.

A's Sun Conjunct B's Sun (A's ☉ ♂ B's ☉)

This comparative conjunction indicates that each individual concerned identifies strongly with the other's drive for creative self-expression. They understand each other. However, both may try to play the starring role in the relationship, with competition instead of cooperation as the result. This problem would become increasingly evident as time went on. Much depends on the sign in which the conjunction is found. Individuals with cooperation-oriented signs such as Aquarius or Libra have an easier time making a success of this conjunction than those whose signs are Leo or Aries, for example. The houses which the natal Suns occupy in each horoscope may help to provide enough difference in perspective so that the individuals can balance each other's drive for significance. This is especially true if the Suns are found in opposite houses. There is also the danger that individuals with the same Sun sign will goad each other to an excessive display of the characteristics of this sign.

The individuals will certainly have a significant effect on each other, but whether this is ultimately constructive or destructive will depend on their basic individual levels of maturity and the overall nature of the comparison, especially the aspects made by other planets to their Suns.

A's Sun Conjunct B's Moon (A's ☉ ☌ B's ☽)

In this comparative conjunction is found a natural yin-yang polarity of creative and receptive principles. The Sun person tends to have a strong effect on the Moon person, influencing or molding unconscious emotional attitudes. This relationship works better if the Sun person is naturally in a role of leadership, such as an employer with respect to an employee; otherwise, the Moon individual may feel his position is threatened. In a marriage relationship, this comparative aspect can indicate a strong sexual attraction, especially if the conjunction is made by the man's Sun to the woman's Moon. If the situation is reversed, the woman may tend to psychologically dominate the man and threaten his masculine self-image. If the relationship is a physical or emotional one, it tends to be more difficult in this respect than otherwise.

In most cases, the individuals tend to be natural friends. Mutual creative endeavors help to bring about an emotional understanding between the individuals, and a spirit of cooperation.

A's Sun Conjunct B's Mercury (A's ☉ ☌ B's ☿)

This comparative combination indicates a strong tendency for the Sun person's will and power potential to stimulate the Mercury person's thinking. At the same time, the Mercury person's ideas will inspire the Sun person to greater effort toward creative, positive self-expression. The two individuals have common intellectual interests, and their relationship is likely to be characterized by discussion about their work and all topics of mutual interest. The ability to communicate with each other is usually a positive factor. However, because of the neutral nature of Mercury, much depends on the nature of other aspects made to the Sun and Mercury in the comparison.

A's Sun Conjunct B's Venus (A's ☉ ☌ B's ♀)

Strong mutual attraction is indicated by this comparative combination. The individuals enjoy each other's company and have fun together. They are likely to share esthetic and cultural values and to go to concerts, plays, shows, and movies together. This can be a good comparative combination for partnerships pertaining to business, especially if the business relates to art, luxury items, entertainment, music, or the performing arts. There can also be a strong emotional, intuitive link, because of Venus's exaltation in Pisces. If other factors are favorable, this comparative aspect contributes greatly to romantic attraction and may indicate marriage.

A's Sun Conjunct B's Mars (A's ☉ ☌ B's ♂)

This is a dynamic comparative combination, which can lead to much mutual accomplishment. It can also produce severe ego conflicts. If the individuals are to get along harmoniously, they must respect each other's independence and free will. If this comparative combination occurs in an otherwise favorable comparison, the individuals can spark each other's energy and enthusiasm with constructive action and meaningful adventure. There is apt to be a sense of competition on a friendly sportsmanlike basis. In cases of severe afflictions to the conjunction, the competition can become quite vicious. This comparative combination can indicate a sexual attraction, but does not by itself indicate love or tenderness.

A's Sun Conjunct B's Jupiter (A's ☉ ☌ B's ♃)

This comparative combination is usually indicative of mutual generosity and kindness, especially on the part of the Jupiter person. The individuals find each other stimulating and bolster each other's self-confidence. They share many spiritual, philosophic, and cultural values, and enjoy each other's company in pleasurable pursuits and social gatherings.

This is one of the best of all comparative combinations for constructive cooperation. These individuals not only help each other out in time of need, but also join forces to help others. They support each other's efforts at self-improvement and ethical or spiritual growth. Usually, ulterior motives are put aside and the individuals deal with each other in an honorable, honest, and aboveboard manner. In a marriage relationship, this comparative combination indicates cooperation in handling domestic responsibilities, especially the raising of children.

A's Sun Conjunct B's Saturn (A's ☉ ☌ B's ♄)

This is a difficult comparative combination. The Saturn individual may tend to be jealous, dampening the Sun person's self-confidence and enthusiasm. If the rest of the comparison is favorable, this comparative aspect has the positive effect of enabling the individuals to work effectively together in business and professional matters or other areas of serious work and responsibility. The Sun person can boost the other's self-confidence, while the Saturn person can help the Sun person to be more practical, patient, and self-disciplined.

This comparative aspect does not favor romantic relationships or parent–child relationships, especially if the parent is the Saturn individual; the parent may discipline the child severely and lack emotional warmth. However, much depends on other aspects in the comparison.

A's Sun Conjunct B's Uranus (A's ☉ ♂ B's ♅)

This comparative combination produces exciting and unique relationships. A sudden magnetic fascination is not uncommon at the first meeting. The Uranus individual is apt to have many surprises in store for the Sun person, and, at times, the Sun person will find him very unpredictable. The Sun person helps to bring out qualities of uniqueness and originality, and each encourages the other's novel and highly individual approaches to self-expression. They are likely to share many exciting experiences and adventures in occult realms and unusual physical activities. There will be provocative exchanges in scientific, intuitive, or metaphysical areas. The individuals must respect each other's need for independence and free will or the relationship will break off as suddenly as it began. While this comparative combination often indicates sexual attraction, it does not, of itself, produce stability in a marriage or romantic relationship.

A's Sun Conjunct B's Neptune (A's ☉ ♂ B's ♆)

This comparative combination can produce a strong psychic link. Although the Sun person tends to perceive the Neptune individual as peculiar, elusive, mysterious, or even deceptive, the Neptune person can bring out the psychic, intuitive, and sometimes the spiritual levels of the Sun person's consciousness. The Sun individual can, in turn, help the Neptune individual to achieve intuitive awareness. Often, the individuals sense a karmic link or feel that they have known each other in a previous incarnation.

In a difficult comparison, the Sun person may attempt to dominate the

Neptune person, who may, in turn, become deceitful to circumvent this. The individuals may have a difficult time understanding each other. Vagueness, elusiveness, or problems of the unconscious mind of the Neptune person can stand in the way of an honest, open relationship.

A's Sun Conjunct B's Pluto (A's ☉ ☌ B's ♇)

This comparative combination is dynamic in much the same way as the Sun/Mars combination, only its effects are more subtle. Problems can arise from the Pluto person's attempts to alter the Sun individual's modes of self-expression. A clash of wills can result from the Sun person's attempts to dominate. If they are to get along effectively, each must respect the other's freedom.

If the rest of the comparison is favorable, the individuals can work together effectively to remold their environment in fields of mutual interest. They often participate in metaphysical, occult, or scientific endeavors. Each can encourage the other's determination to act and express himself more effectively. The Pluto person's psychic power in some way directly affects the Sun individual, who, in turn, stimulates and encourages occult tendencies in the Pluto person. This comparative combination can indicate sexual attraction, especially if the Fifth House of one or both individuals is involved in some way (aspects of the Sun or Pluto to rulers of the Fifth House or to planets in the Fifth House, and so on).

A's Sun Conjunct B's North Node Opposition B's South Node (A's ☉ ☌ B's ☊ ☍ B's ☋)

Relationships in which the individuals help each other to express themselves and to advance socially are favored by this comparative combination. The Nodes individual's awareness of social trends helps the Sun individual to receive more social recognition for creativity. The Sun individual may, in turn, give added energy and drive to the social ambitions of the Nodes individual. Each may play a crucial role in the timing of the other's career.

The individuals increase each other's good fortune in the affairs ruled by the houses in their respective natal charts where the Sun and North Node are found. This is an especially good comparative combination for people working in politics, art, theater, or other lines of work that depend upon public recognition.

A's Sun Conjunct B's South Node Opposition
B's North Node (A's ☉ ♂ B's ☋ ☍ B's ☊)

The Nodes individual in this comparative combination acts as a restraining influence on the Sun individual. If the Nodes individual keeps the Sun native from blindly following others and helps that person to be more individualistic in the face of social pressures, the effects of the aspect can be beneficial. In turn, the Sun individual may help the Nodes individual overcome fears of social disapproval that might have been handicapping.

A's Sun Conjunct B's Ascendant Opposition
B's Descendant (A's ☉ ♂ B's Asc. ☍ B's Desc.)

The Ascendant deals with a person's basic awareness of spiritual essence, and the Sun is concerned with basic life energy and self-expression, through its exaltation in Aries and the First House. Consequently, this comparative combination can indicate a strong spiritual link between two people.

Though, on the negative side, there can be danger of competition, these individuals can effectively reinforce each other's self-image, self-awareness, will power, and self-expression. If they take advantage of the positive influence of this comparative aspect, its effect can be very powerful.

A's Sun Conjunct B's Midheaven Opposition
B's Nadir (A's ☉ ♂ B's M.C. ☍ B's Nadir)

The will and creative expressions of the Sun individual can strongly affect the career and social status of the Midheaven/Nadir individual. In turn, the status and social position of the Midheaven/Nadir individual may help the Sun native toward more effective self-expression, especially in regard to improving public standing. This is a good comparative combination for cooperation in business, professional, and political matters. If the egos are allowed to be obstructive forces, however, there may be rivalry for power and importance.

A's Sun Conjunct B's Descendant Opposition
B's Ascendant (A's ☉ ☌ B's Desc. ☍ B's Asc.)

This comparative combination often produces romantic and sexual attractions, and is frequently found in marriages or other close partnerships. The individuals balance each other's self-awareness and self-expressions with opposite or complementary points of view, and thus compensate for each other's deficiencies. There also is likely to be sharing of social, cultural, and esthetic activities.

As in the "A's Sun Conjunct B's Ascendant Opposition B's Descendant," there can be a strong, spiritual link. Each mirrors the other's ego. This may produce conflict if either or both are immature and seek to blame someone else for those traits which they subconsciously dislike within themselves. Used positively, however, this reciprocal mirror effect can be a means of self-discovery for both. It is important for each to respect the other's self-determinism and independence if harmony is to be maintained in the relationship.

A's Sun Conjunct B's Nadir Opposition
B's Midheaven (A's ☉ ☌ B's Nadir ☍ B's M.C.)

The will and self-expressions of the Sun individual may stir up the roots of consciousness of the Midheaven/Nadir individual. The Midheaven/Nadir individual may provide a base of operations for the self-expressions of the Sun individual.

There are likely to be strong emotional ties in family and domestic relationships, which makes this an extremely important comparative aspect in parent–child relationships.

COMPARATIVE SEXTILES

The will, energy, and creative means of self-expression of the Sun individual can arouse new intellectual insights in the other native. The planets which form sextiles with the Sun can give the Sun individual greater insight into new methods and ways of creative self-expression. The Sun individual can encourage and energize the other. These comparative sextiles in a relationship improve the natives' ability to communicate in areas where there is dynamic mutual action. There is less danger of ego clashes here than with conjunctions, squares, and oppositions of the Sun in horoscopic comparisons. The Eleventh House significance of the sextile indicates that friendship is often the basis of these natives' relationship.

A's Sun Sextile B's Sun (A's ☉ ✳ B's ☉)

Friendship, communication, and cooperation in creative self-expression are favored by this comparative combination. The natives encourage the positive expression of each other's will and power potentials. They usually share pleasurable activities.

A's Sun Sextile B's Moon (A's ☉ ✳ B's ☽)

This comparative combination is good for cooperation and understanding. The Sun person tends to be the more active influence in the relationship. Male–female relationships with this sextile usually have fewer difficulties if the man's Sun aspects the woman's Moon. This is an especially good combination for family and domestic relationships and for business partnerships.

A's Sun Sextile B's Mercury (A's ☉ ✳ B's ☿)

This comparative combination favors communication and intellectual friendships and general cooperation. The Sun person puts power behind the Mercury native's ideas, which enables the Mercury person to both express them more forcefully and put them to practical use. The Mercury individual, in turn, gives the Sun person ideas and information which stimulate power drive and creative self-expression. This is a favorable comparative aspect for cooperation in groups and organizations, working partnerships, and co-worker or employer–employee relationships where communication of ideas and practical know-how is important. The natives' ability to communicate enables them to resolve problem areas in the relationship.

A's Sun Sextile B's Venus (A's ☉ ✳ B's ♀)

Mutual attraction and friendship are indicated by this comparative aspect. The natives enjoy each other's company and share esthetic and cultural values, as well as a sympathetic, emotional understanding. Marriage and romantic attractions are favored when this is confirmed by other influences in the comparison. The natives will share pleasurable activities. Business partnerships involving art, luxury items, entertainment, or social activities are favored.

A's Sun Sextile B's Mars (A's ☉ ✳ B's ♂)

This comparative combination favors energetic cooperation in efforts to improve matters that are of concern to both natives. This makes it a good comparative aspect for business partnerships. Each native stimulates the other's will power, strength, and determination to accomplish something significant. Thus, they further each other's professional goals and efforts toward self-improvement. The Sun native helps the Mars person develop more confidence and will power, and, in turn, receives energy and the impetus to achieve life goals. This comparative combination can help romantic attraction if other factors in the natal horoscopes confirm it. The natives enjoy friendly competition in sports and in games that involve physical exertion.

A's Sun Sextile B's Jupiter (A's ☉ ✳ B's ♃)

This is one of the best comparative combinations for friendship and for cooperation, especially in organizational and group work which has a social, humanitarian, religious, or charitable purpose. The natives encourage each other toward expansion and progress in business, family, cultural, spiritual, or educational areas. The Jupiter native is generous and helpful to the Sun person. The Sun individual helps the Jupiter individual express more confidence and will power. In most instances, the natives' ideas about cultural affairs, religion, philosophy, and education are compatible. This is also a good comparative aspect for cooperation in the home and in family relationships—it favors harmony and durability in the marriage. This is one of the best combinations for a parent–child or teacher–pupil relationship. The natives will also be good traveling companions.

A's Sun Sextile B's Saturn (A's ☉ ✳ B's ♄)

This comparative combination indicates cooperation in business, professional, and organizational matters, and also in serious friendships. The Saturn native will tend to restrain, discipline, and organize the Sun native, especially where the Sun person's creative self-expression is involved. The Sun native will help the Saturn overcome fear, doubt, excessive conservatism, and self-limitation. This comparative aspect works best when the Saturn native is older, especially in employer–employee, teacher–pupil, or parent–child relationships. In such cases, the Saturn individual exercises a maturing and guiding influence on the Sun native. This comparative combination can produce enduring friendships, with a strong sense of mutual purpose and responsibility. Often, this results from the natives' working together. The chances of durability in marriage are increased by this combination, but it does not of itself indicate romantic attraction.

A's Sun Sextile B's Uranus (A's ☉ ✳ B's ♅)

Since this comparative aspect indicates exciting and unusual friendships, natives often meet under extraordinary circumstances, and they seem to have an immediate and inexplicable attraction for each other. Although this comparative aspect can indicate romantic attraction, it does not, of itself, indicate an enduring relationship. Often, there is a strong intuitive link. The natives share interests in science, humanitarianism, or the occult, and they can work together effectively in groups and organizations in these fields. The Uranus native's originality helps the Sun native to be more open and creative in self-expression. The Sun native encourages the Uranus person's originality and efforts to attain freedom and independence. There is much mutual energizing without competition or interference with the other's self-determination or freedom.

A's Sun Sextile B's Neptune (A's ☉ ✳ B's ♆)

This comparative aspect can indicate a subtle intuitive link between the natives. The Neptune native's intuition and imagination can help the Sun person's creative self-expression. The Sun individual can, in turn, give the Neptune native more self-confidence in expressing and utilizing imagination and intuition. Together, they tend to expand each other's creative vision. They are likely to share many spiritual values and perceptions. This is a good comparative combination for cooperation in theatrical, artistic, psychic, and spiritual endeavors. There can also be great sensitivity and emotional rapport in family and domestic relationships. This aspect, by itself, is not a major factor in romantic attraction, but it can increase sensitivity and emotional rapport if other factors in the comparison indicate sexual or romantic attraction.

A's Sun Sextile B's Pluto (A's ☉ ⚹ B's ♇)

Natives with this comparative aspect will stimulate each other's will to accomplish something significant in the areas of creative self-expression and self-improvement. The natives will support each other in efforts to improve conditions and to exert constructive leadership in worthwhile endeavors. This is a favorable comparative aspect for mutual artistic endeavors, especially in areas related to the performing arts. The Pluto person can intensify the awareness of the Sun native, and the Sun person will help the Pluto bring insights out into the open. Often, they share an interest in science or the occult.

A's Sun Sextile B's North Node Trine
B's South Node (A's ☉ ⚹ B's ☊ △ B's ☋)

This comparative combination favors mutual creative expression that takes advantage of current beliefs and styles. This is particularly true if the natives are working in fields related to art or product design, politics, or public relations. The Nodes individual can give the Sun individual valuable insights into how to take advantage of current trends in creative self-expression, while the Sun individual gives the Nodes individual the enthusiasm and impetus to work with these trends.

A's Sun Sextile B's South Node Trine
B's North Node (A's ☉ ⚹ B's ☋ △ B's ☊)

Basically, this comparative combination has the same interpretation as "A's Sun Sextile B's North Node Trine B's South Node." Natives with this aspect, however, will be intellectually critical of prevailing social trends and popular beliefs.

A's Sun Sextile B's Ascendant Trine B's Descendant
(A's ☉ ⚹ B's Asc. △ B's Desc.)

This comparative combination indicates that the natives are able to direct their wills effectively in working together. They can combine their creative self-expression to achieve mutual goals and will help each other develop more confidence and better self-images. This comparative aspect can indicate romantic and sexual attraction. It is also favorable for harmony in a marriage relationship.

A's Sun Sextile B's Midheaven Trine B's Nadir
(A's ☉ ✶ B's M.C. △ B's Nadir)

Professional, political, domestic, and family cooperation are favored by this comparative combination. The Sun individual will encourage the Midheaven/Nadir individual to greater ambition and effort to achieve social status and professional success. Sometimes, the Midheaven/Nadir person provides a home and base of operations for the Sun person, and is instrumental in helping the Sun person to gain official support and recognition for creative endeavors. This is particularly true if the Sun individual is involved in artistic creativity. In family and marital relationships, this comparative combination confers financial and emotional security.

A's Sun Sextile B's Descendant Trine B's Ascendant
(A's ☉ ✶ B's Desc. △ B's Asc.)

This comparative combination has basically the same significance as "A's Sun Sextile B's Ascendant Trine B's Descendant." These natives, however, are more intellectually interested in the psychology of their relationship.

A's Sun Sextile B's Nadir Trine B's Midheaven
(A's ☉ ✶ B's Nadir △ B's M.C.)

This comparative combination has basically the same significance as "A's Sun Sextile B's Midheaven Trine B's Nadir." However, these natives will be more intellectually interested in the family and domestic aspects of their relationship and less interested in the professional aspects.

COMPARATIVE SQUARES

Contacts between natives with squares of the Sun in horoscopic comparisons usually produce ego conflicts. The Sun individual tends to be bossy or authoritarian. The natives can differ over ways of organizing and handling activities. Other obstacles and impediments can make it difficult for the natives to relate to each other, especially in career and domestic affairs. If these natives are to get along, they must practice patience and mutual respect. If both natives are mature and capable of self-discipline, these comparative aspects can produce effective and dynamic mutual action and solid accomplishment.

A's Sun Square B's Sun (A's ☉ □ B's ☉)

The ego conflicts often produced by this comparative aspect take the form of the natives' interfering with each other's creative self-expression. Their tendency to try to boss each other around generally meets with resistance and resentment. There can be serious differences of attitude in major areas. This is a particularly difficult comparative aspect for persons who must work together in the arts or the theater. It also indicates problems in romance and courtship. In a marriage relationship, raising children is often a problem area.

A's Sun Square B's Moon (A's ☉ □ B's ☽)

This is a difficult comparative combination for family, marital, and romantic relationships. The Moon native will see the Sun individual as overbearing and insensitive. The Sun person will see the Moon native as moody, emotionally temperamental, and lazy. The natives' ability to adjust to each other's temperaments, as well as general pace and style of living, is doubtful. Major disagreements about the handling of finances, business affairs, and the raising of children often arise. Frequently, these are the results of differences in family background or deep-seated emotional habit patterns, especially on the part of the Moon native.

A's Sun Square B's Mercury (A's ☉ □ B's ☿)

This comparative combination tends to cause communication difficulties in a relationship. The Mercury person sees the Sun native as domineering. The Sun person sees the Mercury individual as inconsistent, vacillating, scatterbrained, and evasive. The Mercury person's ideas can confuse the Sun person or in some way threaten pride. The Sun native's bossiness may cause the Mercury person to feel put upon or interfered with. Employer–employee, friend, teacher–pupil, or parent–

child relationships are often disrupted because of the major differences in intellectual or work-related matters.

A's Sun Square B's Venus (A's ☉ □ B's ♀)

This comparative aspect indicates difficulties in emotional adjustment between the natives. The Venus person may see the Sun person as overbearing, bossy, or lacking in emotional sensitivity. The Sun native may see the Venus as frivolous or emotionally hypersensitive. Although this combination can produce romantic and sexual attraction, it is not favorable for marriage or serious romantic relationships. Real emotional sensitivity and caring are likely to be lacking, and the relationship will probably be based on pleasure-seeking and sensuality, unless other factors in the comparison compensate. Competition or serious differences in taste can arise in esthetic, social, and cultural matters. The natives can disagree about handling finances, or encourage each other's tendencies to make unwise expenditures. Sometimes, they bring out each other's laziness and hedonistic qualities. In parent–child relationships, there is danger of overindulgence.

A's Sun Square B's Mars (A's ☉ □ B's ♂)

One of the most difficult of all comparative aspects, this can produce the most violent conflicts and disagreements. The level on which these are expressed depends on the nature of the individuals involved and on the overall comparison of the horoscope. In extreme cases, there can be physical combat. In general, the Mars native's aggressiveness and desires pose a threat to the Sun native's ego, while the Sun native's bossiness arouses rebellion and resentment in the Mars person. This is not a good comparative combination for business, professional, romantic, or marital relationships: the natives are likely to react to each other impulsively rather than thoughtfully, and a sense of competition can cause them to goad each other to extremes. However, if one native becomes passive and allows domination by the other, that person's psychological well-being or health may suffer.

A's Sun Square B's Jupiter (A's ☉ □ B's ♃)

In this comparative combination whatever tendency the natives may have to extravagance, overconfidence, and overextending themselves can be increased. They tend to encourage each other's tendencies to self-indulgence and impracticality. There can be serious differences of opinion regarding religion, philosophy, education, ethics, or politics. This is not a favorable combination for family and domestic relationships, since one or both natives are apt to take too much for granted. Permissiveness is a problem in parent–child relationships. In romantic relationships, difficulties can arise over different philosophic, religious, or moral viewpoints. Neither is this a good combination for business and professional relationships: as a rule, the natives are not disciplined or practical in their influence on each other; they tend to ignore responsibility and let things take care of themselves, which, of course, does not happen.

A's Sun Square B's Saturn (A's ☉ □ B's ♄)

This comparative combination is one of the most difficult to work with in a relationship. The Sun native feels repressed and squelched by the negativity of the Saturn person. The Saturn person is likely to feel that the Sun native is too impulsive and impatient and a threat to position and authority. This combination can produce ego conflicts and a clash of wills. In some cases, the Saturn native will be jealous and try to hold the Sun person back. This is not a good comparative combination for business and professional relationships or for parent–child relationships, especially if the parent is the Saturn person. It also tends to create coldness and difficulty in marriage and friendships. In a marriage relationship, the Saturn person will make things difficult for the Sun person and cause him to be discouraged. In some cases, the natives may feel their responsibility to each other as a burden and find it difficult to be fun-loving and spontaneous in each other's presence.

A's Sun Square B's Uranus (A's ☉ □ B's ♅)

Strong attractions of short duration and strong ego conflicts can be produced in this comparative combination. The Uranus person rebels against the authoritarian attitude of the Sun native. The Sun native finds the Uranus native unpredictable, unreliable, and touchy. The natives must work hard to respect each other's freedom if they are to get along. There can be disagreements over friends, group activities, and pleasurable pursuits. The Sun person will be likely to consider the Uranus person "way out" and perhaps even unbalanced, and will be unable to appreciate the Uranus person's interest in unusual scientific pursuits or in the occult. This is not a good comparative aspect for business relationships; cooperation is very difficult.

A's Sun Square B's Neptune (A's ☉ □ B's ♆)

This comparative combination can produce many confusions and misunderstandings in a relationship. The Neptune person is likely to be unreliable and deceptive toward the Sun native. The Sun person tends to be bossy and authoritarian toward the Neptune native, and the Neptune native's defense will be evasiveness. There is often an element of dishonesty in the relationship, whether on a conscious or subconscious level. The Sun person is likely to regard the Neptune person as off in a dream world or spaced out. The Sun person may stimulate unhealthy subconscious emotional reactions in the Neptune native by subconsciously reminding him of painful experiences of the past. In some cases, the natives encourage unhealthy escapist tendencies in each other—drinking, drug-taking, or idle pursuits of pleasure. The Neptune individual tends to drain the energy of the Sun native. This comparative combination can also produce ego conflicts on a very subtle level.

A's Sun Square B's Pluto (A's ☉ □ B's ♀)

This comparative combination can produce a power struggle. The Pluto native resists the Sun native's authoritarian tendencies, and the Sun native resents and resists the Pluto individual's attempts to try to mold or reform him. They can disagree over the handling of joint finances, inheritances, insurance, alimony, or corporate money. Animosity can arise over different approaches to the occult or metaphysical. The Sun person may feel interfered with or invaded by the psychic power of the Pluto person. They are likely to vie with each other for power in some situation of mutual importance. Marital or romantic relationships can suffer from sexual difficulties, often as a result of the Pluto individual's aggressiveness or demands.

A's Sun Square B's North Node Square B's South Node
(A's ☉ □ B's ☊ □ B's ☋)

The will and dynamic self-expression of the Sun individual can conflict with the sense of social timing and propriety of the Nodes individual. The Nodes individual may feel that the Sun individual is on an ego trip, forcing personal modes of self-expression on the prevailing social scene in socially unacceptable, inappropriate ways. The Sun individual is apt to feel that the Nodes person lacks individuality and is a programmed robot of the culture. How serious these problems are depends on the rest of the comparison.

A's Sun Square B's South Node Square B's North Node

See A's Sun Square B's North Node Square B's South Node.

A's Sun Square B's Ascendant Square B's Descendant
(A's ⊙ □ B's Asc. □ B's Desc.)

This comparative combination is likely to produce a clash of wills. The Ascendant/Descendant individual may feel that the Sun person is overbearing, bossy, or unreasonable. The individuals can regard each other as too self-centered, and can threaten each other's independence and authority. On the positive side, if the overall comparison is good and both individuals are sufficiently mature, there can be a dynamic cooperation in their mutual activities.

A's Sun Square B's Midheaven Square B's Nadir
(A's ⊙ □ B's M.C. □ B's Nadir)

The self-expression, power, and authority of the Sun individual can be a threat to the status, professional position, and domestic security of the Midheaven/Nadir individual. The Midheaven/Nadir person's entrenched position or need for security can block the Sun person's self-expression. The Sun native's need for social, romantic, and artistic expression may conflict with the Midheaven/Nadir person's more practical concerns for status and domestic security. The Sun individual seeks change as a means of personal advancement, while the Midheaven/Nadir individual has vested interests in maintaining the status quo.

A's Sun Square B's Descendant Square B's Ascendant

See A's Sun Square B's Ascendant Square B's Descendant.

A's Sun Square B's Nadir Square B's Midheaven

See A's Sun Square B's Midheaven Square B's Nadir.

COMPARATIVE TRINES

These comparative combinations make for dynamic, positive, creative relationships. They are especially good in parent–child, teacher–student, and romantic relationships, and they favor collaboration in creative, artistic endeavors, especially in the performing arts. The Sun individual will energize the other native, helping him or her to greater self-confidence, energy, and will power. There will be cooperation in the affairs ruled by the planet which the Sun trines.

A's Sun Trine B's Sun (A's ☉ △ B's ☉)

This is an excellent comparative combination for general mutual compatibility. The natives have many similar values and, hence, tend to be natural friends. This is a helpful influence in romantic attraction and marriage, and it is a particularly good combination for parent–child relationships and for cooperation in artistic endeavors, especially those related to the performing arts. The natives will support each other's creative self-expression and strengthen each other's will. There is enough similarity in their creative self-expression to make for compatibility, but not so much as to cause competition. The emphasis of the relationship will be strongly influenced by the quality of the element (Fire, Air, Earth, or Water) in which the two natal Suns are found. For instance, if one person has Sun in Taurus trine the other person's Sun in Capricorn, the relationship would tend to center around practical business affairs characteristic of Earth signs.

A's Sun Trine B's Moon (A's ☉ △ B's ☽)

This is an excellent comparative combination for romantic and marital relationships, especially if the man's Sun is trine the woman's Moon. It is also a good combination for parent–child relationships, family and domestic relationships, and business relationships. The Moon individual is receptive to the energy and creative self-expression of the Sun individual, while the Sun individual can benefit by the practical, domestic abilities of the Moon individual. The Sun individual tends to initiate action and take on the leadership role in the relationship, unless other factors in the comparison indicate otherwise. The Moon person can have an emotionally calming effect on the Sun person. As with the Sun trine Sun aspect, this combination will take on the coloring of whatever element (Fire, Air, Earth, or Water) this trine occurs in.

A's Sun Trine B's Mercury (A's ☉ △ B's ☿)

Excellent communication between the individuals is indicated by this comparative combination. It is a good combination for employer–employee relationships, co-worker relationships, parent–child relationships, teacher–student relationships, friendships, and sibling relationships. The natives stimulate each other intellectually and share many cultural, educational, scientific, or literary interests. They can work effectively together as members of a group which has a cultural, educational, or scientific purpose. The ability of these natives to communicate and talk over any mutual difficulties can to some extent offset adverse aspects in the rest of the comparison. The Mercury individual can act as an adviser to the Sun native, giving him ideas for more effective forms of creative self-expression and the exercise of leadership. The Sun person inspires the Mercury native to more self-confidence and will power in the creative expression of ideas.

A's Sun Trine B's Venus (A's ☉ △ B's ♀)

This is a good comparative combination for romantic and sexual attraction and marriage. The natives enjoy each other's company and have fun together. There is good emotional rapport and mutual sensitivity and generosity. The natives are likely to share artistic, cultural, musical, or theatrical interests. This is also a good combination for business cooperation, especially in the areas of art, luxury items, or entertainment. Married couples with this combination enjoy raising children together, and parent–child relationships are favored. The natives will encourage each other to be more outgoing and self-expressive socially.

A's Sun Trine B's Mars (A's ☉ △ B's ♂)

In this dynamic comparative combination the natives support each other's efforts toward self-improvement. Both will be ambitious and energetic in improving the conditions of their lives. This is a good combination for business and professional relationships, especially in fields related to engineering, construction, or corporate finance. The natives often have a strong sense of camaraderie and friendly competition, and share interest in outdoor, physical sports and games. This combination can also contribute to sexual attraction in a romantic relationship.

A's Sun Trine B's Jupiter (A's ☉ △ B's ♃)

This comparative combination endows all types of relationships with a harmony and mutual helpfulness found nowhere else in horoscopic comparisons. Relationships are characterized by a strong sense of trust. The Jupiter individual is generous, benevolent, and optimistic toward the Sun person, while the Sun person vitalizes and encourages the Jupiter. Cultural, religious, spiritual, family, and domestic values are shared. This is an excellent comparative aspect for family relationships in general, especially parent–child relationships. In a romantic or marital relationship, it produces cultural and spiritual values that give durability and lasting value to the relationship. The natives can be excellent traveling companions.

A's Sun Trine B's Saturn (A's ☉ △ B's ♄)

This is a good comparative combination for business and professional relationships. The Saturn person steadies, disciplines, and organizes the Sun person, while the Sun person encourages and gives more self-confidence to the Saturn native. This comparative combination works best in relationships where there is a sharing of work and practical responsibilities, especially when the Saturn individual is older and can act in a natural teacher, boss, or parental role. This comparative aspect, of itself, does not produce romantic attraction, but it can greatly increase the stability and durability of a marriage. The natives are usually conscientious about their practical and moral responsibilities toward each other. They work together well in groups and organizations and generally make steadfast and loyal friends.

A's Sun Trine B's Uranus (A's ☉ △ B's ♅)

Since this comparative combination makes for exciting friendships and romances, the natives often meet under extraordinary circumstances and have a strong magnetic attraction for each other. The Uranus person inspires the Sun person with original, creative ideas, while the Sun individual energizes and gives more self-confidence to the Uranus individual's efforts to achieve personal freedom and self-expression. The natives often share interests in scientific, occult, astrological, or esoteric studies and are likely to participate together in organizations in those fields, and in other organizational and group activities. Although this comparative combination contributes to sexual attraction and romantic excitement, other factors in the comparison must be looked to for stability in this kind of relationship. The natives always maintain a strong feeling of mutual friendship and generally respect each other's need for freedom and independence.

A's Sun Trine B's Neptune (A's ☉ △ B's ♆)

Interesting and sometimes psychic relationships are produced by this comparative combination. It can improve mutual psychological insight in a relationship, especially in the realm of the subconscious and past conditioning. The Neptune person's imagination and intuition can bring out the Sun person's creativity and self-expression, while the Sun native can help the Neptune individual express imagination and intuition openly and self-assuredly. The Neptune individual, especially, has a high degree of emotional sensitivity toward the other. This comparative aspect can increase romantic feelings and idealism in a romantic or marital relationship, but it does not, of itself, guarantee stability or practicality in such a relationship. The natives share musical, artistic, spiritual, religious, or psychic interests.

A's Sun Trine B's Pluto (A's ☉ △ B's ♀)

The comparative combination is excellent for mutual reinforcement in creativity, self-improvement, and improving the environment. The natives have a positive effect on each other's will power and determination to bring about constructive change. They often share an interest in occult, metaphysical, or scientific subjects. This can be an effective comparative combination for corporate and mutual financial speculation. Because of the double-Fifth House connotation, it also favors mutual artistic, creative endeavors, especially in the performing arts. It increases sexual attraction in romantic relationships. There is often a strong intuitive link between the natives.

A's Sun Trine B's North Node Sextile B's South Node

See A's Sun Sextile B's South Node Trine B's North Node.

A's Sun Trine B's South Node Sextile B's North Node

See A's Sun Sextile B's North Node Trine B's South Node.

A's Sun Trine B's Ascendant Sextile B's Descendant

See A's Sun Sextile B's Descendant Trine B's Ascendant.

A's Sun Trine B's Midheaven Sextile B's Nadir

See A's Sun Sextile B's Nadir Trine B's Midheaven.

A's Sun Trine B's Descendant Sextile B's Ascendant

See A's Sun Sextile B's Ascendant Trine B's Descendant.

A's Sun Trine B's Nadir Sextile B's Midheaven

See A's Sun Sextile B's Midheaven Trine B's Nadir.

COMPARATIVE OPPOSITIONS

These comparative oppositions make for strong and dynamic personal interaction in the affairs ruled by the planet which the Sun opposes and by the houses occupied and ruled by the Sun. Oppositions of the Sun are frequent in marriages and other partnerships because of the natural Seventh House/Libra significance of the opposition aspect. If Venus or the ruler of the Fifth House is involved in the opposition, romantic attraction can result. If both natives are mature, they can cooperate effectively and dynamically, but, if they are not, ego conflicts are likely to arise. Neither native should try to dominate the other.

A's Sun Opposition B's Sun (A's ☉ ☍ B's ☉)

This comparative combination is often found in marriages and other close personal relationships, inasmuch as the opposition aspect is basically a relationship aspect. The natives can balance each other and complement each other's deficiencies. There can be a strong attraction, and the natives are important to each other. However, there can also be a clash of wills and egos, and the natives must respect each other's personal autonomy if they are to get along. Any attempt on the part of either to boss the other around will meet with resistance and resentment. Because the Sun is the natural ruler of the Fifth House, this combination indicates sexual and romantic attraction. It also favors parent–child relationships.

A's Sun Opposition B's Moon (A's ☉ ☍ B's ☽)

In this comparative aspect, found in many marital and other important relationships, the Sun individual is the more dynamic influence, while the Moon person is receptive. Consequently, in terms of traditional concepts of a marriage relationship, it is better if the man's Sun is in opposition to the woman's Moon than otherwise. This comparative combination intensifies emotional issues in family, domestic, and financial areas. In some cases, the Moon individual feels overpowered by the Sun individual, who tends to view the other as weak, indecisive, or hung up in the past. The Moon individual can sometimes be vague and behave inconsistently toward the Sun individual, and the Sun native becomes irritated by the Moon individual's moodiness and may hurt feelings.

A's Sun Opposition B's Mercury (A's ☉ ☍ B's ☿)

Extensive communication between two people is indicated by this comparative aspect. The quality and kind of communication and the fields in which it is concentrated are determined by whatever planets most strongly aspect the Sun and Mercury in the natives' natal horoscopes. Problems in communication can result from the natives' widely varying ideas and viewpoints, but if communication is successful, the individuals arrive at a balanced and comprehensive understanding of their relationship and of life in general. Because Mercury is a neutral planet, this comparative aspect, of itself, does not indicate a romantic attraction unless it is involved in some way with the Fifth House or its ruler. This can be an effective comparative combination for business, professional, or scientific relationships, if other factors in the comparison agree.

A's Sun Opposition B's Venus (A's ☉ ☍ B's ♀)

This comparative aspect is frequently found in romantic attractions and marriages. If other factors in the comparison indicate a harmonious relationship, the natives will enjoy deep friendship and be fond of each other's company. When the negative side of the opposition comes out, however, the Venus individual can feel dominated and overpowered by the Sun individual's ego and power drive, and the Sun individual may feel that the Venus individual is lazy and self-indulgent or else overly sensitive or effete. Much depends on the relative strength of the Sun and Venus in the natives' natal horoscopes. There can be a mutual enjoyment of and participation in social activities such as parties, theater, concerts, or other esthetic, cultural activities. Business partnerships related to art, music, luxury items, and show business are favored. In some cases, this comparative combination contributes to sympathetic, emotional understanding between the natives, especially on the part of the Venus individual.

A's Sun Opposition B's Mars (A's ☉ ☍ B's ♂)

The conflict of wills often produced by this comparative aspect can result in competition, arguments, fights, or power struggles. The Sun native is likely to resent the Mars individual's impulsiveness and agressiveness, while the Mars native resents the Sun native's bossiness and authoritarian tendencies. If the rest of the comparison shows a potential for cooperation, and if the natives have sufficient psychological maturity, they can work together energetically and effectively. However, they must respect each other's free will.

A's Sun Opposition B's Jupiter (A's ☉ ☍ B's ♃)

This comparative combination can be a mixed blessing. The natives are usually kindly disposed and generous toward each other, but they can encourage each other to various excesses and overindulgences that can be very harmful to one or both. Sometimes the Jupiter native's moralizing or preaching antagonizes the Sun person, while the Sun native can seem overly proud and egotistical to the Jupiter individual. There may be differences over religious and philosophic beliefs, as well as practical difficulties in family and domestic matters.

A's Sun Opposition B's Saturn (A's ☉ ☍ B's ♄)

The probability of mutual jealousy and clashes of personal authority make this a difficult relationship. The Saturn native tends to squelch the Sun individual's enthusiasm and self-expression, while the Sun native may threaten the Saturn native's authority and position and seem proud and conceited. The natives must respect each other's autonomy and not boss each other around if the relationship is to be worthwhile. The handling of serious mutual responsibilities will be a major issue. If both parties are sufficiently mature and the rest of the comparison is favorable, they can work together effectively in business and professional relationships and have rewarding friendships. This is not a favorable comparative aspect for romantic attraction. It also indicates difficulties in parent–child relationships, particularly if the parent is the Saturn individual: the child is likely to feel unloved and too severely disciplined. Contestants in lawsuits frequently have this aspect in their horoscopic comparisons.

A's Sun Opposition B's Uranus (A's ☉ ☍ B's ♅)

This comparative combination can produce a clash of wills. The Uranus individual's desire for freedom and independence is likely to clash with the Sun native's authoritarian tendencies. The natives must show absolute respect for each other's freedom if they are to get along. The Sun individual may regard the Uranus person as eccentric, impractical, unreasonable, or unreliable. This comparative combination can produce sudden romantic infatuations, but they are usually not stable or longlasting. The natives often meet suddenly and under unusual circumstances and are involved in many exciting adventures together. If both individuals are mature and there are many other good aspects in the comparison, a dynamic, interesting friendship and mutual sharing of humanitarian, scientific, or occult interests are possible. The natives can act as catalysts for change in each other's lives.

A's Sun Opposition B's Neptune (A's ☉ ☍ B's ♆)

This tends to be a difficult comparative combination: the Neptune individual is confusing and evasive toward the Sun individual, while the authoritarian tendencies of the Sun individual can disturb the more delicate psychic, esthetic, and emotional sensitivities of the Neptune individual. Although this comparative combination indicates a peculiar type of romantic attraction, such a relationship is likely to suffer from much confusion and misunderstanding. The Neptune individual has a subtle psychic effect on the Sun individual. Subliminal messages and conscious or unconscious telepathic interchanges are a definite factor in the relationship. The natives can share and exchange musical, theatrical, esthetic, and psychological or psychic perceptions and appreciations. Their association can have an element of fascination, romance, and intrigue. However, deceptiveness or evasion of honest confrontation in important areas of the relationship can cause a breakdown of the relationship. Even with the best of intentions, there can be confusion and misrepresentation. Both individuals must be mature and willing to work at the relationship for it to be successful.

A's Sun Opposition B's Pluto (A's ☉ ☍ B's ♀)

A dynamic comparative combination, this often produces, however, a clash of wills. If the Pluto individual is more dynamic and has a more powerful will than the Sun individual, the Pluto may try to dominate the Sun individual psychically. The Sun individual may resent the Pluto individual's attempts to reform or change his character. In turn, the authoritarian or egotistical tendencies of the Sun individual can cause the Pluto individual to react negatively.

A's Sun Opposition B's North Node Conjunct B's South Node

See A's Sun Conjunct B's South Node Opposition B's North Node.

A's Sun Opposition B's South Node Conjunct B's North Node

See A's Sun Conjunct B's North Node Opposition B's South Node.

A's Sun Opposition B's Ascendant Conjunct B's Descendant

See A's Sun Conjunct B's Descendant Opposition B's Ascendant.

A's Sun Opposition B's Midheaven Conjunct B's Nadir

See A's Sun Conjunct B's Nadir Opposition B's Midheaven.

A's Sun Opposition B's Descendant Conjunct B's Ascendant

See A's Sun Conjunct B's Ascendant Opposition B's Descendant.

A's Sun Opposition B's Nadir Conjunct B's Midheaven

See A's Sun Conjunct B's Midheaven Opposition B's Nadir.

VIII
Moon

Comparative influences of the Moon indicate the means by which the Moon individual's automatic habit responses, family upbringing, and cultural conditionings will affect a relationship. The specific nature of these effects will depend upon both natal and comparative aspects of the sign and house placement of the Moon.

Harmonious comparative influences can provide the natives with an emotional understanding of one another. The Moon native will lend domestic support to the activities and endeavors of the other native in the affairs designated by the Moon's comparative position.

Stress aspects to the position of the Moon in the comparison can cause the subconscious emotional hangups, inhibitions, and family conditionings of the Moon native to be a source of irritation and annoyance to the other individual in the relationship. The domestic habits of the Moon native can also become a source of conflict.

COMPARATIVE HOUSE PLACEMENTS

Comparative house placements of the Moon indicate the way in which the emotional habits, the family conditioning, and the domestic affairs of the Moon individual influence the practical affairs of the other native's life. The affairs ruled by the house in which the Moon falls will be the source of emotional confrontations, and the families of one or both natives may influence or interfere in these affairs.

A's Moon in B's First House

A close emotional link in important relationships is indicated by this combination. The self-expression of the First House individual will strongly affect the emotional reactions of the Moon individual. If the Moon is linked with the Fifth House in any way in either horoscope, this combination can be a strong indicator of romantic attraction.

Family and domestic affairs will be one of the major issues in the relationship. The Moon individual's domestic life is likely to be affected by the First House individual. This comparative placement can indicate strong emotional ties in family relationships. In a parent–child relationship, this can be too much of a good thing, and the child may find it difficult to be emotionally independent of the parents in later years. The natives tend to remind each other of their family upbringing and early childhood, and thus bring out each other's habitual psychological responses. Whether this effect is positive or negative depends on other factors in the comparison and on how the Moon is aspected. In some cases, the Moon individual may irritate the First House individual with moodiness and emotional problems, and, if the Moon is unfavorably aspected or the overall comparison is difficult, the First House individual could emotionally upset the Moon individual.

A's Moon in B's Second House

This combination frequently occurs in mutual business activities relating to food, restaurants, real estate, or domestic products and services, especially in family businesses. The family and domestic affairs of the Moon individual are likely to influence the financial affairs of the Second House individual, and in turn, the financial fortunes of the Second House individual can have an emotional impact on the Moon individual. This can be a good combination for business partnerships, because of the Moon's accidental exaltation in the Second House, which corresponds to Taurus in the natural Zodiac. In some cases, the natives will share an enjoyment of luxuries or other sensuous pleasures, such as dining together.

A's Moon in B's Third House

Communication about personal, emotional, family, and domestic issues and about small everyday occurrences is characteristic of this combination. The emotional reactions of the Moon individual influence the thinking and manner of communication of the Third House individual, while the ideas and communications of the Third House individual can have an emotional impact on the Moon individual. Too much useless talk about petty inconsequential affairs can be a problem in these relationships, and can interfere with work efficiency or with real communication in areas of vital importance. There can be sharing of educational and intellectual activities in the home. The Third House individual can help the Moon individual with business and financial ideas and plans.

If this combination is favorably aspected, it can improve communication about family, domestic, and personal emotional issues.

A's Moon in B's Fourth House

This combination makes for a close personal relationship where family and domestic issues are concerned. The natives are often members of the same family or live in the same household. They have a strong emotional connection based on family ties or similar family experiences. There is a sort of psychic attunement of the feelings, based on early childhood conditioning and ingrained emotional attitudes.

The natives will nurture each other emotionally and in matters of food and domestic comfort. They may supply each other financially with the necessities and comforts of life, and they could be involved together in financial affairs related to real estate, food, domestic products, and perhaps farming. The family and domestic conditions of the Fourth House individual will affect the emotional responses of the Moon individual. The Moon individual will reinforce and encourage the Fourth House individual's domestic tendencies.

A's Moon in B's Fifth House

This comparative placement can indicate emotional, romantic attraction. If the relationship is a romantic one, domestic and family affairs will play an important part. The natives may choose to live together without marriage. In some romances, one individual may play a parental role toward the other. Married or not, these natives often have a strong mutual interest in establishing a family and having children, and this can strengthen and make more meaningful their romantic and sexual attraction. Parents and children with this combination can have unusually strong emotional ties.

The natives will tend to stimulate each other's artistic and creative imaginations. They will enjoy pursuing social activities and pleasure-oriented activities together. They will enjoy having meals and dining together. If the Moon is favorably aspected, this can be a good combination for business partnerships related to art and entertainment. The imagination of the Moon individual will bring out the creative abilities in the Fifth House individual. In turn, the Fifth House individual will bring social and artistic activities into the Moon individual's home.

A's Moon in B's Sixth House

In all relationships with this placement, which is often found in employer–employee relationships or in other relationships related to work and service, proper performance of everyday small duties and responsibilities will be significant. The Sixth House individual will bring improved methodology and efficiency to the domestic activities and dietary habits of the Moon individual. The Moon individual will, in turn, make the working environment or dietary habits of the Sixth House individual more pleasant and enjoyable. Both natives will be interested in matters of diet and family health. Neatness and cleanliness in housekeeping can become an important issue. If the Moon is afflicted, the personal hygiene and housekeeping habits of the Moon individual can irritate the Sixth House individual.

A's Moon in B's Seventh House

This comparative combination is frequently found in romantic and marital relationships. The possibility of romantic attraction is especially strong if the Moon individual's Moon conjuncts the other native's Descendant. The families of one or both parties can play an important part in the relationship. Because the natives often live under the same roof, domestic issues can be of consequence in how they get along. Marriage can be entered into for the purpose of establishing a home and family or achieving domestic security.

The relationship of these individuals will be subject to many ups and downs, according to changing moods and emotional reactions. They are usually keenly aware of each other's moods and feelings. This can be a good combination for business partnerships involved in family businesses or for businesses related to farming, real estate, food, or domestic products.

The Seventh House individual will bring social activities into the home of the Moon individual. The Moon individual can provide the Seventh House individual with emotional support and understanding.

A's Moon in B's Eighth House

This combination can be important in business relationships or family relationships where inheritances or the financial settlements of divorce are issues. If the Moon is afflicted in the Moon individual's natal horoscope or in the comparison, there can be struggle and conflict over these issues. On the positive side, this can be a good combination for business relations or partnerships dealing with real estate, farming, food, building, restaurants, or home and domestic products. Business and financial affairs of the relationship can be related to the family affairs of one or both natives. All these affairs will be subject to difficult emotional factors, especially for the Moon individual. The Eighth House individual can influence the domestic affairs of the Moon individual through joint finances and related business activities. The Moon individual will give emotional support to the business activities of the Eighth House individual. In some cases, the natives may stimulate each other's interest in occult or psychic phenomena.

A's Moon in B's Ninth House

Family influences, especially early childhood conditioning, are likely to affect, favorably or unfavorably, the natives' ability to agree on or accept each other's religious, ethical, social, and moral values. In a family or marital relationships, how these matters are incorporated into the natives' family life will be of major concern. Mutual business and financial concerns are likely to relate to education or mutual travel plans.

If the overall comparison is good, these natives can enjoy each other as traveling companions. The Moon individual can help the Ninth House individual to incorporate his religious, educational, and cultural values into everyday affairs, and the Ninth House individual can help the Moon individual to overcome limited habitual points of view toward religion, philosophy, culture, and education.

A's Moon in B's Tenth House

The career and status of the Tenth House individual in this combination will affect the home and domestic conditions, as well as the emotional well-being, of the Moon individual, either favorably or unfavorably. The Tenth House individual will, through professional activities, provide status and financial security for the Moon individual. The Moon individual can, in turn, help the Tenth House individual by providing a home or base of operations.

This combination is often found in professional or business relationships, especially where finances are concerned. The natives' business associations can relate to food, real estate, building, and household items or domestic goods and services.

The natives may be brought together through similar family backgrounds or through family connections, and the parents of one or both natives may be a significant factor in the relationship. Some relationships with this placement are entered into because of a desire on the part of one or both natives for security and status.

A's Moon in B's Eleventh House

This combination is good for friendships and group associations. The natives will treat each other like members of their own families. They will be able to share their feelings and emotional reactions, and are likely to spend a great deal of time in each other's homes. There can also be cooperation in social activities centered around family or domestic issues or around cooking and entertaining for group and organizational gatherings. The natives will have a common interest in everyday family and business occurrences, and they will often form friendships as a result of family connections or everyday business transactions.

The Eleventh House individual can help the Moon person expand intellectual and social horizons and will introduce new and interesting friends and acquaintances. The Moon individual can, in turn, provide a home or meeting place for the friendly get-togethers or group and organizational activities of the Eleventh House individual.

A's Moon in B's Twelfth House

Because this combination makes for a strong emotional and intuitive link, the natives will be intensely aware of each other's subconscious moods and feelings. On the positive side, this will make for sympathetic understanding, empathy, and mutual compassion. However, if the overall horoscopic comparison is unfavorable and if the Moon is afflicted, the natives may stimulate each other's self-destructive tendencies and encourage each other's subconscious self-deceptions and hangups. There can be a psychic link between them which can influence their attitudes toward each other through a process of subconscious telepathy. They may have a karmic relationship in their family or financial affairs. The Moon individual can stimulate the deep-seated subconscious memories of the Twelfth House individual, but whether this is positive or negative depends upon the overall comparison. The Twelfth House individual can awaken the Moon individual to a deeper level of intuitive awareness. Deception and dishonesty in feelings and attitudes should be avoided at all costs in these relationships.

COMPARATIVE CONJUNCTIONS

Comparative conjunctions of the Moon indicate the ways in which the natives will influence each other dynamically in their financial, family, and domestic affairs. These influences usually have considerable emotional impact, especially when they relate to deep-rooted unconscious emotional habits that are based on family conditioning and early childhood experiences.

These comparative aspects are especially important if the natives belong to the same family or live together in the same household. They are also a significant factor in business partnerships or other financial relationships. The natives can influence each other to display more initiative in business affairs related to farming, real estate, food, the home, and domestic products and services.

The Moon individual can provide a home or base of operations for the activities of the other native that are related to the affairs ruled by the planet which the Moon conjuncts in the comparison.

If comparative conjunctions of the Moon are afflicted by other comparative aspects, the Moon individual is likely to indulge in moodiness and emotional outbursts, and this can have an annoying effect on the other native.

The emotional nature of affairs of the relationship will be indicated by the signs and houses ruled and occupied by the Moon in A's horoscope and the conjuncting planet or planets in B's horoscope.

A's Moon Conjunct B's Sun

See A's Sun Conjunct B's Moon.

A's Moon Conjunct B's Moon (A's ☽ ☌ B's ☽)

This comparative combination often indicates emotional empathy in a relationship; the natives go through moods and emotional changes simultaneously. This can aid their mutual understanding, but it also presents the danger of bringing out each other's emotional extremes or excesses. There are apt to be strong emotional bonds in family relationships. The two individuals are apt to have similar attitudes and values in home and domestic affairs, diet, and family matters.

This can be an effective combination for cooperation in business and financial affairs, especially if the Moons are well-aspected by other planets in the natives' natal horoscopes. This is particularly true for family businesses and businesses related to real estate, home and domestic products and services, restaurants, farming, or food.

A's Moon Conjunct B's Mercury (A's ☽ ☌ B's ☿)

This is a good comparative aspect for communication between the natives about family and domestic matters—food, clothing, diet, personal hygiene, and cleanliness and organization in the house. It also helps the natives communicate about and work out emotional problems in a relationship. The Mercury individual will take an analytical approach to the moods, feelings, and emotional responses of the Moon individual. This can aid understanding, but the feelings of the Moon individual can be hurt if the Mercury individual is too critical. The Moon individual can provide the Mercury individual with a base of operations for work-oriented or intellectual activities, and the Mercury individual can, in turn, help the Moon individual to be more scientifically and intellectually aware of dietary and emotional habits.

Some natives with this combination may talk incessantly about trivial inconsequential matters to the point of boring or annoying others or becoming inefficient in their work.

This can be a favorable combination for business partnerships, especially in working out detailed methodologies and responsibility. It does not, of itself, indicate sexual or romantic attraction.

A's Moon Conjunct B's Venus (A's ☽ ☌ B's ♀)

In general, this is one of the best of all comparative aspects. The Moon individual can provide domestic and emotional security for the Venus individual, and the Venus individual can express love and emotional understanding to the Moon individual. There is usually a strong emotional link. The natives are often sexually and romantically attracted to each other, if other factors are favorable. They are sensitively attuned to each other's moods and subconscious emotional responses and respond to each other in a way that is both sympathetic and soothing. They will be able to share many sympathetic tender feelings and will enjoy esthetic, musical, social, and artistic pursuits together.

This can be a good combination for financial partnerships, if other factors in the horoscope indicate practical organizing ability, such as good comparative aspects involving Saturn and Mercury. The natives can work in business partnerships related to art, music, food, entertainment, restaurants, or luxury items such as fine furniture, jewelry, or expensive clothing, gourmet foods, or catering.

This is an excellent combination for marriage, family relationships, or all relationships of people who live together under the same roof. It permits happiness, mutual sharing, and harmonious relationships in the home. The natives will enjoy entertaining together and giving parties for their friends.

If this aspect is afflicted in the comparison, the natives could encourage each other's self-indulgences and weaknesses in regard to food and drink, as well as each other's nonproductive, hedonistic pursuits.

A's Moon Conjunct B's Mars (A's ☽ ☌ B's ♂)

This tends to be a difficult comparative aspect. The aggressiveness of the Mars individual emotionally irritates and upsets the Moon individual, and the moodiness and hypersensitivity of the Moon individual makes the Mars individual annoyed and impatient. The Moon individual regards the Mars individual as crude and insensitive, while the Mars individual sees the Moon individual as weak, lazy, and self-indulgent.

In a good overall comparison, this comparative aspect can produce constructive, energetic mutual action in home improvement, business, family, and domestic areas. It can indicate sexual attraction, but is no guarantee of compatibility. The Mars individual may try to change or improve the habits of the Moon individual or motivate the Moon individual to greater career ambition. The initiative and ambition of the Mars individual can, in some cases, provide security for the Moon individual, who, in turn, can provide domestic comfort for the Mars individual. Relationships with this comparative aspect work best if the Mars individual is a man and the Moon individual is a woman. This is generally a difficult combination for marriage, family relationships, or for people who live together, since it is likely to produce domestic disagreements.

A's Moon Conjunct B's Jupiter (A's ☽ ☌ B's ♃)

This comparative aspect greatly increases the chances of harmony in a relationship. There is usually a feeling of trust and mutual confidence. The natives will have compatible religious, social, and ethical values where running a family and maintaining a worthwhile home life are concerned. They will be emotionally sympathetic toward each other and will share many cultural activities and values. The Jupiter individual will encourage optimism and emotional serenity in the Moon individual. The Moon individual can provide the Jupiter individual with a home or base of operations for social, religious, philosophical, or educational activities.

This aspect, by itself, does not indicate romantic attraction, but it will increase the durability and stability of a romantic or marital relationship, because it gives the natives the capacity to share educational, spiritual, and social values and ideals which go beyond mere sexual and emotional attraction. This is also an excellent combination for parent–child relationships, especially if the parent is the Jupiter individual. It also favors business partnerships. Often, the natives have similar social or family backgrounds or, at least, an interest in these aspects of each other's backgrounds. The association may bring about moving or traveling.

A's Moon Conjunct B's Saturn (A's ☽ ☌ B's ♄)

Generally this is a difficult aspect for all relationships, except, perhaps, business and professional ones. The Saturn person has an emotionally depressing, wet-blanket effect on the Moon individual, while the Moon individual seems moody, unstable, and irresponsible to the Saturn individual. The Moon individual is likely to feel that the Saturn individual is insensitive. The natives may also reinforce any mutual tendency toward negative emotional outlook or emotional depression.

In family, parent–child, marital, and romantic relationships, this combination can produce emotional coldness and estrangement. In some cases, the relationship is entered into for monetary reasons or out of a need for security rather than any genuine sympathetic understanding between the natives.

The career concerns of the Saturn individual can conflict with the domestic and family concerns of the Moon native. Financial problems can also put a strain on the relationship. One or both individuals may be so busy trying to achieve financial security that there is no time for developing the personal side of the relationship. On the positive side, there can be a strong sense of mutual responsibility and the natives can work effectively together in business.

A's Moon Conjunct B's Uranus (A's ☽ ☌ B's ♅)

This combination produces unusual and exciting, but not always stable, relationships. Much depends on the nature of the rest of the comparison. Unless other aspects in the comparison, such as good Saturn aspects, balance this comparative conjunction, the relationship is likely to be unstable and the natives' feelings about each other are apt to be subject to sudden and unpredictable changes. In some cases, there will be a psychic link between the natives, and they can have occult or astrological interests in common. The Uranus individual can have a stimulating, exciting effect on the feelings of the Moon individual. He brings unexpected changes and unusual people into the domestic and family affairs of the Moon individual.

In romantic relationships, the natives often live together without being married. In some cases, there are communal living arrangements, or the home may be a place where friends gather and group activities take place.

The Moon individual can provide a base of operations or a home for the unusual activities of the Uranus individual. This can be a good combination for business partnerships or corporate enterprises of an unusual nature.

A's Moon Conjunct B's Neptune (A's ☽ ☌ B's ♆)

Usually this combination produces relationships with a strong psychic link. The natives will be sensitively attuned to each other's moods and feelings. However, if they are immature, or if the overall comparison is unfavorable, there can be deception, especially on the part of the Neptune individual. Emotional problems stemming from the subconscious mind and memories of past experiences can also stand in the way of a successful relationship. On the positive side, there can be a great deal of empathy and mutual sympathy between the natives. There can be a sharing of interest in mysticism, psychic studies, or practices in religious beliefs. Mutual psychic attunement can aid psychological understanding in the relationship. The home will be used as a place of retreat, meditation, and introspection. Mutual domestic needs and appreciations can also lead to an appreciation of esthetic values in music, art, home decor, etc. The natives can enter into private and somewhat secretive activities together. This comparative aspect can be good for business partnerships involving esthetic values where intuitive awareness is needed, or in fields related to psychology or psychic matters.

A's Moon Conjunct B's Pluto (A's ☽ ☌ B's ♀)

In this sensitive and dynamic comparative aspect the intense energy of the Pluto individual can sometimes overpower the feelings and emotional sensitivities of the Moon individual and cause him or her to retreat or react in an emotionally unstable way. The Pluto individual is likely to try to mold or remake the Moon individual, and can drastically alter the home and domestic circumstances, as well as family relationships, of the Moon person.

In some cases, this combination can produce sexual attraction, but durability in the relationship and overall ability to get along depend upon the rest of the comparison. If the overall pattern of both horoscopes reveals that the Pluto individual has a much stronger will than the Moon individual, then the latter is in danger of being psychically dominated. The Moon individual can provide domestic security for the Pluto individual. In turn, the Pluto individual attempts to improve existing conditions. This can be an effective combination for partnership in corporate business enterprises if the Moon and Pluto are well aspected. In some cases, there is a psychic or intuitive link between the natives. There can also be a mutual interest in occult studies or various occult methods of self-improvement, such as yoga.

A's Moon Conjunct B's North Node Opposition
B's South Node (A's ☽ ☌ B's ☊ ☍ B's ☋)

This comparative combination indicates compatible emotional attitudes toward the prevalent social attitudes and popular beliefs of the society in which the natives live. The natives are likely to have similar family backgrounds and social upbringings, which result in compatible cultural and moral values. There could be an interest in the commercial aspects of cultural trends and fads, and these trends could become an important part of their domestic life.

A's Moon Conjunct B's South Node Opposition
B's North Node (A's ☽ ☌ B's ☋ ☍ B's ☊)

This comparative combination indicates differences in values regarding popular trends, fads, social beliefs, and economic policies. The Nodes individual is likely to consider the Moon individual as superficial and blindly following the current vogue, while the Moon individual may regard the Nodes individual as negative and antisocial. The Nodes individual can be emotionally oppressive toward the Moon individual.

A's Moon Conjunct B's Ascendant Opposition
B's Descendant (A's ☽ ☌ B's Asc. ☍ B's Desc.)

Much as "A's Moon in B's First House," this comparative combination indicates that the actions and self-expression of the Ascendant/Descendant individual will have a strong emotional impact on the Moon individual. This influence will be particularly felt in the Moon individual's family and domestic affairs.

The Moon individual can in turn provide a home and base of operations for the expressions of the Ascendant/Descendant individual. There will be strong emotional ties in the family relationships. If the conjunction is afflicted, however, family problems of an emotional nature can cause difficulties in the relationship.

A's Moon Conjunct B's Midheaven Opposition B's Nadir
(A's ☽ ☌ B's M.C. ☍ B's Nadir)

This comparative combination has basically the same significance as "A's Moon in B's Tenth House," except that its effects will be more dynamic and immediate.

Natives in family relationships are often involved in a family business. In parent–child relationships, the child is apt to follow in the professional footsteps of the parent. The Moon individual can provide a home or base of operations for the career activities of the Midheaven/Nadir individual, and the professional activities of the Midheaven/Nadir individual can provide security and status for the Moon individual. The professional activities of the Midheaven/Nadir individual can have a strong effect on the emotional aspect of the family and domestic affairs of the Moon individual. There can be mutual involvement in professions related to food, real estate, mining, farming, domestic products, and services.

If the conjunction is afflicted by other comparative aspects, there could be conflict between the professional responsibilities of the Midheaven/ Nadir individual and the domestic responsibilities of the Moon individual.

A's Moon Conjunct B's Descendant Opposition B's Ascendant
(A's ☽ ☌ B's Desc. ☍ B's Asc.)

This comparative combination has basically the same significance as "A's Moon in B's Seventh House," except that its effects will be stronger and more immediate. It can indicate sexual attraction if other factors in the comparison concur. Domestic and family affairs will have a more significant effect than would ordinarily be the case on the success of marital relationships. The proverbial in-law problem could be a serious matter if this comparative combination is afflicted.

The family background and emotional habit patterns of the Moon individual will strongly influence the relationship. The Moon individual can provide a home or base of operations for the Ascendant/Descendant individual, who, in turn, can provide emotional and domestic companionship to the Moon individual.

Business partnerships could relate to food, farming, building, real estate, and home and domestic products. The natives could be mutually involved in public relations in some manner.

A's Moon Conjunct B's Nadir Opposition B's Midheaven
(A's ☽ ☌ B's Nadir ☍ B's M.C.)

This comparative combination has the same basic significance as "A's Moon in B's Fourth House," except that its effects will be stronger and more immediately felt, especially after the natives' fortieth year. These natives will have a strong mutual interest in family and domestic affairs, and there will be strong mutual emotional ties in family relationships. Family background and emotional conditioning will be important factors in their ability to get along. The natives could be involved in business related to real estate, farming, food, and products and services used in the home.

COMPARATIVE SEXTILES

These comparative aspects aid communication in emotional, family, domestic, and financial affairs. The natives will be able to discuss these issues intelligently, and this will contribute to the development of a friendship between them. These comparative aspects are especially helpful for people who live together or who are members of the same family.

A's Moon Sextile B's Sun

See A's Sun Sextile B's Moon.

A's Moon Sextile B's Moon (A's ☽ ✶ B's ☽)

This comparative aspect indicates that the natives will have good emotional empathy and communication. They will be able to cooperate in family, domestic, and business affairs, unless other factors in the comparison indicate otherwise. They will be able to communicate with each other about their feelings and emotional responses, and this will improve their compatibility even further.

This is a favorable influence for all types of family relationships, as well as other associations of people who live together in the home.

A's Moon Sextile B's Mercury (A's ☽ ✶ B's ☿)

The Mercury individual can come up with worthwhile, constructive ideas to improve the Moon person's efficiency and hygiene in domestic and home affairs. The Mercury person can help the Moon individual gain a more rational understanding of automatic feeling responses and subconscious emotional attitudes. The Moon individual will, in turn, provide the Mercury individual with a home or base of operations for intellectual pursuits and for communications among friends and relatives.

There is apt to be a mutual sharing of intellectual and educational activities in the home. This comparative aspect helps communication in family, domestic, financial, and emotional issues, especially in areas of diet and hygiene.

This comparative aspect can help the natives to resolve any emotional difficulties in the relationship through the ability it confers to communicate and talk about problems. This is a good comparative aspect for cooperation in business, especially businesses related to food, home and domestic products.

A's Moon Sextile B's Venus (A's ☽ ✳ B's ♀)

This is a good comparative aspect for romantic attraction and marriage. The natives tend to be sympathetic toward and considerate of each other and to share social, musical, artistic, and other refined cultural activities and appreciations. They will share an interest in creating a harmonious, beautiful home and domestic life, and they are likely to have many friends in common.

If other factors in the comparison are agreeable, the natives will generally have a sympathetic, emotional understanding of each other's moods and feelings, which can border on the intuitive level. The Venus individual can bring social and artistic activities into the home and family life of the Moon individual. The Moon individual can provide domestic security and emotional support for the social and artistic expressions of the Venus individual.

This is a good combination for parent–child relationships; it increases love and sympathetic understanding. It can contribute to sexual and romantic attraction if other factors are favorable. It is also a good combination for business partnerships pertaining to luxury items, art, fine clothing, perfumes, flowers, and luxury items for the home.

A's Moon Sextile B's Mars (A's ☽ ✳ B's ♂)

This is a good combination for dynamic cooperation in action, especially in areas of business and home improvement. It favors enterprise in business partnerships and cooperation in corporate affairs.

The Mars individual can help the Moon individual overcome psychological inertia and fear based on past experiences, while the Moon individual can have a calming effect on the Mars individual. The Mars individual can also help the Moon individual overcome inertia and inactivity.

This comparative aspect can contribute to sexual attraction in romantic relationships.

A's Moon Sextile B's Jupiter (A's ☽ ✶ B's ♃)

Mutual generosity and good will in all relationships are indicated by this combination. It works best in family relationships, although it is also good for business partnerships, since the natives will be honest and considerate toward each other. It is especially good for cooperation in businesses related to home and domestic products, food, and real estate. There will be constructive cooperation to bring religious, educational, philosophical, and cultural values into the family and domestic life.

The Jupiter individual is usually generous, encouraging, and benevolent toward the Moon individual and helps the latter to develop more self-confidence and assurance. The Moon individual can, in turn, provide the Jupiter individual with a home or base of operations for his religious, cultural, and educational activities. The natives will usually have a sympathetic understanding for each other, along with mutual trust and loyalty.

A's Moon Sextile B's Saturn (A's ☽ ✶ B's ♄)

This sextile combination is helpful for business and professional relationships. The natives will have a sense of responsibility toward each other. The Saturn individual can be a constructive, disciplining influence, helping the Moon individual to achieve greater efficiency and organization in business, financial, home, and domestic affairs. The Moon individual can, in turn, help the Saturn individual achieve greater emotional sensitivity to family and domestic affairs. If the Saturn individual is older, he or she may act as a parental figure toward the Moon individual.

This comparative aspect works best where thrift, resourcefulness, practicality, discipline, and responsibilities are necessary. It does not contribute to romantic attraction or even mutual excitement, but it does indicate mutual respect, loyalty, and durability in a relationship where friendship and romantic attraction are indicated.

A's Moon Sextile B's Uranus (A's ☽ ✳ B's ♅)

Interesting, exciting, unusual friendships occur with this comparative aspect. The natives may meet under unusual circumstances and be intuitively attracted to each other. This comparative aspect can do a great deal to keep a relationship lively and interesting. There can be an intuitive link between the natives, especially with respect to moods and feelings. The Uranus individual can help the Moon individual overcome negative, emotional habit patterns based on experiences of the past, and the Moon individual can provide a home or base of operations for the Uranus individual's unusual or creative interests and self-expression.

There can be a sharing of friends, hobbies, and occult or astrological interests, and often the home is the place where these and other group and organizational activities are pursued.

A's Moon Sextile B's Neptune (A's ☽ ✳ B's ♆)

This comparative aspect can indicate an intuitive link between the natives. They will be telepathically sensitive to each other's moods and feelings, and they can help each other gain insight into their subconscious feelings and motivations. Their intuitive, emotional rapport will help them understand each other's feelings and work out differences when they arise. There can be mutual involvement in psychic or spiritual pursuits.

This is a good comparative combination for harmony in family and domestic relationships. The natives can encourage each other to use the home as a place for meditation, introspection, and intuitive inspiration.

A's Moon Sextile B's Pluto (A's ☽ ✳ B's ♀)

The Pluto individual can energize the Moon individual, helping to overcome inertia and negative emotional habit patterns. The Moon individual will cooperate with the Pluto individual in efforts to regenerate and improve family and domestic conditions. The strength and determination of the Pluto individual can be an encouragement and positive impetus to the Moon individual. The natives can encourage each other to improve dietary habits and personal hygiene.

This can be a good combination for cooperation in psychology and in efforts to attain a higher level of awareness. The individuals may also share an interest in occult, mystical, or psychic matters.

This combination is helpful in business and corporate associations. The natives can be effective and resourceful in the management and sharing of resources and financial assets.

A's Moon Sextile B's North Node Trine B's South Node
(A's ☽ ✶ B's ☊ △ B's ☋)

The Nodes individual can help the Moon individual adjust emotionally to and fit in with popular trends and prevailing social customs. The Moon individual will support the social and economic activity of the Nodes individual.

A's Moon Sextile B's South Node Trine B's North Node
(A's ☽ ✶ B's ☋ △ B's ☊)

This comparative combination has basically the same significance as "A's Moon Sextile B's North Node Trine B's South Node," except that these natives will be intellectually critical of popular trends and social beliefs.

A's Moon Sextile B's Ascendant Trine B's Descendant
(A's ☽ ✶ B's Asc. △ B's Desc.)

The Moon individual will adjust well to the Ascendant/Descendant individual's manner of self-expression and basic outlook on life and can have a comforting and soothing effect on him. The Ascendant/Descendant individual can help the Moon individual overcome emotional problems and difficulties so as to achieve financial and domestic security. This is a good combination for cooperation in family and domestic matters. It helps family and domestic compatibility in marriage, and improves prospects for the natives' emotional compatibility and understanding of each other's basic modes of self-expression.

A's Moon Sextile B's Midheaven Trine B's Nadir
(A's ☽ ✶ B's M.C. △ B's Nadir)

The Moon individual can provide money, domestic security, and emotional support for the Midheaven/Nadir individual's attempts to achieve domestic and career security and success. The status, career, and domestic security of the Midheaven/Nadir individual can also be the means of providing money, domestic security, and well-being to the Moon individual.

A's Moon Sextile B's Descendant Trine B's Ascendant
(A's ☽ ✳ B's Desc. △ B's Asc.)

This comparative combination has basically the same significance as "A's Moon Sextile B's Ascendant Trine B's Descendant." These natives, however, will be more intellectually concerned with the emotional aspects of their relationships and less with separate self-expression.

A's Moon Sextile B's Nadir Trine B's Midheaven
(A's ☽ ✳ B's Nadir △ B's M.C.)

This comparative combination has basically the same significance as "A's Moon Sextile B's Midheaven Trine B's Nadir," except that these natives will be more intellectually concerned with family and domestic affairs and less with professional matters.

COMPARATIVE SQUARES

These comparative combinations make for emotional difficulties in a relationship, especially with regard to the affairs ruled by the Moon in A's horoscope and the planet being squared in B's horoscope. If the square is in a Cardinal sign (Aries, Cancer, Libra, or Capricorn), impulsive action can cause squabbles. If it is in a Fixed sign (Taurus, Leo, Scorpio, or Aquarius), inflexible emotional attitudes and habits will tend to stand in the way of mutual harmony. If the square falls in a Mutable sign (Gemini, Virgo, Sagittarius, or Pisces), the natives will tend to be restless, irritable, and bored with each other.

The Moon individual's irrational emotional attitudes, which stem from experiences, often childhood experiences, that he remembers only subconsciously, can be difficult or exasperating to the other native. There can be disagreements and conflicts over the handling of family, domestic, financial, and professional matters.

A's Moon Square B's Sun

See A's Sun Square B's Moon.

A's Moon Square B's Moon (A's ☽ □ B's ☽)

Natives with this comparative aspect are apt to have difficulty under-standing each other's feelings and emotional responses. This sometimes is a result of differences in family and cultural background. The natives' moods may tend to be out-of-phase, so that it is difficult for them to do the same thing at the same time. They may not see eye-to-eye about the handling of family, domestic, dietary, and financial affairs.

If this comparative square occurs between planets in Cardinal signs (Aries, Cancer, Libra, or Capricorn), the natives may act impulsively without consulting each other. If it occurs between planets in Fixed signs (Taurus, Leo, Scorpio, or Aquarius), the natives can disagree over stub-bornly held emotional attitudes and habits. If it occurs between planets in Mutable signs (Gemini, Virgo, Sagittarius, or Pisces), the natives will feel nervous and irritable in each other's presence and will bring out each other's unpleasant memories.

A's Moon Square B's Mercury (A's ☽ □ B's ☿)

Individuals with this comparative combination are apt to have diffi-culty communicating with and understanding each other where everyday practical domestic affairs and family matters are concerned. They can disagree over matters of diet, personal hygiene, neatness and order in the home, and the handling of practical affairs. The Mercury individual operates on a rational, intellectual level, while the Moon individual responds on an instinctual emotional level, and this contributes to their difficulties in understanding each other. The Mercury individual is likely to regard the Moon person as overly emotional, irrational, lazy, and unre-liable, while the Moon individual will regard the Mercury person as hypercritical, nit-picking, and insensitive. The Mercury individual can regard the Moon individual as dull, overly attached to material comforts and possessions, or hung up in emotional habit patterns based on past experiences and conditioning. The Moon individual can regard the Mer-cury individual as hung up in intellectual games and issues which are beside the point.

In some cases, the natives will engage in endless, meaningless idle chit-chat without ever dealing with the really important issues of their rela-tionship and the problems they face. There can be disagreement over the friends of the Mercury individual, who pose a threat to the domestic tranquility or emotional security of the Moon individual. Often, there is confusion in the coordination of everyday activities.

A's Moon Square B's Venus (A's ☽ □ B's ♀)

Persons with this comparative combination are likely to have a hard time understanding each other's moods and feelings and expressing real sympathy and understanding. They are likely to experience emotional misunderstandings and confusion in romantic relationships. This comparative combination can also produce one-sided romantic attractions, and subsequent emotional pain and misunderstanding for one or both parties. In some cases, the attraction is only sexual or emotional, without real understanding or overall mental and spiritual compatibility. Marriages may be contracted for reasons of financial or domestic security, or as a result of family pressure, rather than because of real affinity. This is not a good combination for business partnerships, since the natives tend to encourage each other to be extravagant, lazy, and unrealistic in their expectations. The natives can encourage each other's self-indulgence. The association often tends to be a hedonistic one, based on social activities, parties, and luxurious pursuits, without dealing with the practical responsibilities of life. The natives can also have a hard time understanding each other's moods and feelings and expressing real sympathy and understanding.

A's Moon Square B's Mars (A's ☽ □ B's ♂)

This is one of the most difficult and emotionally explosive of all comparative aspects. The Mars individual tends to be impatient with what he considers the weak, indecisive, lazy, and materialistic nature of the Moon individual. The Moon individual resents and is hurt by the emotional insensitivity of the Mars individual. There will be a general lack of domestic harmony and many emotional misunderstandings. The Moon individual regards the Mars native as rude, overbearing, impatient, and crude in social manners and domestic behavior.

This combination typically produces clashes and angry emotional scenes. It is certainly unfavorable for marriages or for people who must live in close proximity. The Mars individual's career ambitions can clash with the domestic and family concerns of the Moon individual. This combination can also produce quarrels and fighting over financial management, inheritances, and alimony settlements. In some cases, the natives can goad each other to unwise speculation, extravagance, and excess.

A's Moon Square B's Jupiter (A's ☽ □ B's ♃)

This comparative combination indicates the possibility of an insincere or somewhat hypocritical relationship between two people. The natives can pander to each other's weaknesses and self-indulgent tendencies, especially in matters of food and domestic comfort. In parent–child relationships, the parent can have a tendency to be overly protective and indulgent. There can be difficulties over differences in religious background and social upbringing. The natives may feign generosity and concern for each other's welfare, while they are secretly concerned about security, money, or other material advantages. In business relationships, the natives can encourage each other to extravagances and unwise financial risks in their attempt to appear more enterprising than they really are. The natives can also encourage each other's subconscious psychological difficulties and weaknesses, often through emotional dishonesty and overprotectiveness.

A's Moon Square B's Saturn (A's ☽ □ B's ♄)

In this very difficult and emotionally restrictive comparative combination, one of the natives is often an emotional and/or financial burden on the other. In some cases, there will be a neurotic mutual dependency.

The association is often forced by family obligations or economic necessity. This results in drudgery and lack of emotional freedom for one or both parties. Often, the association is based on ulterior motives of money and status, and has little to do with real friendship or affection.

The natives tend to amplify each other's fears and remind each other of past misfortunes. In business relationships, each tends to encourage the other's negative attitudes and block creative initiative with an "it-won't-work" attitude. The career and status ambitions and responsibilities of the Saturn individual tend to conflict with the family and domestic concerns of the Moon individual. The Saturn individual may be so wrapped up in career activities as to have no time to devote to the emotional needs of home and family.

In general, the natives tend to have an oppressive, emotionally stifling influence on each other. This can result from excessive severity in the Saturn individual or excessive dependency in the Moon individual or both. The Saturn individual tends to have an emotionally depressing, wet-blanket effect on and to be overly severe toward the Moon individual. Often, the natives will seek to control each other through guilt, especially in parent–child and marital relationships.

A's Moon Square B's Uranus (A's ☽ □ B's ♅)

In some cases, this comparative combination produces sudden and temporary attractions and infatuations. The Moon individual can seem commonplace and uninteresting to the Uranus individual, and the Uranus individual can be too way-out and undependable for the basic concerns and everyday affairs of the Moon individual. The Uranus individual's eccentric behavior and strange friends can upset the domestic harmony and security of the Moon individual who is emotionally tied to established habit patterns. Both natives will tend to trigger emotional upsets and immature behavior in the other. They tend to make each other nervous, upset, and irritable. There can also be disagreements over approaches to and involvement with occult or psychic interests.

A's Moon Square B's Neptune (A's ☽ □ B's ♆)

Mutual deception and dishonesty, often based on subconscious psychological hangups, are frequently characteristic of relationships with this comparative combination. One or both of the natives can have a parasitical psychological effect on the other. The natives can encourage each other's tendencies to get hung up in negative emotional memories, to the point of being incapable of acting appropriately in their present circumstances. They can become so involved in their own private dream worlds that they are no longer able to communicate or take care of practical family, domestic, business or other mutual responsibilities. They may encourage each other's neuroses, psychological weaknesses, and subconscious self-destructive tendencies, such as alcoholism, drug-taking, or other destructive escapist tendencies.

This is not a good combination for business partnerships. The natives will tend to be unreliable toward each other and make foolish, unwise expenditures.

The Neptune individual is likely to be emotionally deceptive toward the Moon individual and the Moon person often finds the other hard to understand.

A's Moon Square B's Pluto (A's ☽ □ B's ♀)

This comparative combination is prone to many of the difficulties of the "Moon Square Mars" comparative combination, but on a more subtle and psychological level. The Pluto individual can take advantage of the impressionability of the Moon individual to psychically dominate and control him or her. The Moon individual can tend to be hypersensitive, peevish, and unstable in response to the Pluto individual's attempts at mutual self-improvement and regeneration of family and domestic conditions. The Pluto individual can tend to emotionally dominate and bully the Moon individual to the point where the latter becomes resentful and uncooperative. The Moon individual tends to fight the dominating tendencies of the Pluto individual by passive resistance and little acts of subconcious rebellion which, in turn, aggravate and frustrate the Pluto individual. Much depends on the overall nature of the comparison and on which of the natives is the more dominant or has a stronger will.

This is not a good combination for cooperation in business, and there is likely to be lack of harmony and agreement concerning family, domestic, and joint financial affairs.

A's Moon Square B's North Node Square B's South Node
(A's ☽ □ B's ☊ □ B's ☋)

The family upbringing and emotional habits of the Moon individual will tend to be out of harmony with the Nodes individual's idea of how to get along with and make the best social and commercial use of prevailing cultural beliefs, attitudes, fads, and popular trends. In some cases, the natives may encourage each other to exploit these trends at the expense of their own inner feelings and, sometimes, their moral principles.

A's Moon Square B's South Node Square B's North Node

See A's Moon Square B's North Node Square B's South Node.

A's Moon Square B's Ascendant Square B's Descendant
(A's ☽ □ B's Asc. □ B's Desc.)

The Moon individual's family upbringing and emotional habit patterns conflict with the Ascendant/Descendant individual's manner of self-expression, self-image, and the concept of cooperation in partnerships. The Ascendant/Descendant individual, in turn, can emotionally upset and disorient the Moon individual. There can be disagreement about how to conduct family, domestic, and business affairs.

A's Moon Square B's Midheaven Square B's Nadir
(A's ☽ □ B's M.C. □ B's Nadir)

The family backgrounds and emotional habit patterns and conditionings of these natives tend to conflict. The families of one or both natives can interfere with the relationship. There can be conflict between the natives' domestic and career ambitions, and they can have serious disagreements over family and domestic matters. The emotional instability of the Moon individual can hamper the career efforts of the Midheaven/Nadir individual, hurting status and prestige.

A's Moon Square B's Descendant Square B's Ascendant

See A's Moon Square B's Ascendant Square B's Descendant.

A's Moon Square B's Nadir Square B's Midheaven

See A's Moon Square B's Midheaven Square B's Nadir.

COMPARATIVE TRINES

These comparative combinations make for good emotional compatibility in romantic, parent–child, business, and family relationships. There will be a natural empathy and harmony of feelings and emotions in the affairs ruled by the Moon in A's horoscope and the planet trining the Moon in B's horoscope. These comparative aspects are also helpful in business, especially those related to food, farming, real estate, home, and domestic products and services. The natives are likely to agree on religious and philosophic values with regard to family life.

A's Moon Trine B's Sun

See A's Sun Trine B's Moon.

A's Moon Trine B's Moon (A's ☽ △ B's ☽)

Good emotional rapport and harmony between the natives are indicated by this comparative combination. It is favorable for those who are members of the same family or who live in the same household. It confers mutual understanding in parent–child relationships and general courtesy and consideration. It can also favor the sharing of cultural and religious values in family and domestic life. This is a favorable influence for business partnerships, especially those relating to food, farming, real estate, or services.

A's Moon Trine B's Mercury (A's ☽ △ B's ☿)

This combination is good for communication about everyday practical affairs, especially those relating to business, work, and domestic matters. The Mercury individual can help the Moon individual to understand emotional habit patterns and automatic responses based on experiences and family conditioning. The Moon individual can provide a home or base of operations for the intellectual activities of the Mercury individual. The ability to communicate about emotional problems can help to offset other difficult factors in the comparison.

This comparative combination does not, of itself, indicate sexual attraction, but it does improve overall compatibility if other aspects in the comparison show romantic or sexual attraction. This is an excellent combination for cooperation in business, especially businesses related to real estate, food, restaurants, and home and domestic products. It is also a good comparative aspect for increasing efficiency and cooperation in work relationships where methodology and attention to practical detail are important.

A's Moon Trine B's Venus (A's ☽ △ B's ♀)

This is one of the best combinations for romantic attraction. The natives enjoy each other's company and pursue artistic, social, musical, and pleasure-oriented activities together. This combination often produces mutual sexual attraction if other factors are appropriate. The natives often have a sympathetic, emotional attunement to each other. A mutual appreciation of the good things in life can lead to a strong mutual involvement in establishing a pleasant and beautiful domestic life. The Venus native can bring social and esthetic influences into the family and domestic affairs of the Moon individual. The Moon individual will help the Venus individual by providing emotional security and a home or base of operations for the Venus individual's social and artistic activities. The double-Taurus connotation of this comparative aspect, combined with the expansive Sun-Jupiter nature of the trine, makes this a good combination for business partnerships, especially those businesses pertaining to art, music, luxury items, food, parties, and home and domestic products. The natives will show mutual consideration and kindness for each other, unless other factors in the comparison strongly contradict this.

A's Moon Trine B's Mars (A's ☽ △ B's ♂)

The Mars individual will energize and encourage the Moon individual into greater self-confidence and constructive action. The Moon individual, in turn, will soothe and calm the Mars individual and provide a base of operations or home for work and activity. This comparative combination is helpful for any mutual endeavor requiring energy, courage, and determination. It is especially effective for cooperation in business enterprises and professional and domestic endeavors, often in the form of mutual involvement in home improvement and do-it-yourself projects.

This combination also contributes to sexual attraction, if other factors are favorable. This kind of relationship works best, however, when the man is the Mars individual and the woman is the Moon individual.

A's Moon Trine B's Jupiter (A's ☽ △ B's ♃)

One of the best comparative aspects for mutual kindness, generosity, and helpfulness in all relationships, this is especially helpful for harmony and mutual consideration in family and domestic relationships. There is often a sharing of religious, social, and ethical values with respect to home and family affairs. The Jupiter individual is kind and generous toward the Moon individual, while the Moon individual is receptive and sympathetic toward the Jupiter individual. In some cases, there may be a psychic or intuitive link between the natives. They will often have cultural interests in common and will use their home as a place for pursuing such activities and as a gathering place and refuge for family and friends. This is also a good combination for business partnerships, parent–child relationships, and teacher–pupil relationships. This combination does not, of itself, indicate romantic or sexual attraction, but it does increase the durability and stability of such a relationship by providing shared cultural, educational, moral, and religious values and interests. This is also a good comparative aspect for traveling companions.

A's Moon Trine B's Saturn (A's ☽ △ B's ♄)

This comparative combination is helpful for cooperation in serious responsibilities, business matters, and domestic affairs. It is not conducive to mutual excitement or romantic attraction, but it will improve the durability of a relationship by conferring a practical, responsible approach to everyday responsibilities and problems. The natives will tend to rely on each other for security and stability. If the Saturn individual is older, he or she will act to some degree as a parental figure to the Moon individual. The Saturn individual can provide professional or financial security for the Moon individual, and the Moon individual can provide domestic comforts and security for the Saturn individual. The Saturn individual can be a disciplining, restraining influence on the emotional instabilities of the Moon person. This is a good combination for cooperation in businesses related to real estate, farming, food, and domestic products.

A's Moon Trine B's Uranus (A's ☽ △ B's ♅)

If other factors are favorable, this combination can indicate sexual attraction. The Uranus individual can bring interest and excitement into the Moon individual's life by introducing the Moon individual to interesting friends, groups, or new interests, often in scientific, occult, or humanitarian areas. The Moon individual can, in turn, give the Uranus individual emotional support in scientific, occult, humanitarian, or other special or unusual interests and provide the Uranus individual with a base of operations for activities. The natives often use their home as a meeting place for friends, organizations, and unusual activities. These relationships generally have a feeling of adventure and excitement. The natives will encourage each other to be more individualistic and creative and allow each other freedom of emotional self-expression, unless other factors in the comparison contradict this.

A's Moon Trine B's Neptune (A's ☽ △ B's ♆)

This comparative combination usually indicates a psychic link between the natives. They can have intuitive sympathetic insight into each other's moods, feelings, and emotional conditionings. They will stimulate each other's imagination and share many esthetic, musical, and psychological perceptions and feelings. In some cases, they may feel a karmic link or sense that they have known each other before, perhaps in some previous lifetime. There can be a mutual interest in incorporating meditative and esthetic or spiritual values into the home life. The natives can share psychic and occult interests and often have a telepathic awareness of what the other is thinking or feeling. They will support each other's need for privacy and sanctuary. The Moon individual can provide the Neptune individual with domestic security, and the Neptune individual's intuitive insights can be helpful to the Moon individual.

A's Moon Trine B's Pluto (A's ☽ △ B's ♀)

The Pluto individual can help the Moon individual overcome psychological inertia and negative habit tendencies of the past. In some cases, the natives can share a mutual psychic awareness; their interaction will be more dynamic than with Moon–Neptune combinations, with the Pluto individual usually taking the lead. The Pluto individual will encourage the Moon individual in efforts toward self-improvement and psychological transformation, especially in letting go of past conditionings. The Moon person will give emotional support and provide a base of operations for the business or occult activities of the Pluto individual. This can be an effective combination for dynamic action in corporate endeavors and business affairs. The natives can bring out each other's resourcefulness.

A's Moon Trine B's North Node Sextile B's South Node

See A's Moon Sextile B's South Node Trine B's North Node.

A's Moon Trine B's South Node Sextile B's North Node

See A's Moon Sextile B's North Node Trine B's South Node.

A's Moon Trine B's Ascendant Sextile B's Descendant

See A's Moon Sextile B's Descendant Trine B's Ascendant.

A's Moon Trine B's Midheaven Sextile B's Nadir

See A's Moon Sextile B's Nadir Trine B's Midheaven.

A's Moon Trine B's Descendant Sextile B's Ascendant

See A's Moon Sextile B's Ascendant Trine B's Descendant.

A's Moon Trine B's Nadir Sextile B's Midheaven

See A's Moon Sextile B's Midheaven Trine B's Nadir.

COMPARATIVE OPPOSITIONS

These comparative combinations often occur in marital relationships and partnerships, because of the natural Libran/Seventh House significance of the opposition aspect. The affairs ruled by the signs and houses occupied and ruled by the Moon in A's horoscope and the planet opposed by the Moon in B's horoscope will be of major emotional concern in the relationship.

The other native may regard the Moon individual as hypersensitive or emotionally hung up in past experiences or family conditioning. Family, domestic, dietary, and financial issues can be of major concern. If these natives are to cooperate effectively, they must be sensitive to each other's moods and feelings and willing to share equal responsibility in everyday household tasks.

A's Moon Opposition B's Sun

See A's Sun Opposition B's Moon.

A's Moon Opposition B's Moon (A's ☽ ☍ B's ☽)

Natives with this comparative combination will tend to mirror and polarize each other's emotional moods, thus triggering strong emotional responses in each other. Difficulties can arise if the natives' moods are out of harmony and they thus find it difficult to do the same thing at the same time. If the natives are to cooperate effectively, they must seek to understand each other's moods, feelings, and past family and emotional conditioning.

A's Moon Opposition B's Mercury (A's ☽ ☍ B's ☿)

This comparative combination often presents communication problems. The Mercury individual responds on a rational level, while the Moon individual reacts on an emotional level; consequently, they find it difficult to understand each other. The Mercury individual can seem nagging and overly critical or nit-picking to the Moon individual, while the Moon individual may seem moody, lazy, overly emotional, and irrational to the Mercury individual. There can be disagreements over diet, everyday practical affairs, business, financial expenditures, and domestic and family issues. In some cases, differences in family background and social upbringing can be an obstacle to close relationships.

This is not a good combination for teacher–student or employer–employee relationships where attention to detail is important. The natives can misunderstand each other and suffer confusion in communication. They often miss appointments with each other.

A's Moon Opposition B's Venus (A's ☽ ☍ B's ♀)

This comparative aspect can indicate strong romantic and sexual attraction, but emotional communication is more delicate and difficult than with other Moon–Venus combinations. One or both of the natives' feelings can easily be hurt, or one or both parties may feel misunderstood or "used" for sexual gratification. If both parties are reasonably mature, such difficulties can be overcome, since the opposition aspect and the planet Venus both deal with relationships. This combination is commonly found in marriages and romantic attractions. The natives can share social, musical, esthetic, and pleasure-oriented activities. In some cases, they may encourage each other to dissipation through too many parties, overeating, financial extravagance, sexual excess, and general avoidance of work and serious responsibilities. This is not a good combination for business partnerships, since the natives are apt to encourage each other to extravagance and unwise expenditures.

A's Moon Opposition B's Mars (A's ☽ ☍ B's ♂)

Usually this combination produces emotional conflict. The Moon individual will regard the Mars individual as overly aggressive, domineering, and insensitive, while the Mars individual is likely to look upon the Moon individual as lazy, weak, moody, and overly emotional. There can be conflict over financial and business affairs. This comparative aspect is not favorable for compatibility in marriage and romance, although it can produce sexual attraction. In marital or romantic relationships, one party may feel that he or she is being exploited for sexual or financial reasons. It is a particularly difficult comparative aspect for domestic harmony and for people who must live under the same roof or in the same family; they will be prone to emotional conflicts and angry scenes.

In some cases, natives will have difficulties over inheritances, joint finances, corporate financial affairs, or alimony. If the natives are to get along, they must work consciously at exercising patience, gentleness, and consideration for each other.

A's Moon Opposition B's Jupiter (A's ☽ ☌ B's ♃)

Natives with this comparative combination tend to have genial relationships and show mutual kindness and consideration. However, hypocritical motives or a tendency for the natives to encourage each other's self-indulgent tendencies can enter into the relationship. In some cases, there can be genuine good will between the natives, but a lack of wisdom and discrimination as to how their good feelings should be expressed. This is especially true in parent–child relationships, where the child is spoiled or the parent uses material gifts as a substitute for real interest and attention.

In some cases, there can be religious or cultural differences. The Jupiter individual may be too sanctimonious. One or both parties can be overly protective of the other and prevent the other from gaining experiences and learning from mistakes. The natives can also encourage each other in excessive eating and drinking. Even with these difficulties, however, the natives can be very helpful to each other. They can share an interest in religious, philosophical, cultural, and educational pursuits. They will tend to increase each other's optimism, and this is good, as long as it does not degenerate into foolish optimism.

Even the opposition between these planets can improve family relationships. It can also be good for business partnerships, as long as the natives do not encourage each other to make unwise and unnecessarily extravagant expenditures.

A's Moon Opposition B's Saturn (A's ☽ ☌ B's ♄)

This is a difficult comparative combination for all kinds of relationships. In many cases, the natives' association is based purely on a need for security or for financial reasons rather than out of any real affinity. The Moon individual is likely to regard the Saturn individual as unkind and unsympathetic, while the latter may regard the Moon individual as weak, indecisive, self-indulgent, and lacking in practicality and discipline. The Saturn individual is likely to be an emotional wet blanket to the Moon individual and will be a harsh disciplinarian and unsympathetic.

There can be conflict between the professional, business, and career ambitions of the Saturn individual and the domestic and family concerns of the Moon individual. On the positive side, this comparative combination can indicate a mutual sense of responsibility and loyalty, as long as other factors in the comparison contribute to overall compatibility. In some cases, differences in family or cultural background can cause difficulties. The natives may tend to make each other overly pessimistic and fearful.

A's Moon Opposition B's Uranus (A's ☽ ☍ B's ♅)

This combination makes for unusual, interesting, exciting relationships, but not necessarily lasting ones. Often, the association is of a revolutionary or unconventional character. In romantic or sexual attractions, the natives may live together without marrying. The natives' emotional response to each other is subject to many sudden changes of mood or attitude. This comparative combination does not make for lasting marriages, unless other factors in the comparison provide durability in the relationship.

The unusual activities and interests of the Uranus individual can stimulate the imagination of the Moon individual. The Uranus individual is likely to introduce the Moon individual to new friendships and interests. However, the Uranus person's many unexpected actions and changes of plans are likely to confuse the Moon individual. The Uranus native's desire for freedom and independence can cause instability in the relationship. If the natives belong to the same family or are married, there can be frequent changes of residence, and this can upset the Moon individual. The natives may share occult, scientific, or humanitarian interests.

A's Moon Opposition B's Neptune (A's ☽ ☍ B's ♆)

Subtle psychological difficulties in a relationship can be indicated by this comparative combination. The Neptune individual may seem vague and elusive to the Moon individual. The natives may aggravate each other's tendency to dwell on emotional psychological hangups based on past experiences. On the positive side, they can stimulate each other's imagination and can have a psychic, telepathic link. They often share interest in psychology, psychic phenomena, occult subjects, astrology, art, and music. They can help each other gain insight into their psychological problems or aid one another in expressing intuitive creative abilities. The natives can use their home as a place to seek privacy or create a special artistic or psychic, meditative environment. If unfavorable indications are present in the comparison, the natives may encourage each other in escapist tendencies or self-destructive habits such as drinking, drug abuse, or unrealistic fantasizing. The Neptune individual can be deceptive toward the Moon individual.

A's Moon Opposition B's Pluto (A's ☽ ☍ B's ♇)

The Pluto individual can tend to psychically dominate or overpower the Moon individual, and these attempts at molding, reforming, or remaking can make the Moon individual resentful. The Moon native may resist the Pluto individual by evasiveness or passive resistance. The Pluto individual may attempt to use the Moon individual for sexual or financial reasons. The Moon individual may regard the Pluto individual as overbearing and insensitive to his feelings. There can be disagreements over financial expenditures, joint finances, inheritances, corporate finances, or alimony in the case of divorce. The natives can have disputes over family and domestic matters. In romantic and marital relationships, sexual incompatibility can be a problem.

A's Moon Opposition B's North Node Conjunct B's South Node

See A's Moon Conjunct B's South Node Opposition B's North Node.

A's Moon Opposition B's South Node Conjunct B's North Node

See A's Moon Conjunct B's North Node Opposition B's South Node.

A's Moon Opposition B's Ascendant Conjunct B's Descendant

See A's Moon Conjunct B's Descendant Opposition B's Ascendant.

A's Moon Opposition B's Midheaven Conjunct B's Nadir

See A's Moon Conjunct B's Nadir Opposition B's Midheaven.

A's Moon Opposition B's Descendant Conjunct B's Ascendant

See A's Moon Conjunct B's Ascendant Opposition B's Descendant.

A's Moon Opposition B's Nadir Conjunct B's Midheaven

See A's Moon Conjunct B's Midheaven Opposition B's Nadir.

IX
Mercury

Comparative influences of Mercury concern the communication between the natives. The exchange of ideas and information relating to work, everyday practical responsibilities, scientific and intellectual concepts, dress, and health are all related to comparative house placements and aspects of Mercury.

If Mercury is well-aspected in the comparison, the ability to communicate can help the natives resolve mutual problems. If Mercury is afflicted in the comparison, inability to communicate or confusion in communication can cause a breakdown in the relationship.

In romantic and marital relationships, the comparative influences of Mercury indicate the ability of the natives to share intellectual interests, and where these interests are shared, the relationship will extend beyond mere physical attraction and emotional factors. The comparative influences of Mercury also indicate short journeys concerning the relationship.

COMPARATIVE HOUSE PLACEMENTS

Comparative house placements of Mercury indicate the practical affairs of life that will be directly influenced by the communication between the natives and by practical work responsibility in the relationship. These affairs will be of mutual intellectual concern to the natives and can bring short-distance traveling and activities related to work methodology.

A's Mercury in B's First House

The Mercury individual will intellectually stimulate the First House individual and provide him or her with ideas for self-expression, and the First House individual will, in turn, give the Mercury person ideas and support for self-expression. The First House individual can encourage the Mercury individual to put ideas into action and will lend energy and support to them. The Mercury individual's opinions and mental attitudes can tend to define and influence the self-image and self-expression of the First House individual, either positively or negatively, depending on how Mercury is aspected in the comparison and in the Mercury individual's horoscope. In any case, the Mercury individual is likely to give the First House individual a great deal of verbal feedback on his or her manner of action, self-expression, and general level of awareness.

A's Mercury in B's Second House

This is an excellent combination for business and professional partnerships, provided Mercury is not badly afflicted in the comparison. The natives are able to communicate about property and financial affairs. The Mercury individual can stimulate the Second House individual mentally in regard to ways of handling business and financial affairs more efficiently and effectively. The Second House individual sometimes provides financial support for implementing the ideas of the Mercury individual. In some cases, cooperative business endeavors are related to Mercury-ruled activities such as writing, news media, communications media, advertising, publishing, lecturing, travel, accounting, and medicine. Joint business affairs may also relate to scientific fields, inventions, and discoveries.

A's Mercury in B's Third House

Natives with this comparative placement of Mercury communicate about all manner of intellectual subjects. Because the Third House is ruled by Mercury in the natural Zodiac, the natives will stimulate each other mentally in many ways and encourage each other's intellectual pursuits. Consequently, this is one of the best combinations for teacher–student relationships. It is also excellent for collaboration in fields related to scientific research, technology, writing, publishing, teaching, traveling, journalism, and the communications media. It is necessary to look to other influences affecting Mercury in A's horoscope and the Third House in B's horoscope to determine primary areas of discussion and mutual concern.

A's Mercury in B's Fourth House

The Mercury individual's ideas are likely to influence the way the Fourth House individual handles domestic and family affairs. The Fourth House individual's family conditioning is likely to influence the mental attitudes of the Mercury individual. The family and domestic affairs of the Fourth House individual can also become a mental concern to the Mercury individual. In some cases, the natives will stimulate each other's interest in things connected with the earth itself and in general environmental, ecological concerns such as food, farming, gardening, real estate, and other things pertaining to the land and its use. The Mercury individual is likely to encourage the Fourth House individual to use his or her home as a place of writing, study, intellectual pursuits, and sharing of ideas among friends. The Mercury individual can also help the Fourth House individual gain insight into emotional issues related to family upbringing and ingrained psychological habits. The Fourth House individual can provide a base of operations for the intellectual activities of the Mercury individual. There will be mutual concern with clothing, family, health, diet, and hygiene.

A's Mercury in B's Fifth House

The ideas and opinions of the Mercury individual are likely to influence the Fifth House individual's ideas and attitudes about romance, sexual behavior, the performing arts, financial speculation, the raising and educating of children, and social activities. The natives are likely to communicate a great deal about these matters. The creative self-expression and artistic activities of the Fifth House individual may be of mental interest to the Mercury individual. Because Mercury is a neutral, sexless planet, this combination does not, of itself, indicate sexual attraction, but it can improve compatibility in a romantic relationship by enabling the natives to communicate effectively about the romantic aspects of their relationship. This is an excellent placement for teacher–student relationships and parent–child relationships. The natives will often have enjoyable discussions about artistic and cultural areas of mutual interest.

A's Mercury in B's Sixth House

This comparative combination indicates good mutual communication about work and health. It is a good comparative placement for employer–employee relationships, co-worker relationships, and business and professional partnerships. The ideas, knowledge, and experience of the Mercury individual can help the Sixth House individual to work more efficiently and effectively and to take better care of his or her health. This is an excellent combination for doctor–patient relationships, especially if the Mercury individual is the doctor. The natives can help each other to work out practical solutions to everyday problems. There can be mutual interest in matters of diet and clothing. If Mercury is badly afflicted in either the individual horoscopes or the comparison, the natives can be nagging, nit-picking, and unnecessarily critical toward each other. This is generally a good comparative placement for relationships involving co-operation in scientific and technological work where order, system, exact knowledge, and intelligence applied to work are critical factors.

A's Mercury in B's Seventh House

Natives with this comparative combination are curious about each other's thoughts and attitudes about the relationship. Marriage, partnerships, human relations, psychology, and how they think and feel about their own relationships are likely to be major topics of discussion. Their ability to communicate about mutual problems can help to offset any adverse indications in the comparison and can provide a lasting basis for the relationship. If Mercury is afflicted, either natally or in the comparison, the natives will have a hard time understanding each other and will probably experience intellectual differences of opinion. If Mercury is well-aspected, however, they will share many intellectual and educational interests; often, these involve mutual friendships and group activities. This is an excellent placement for intellectual partnerships in writing, research, teaching, journalism, and scientific work. The natives are also apt to be traveling companions on excursions and short journeys.

A's Mercury in B's Eighth House

This comparative combination can stimulate a mutual interest in occult or scientific matters. It is also an effective combination for business partnerships and cooperation in corporate enterprises. Joint financial affairs and matters pertaining to the Eighth House individual's insurance, taxes, legacies, inheritances, and alimony can be of mental concern or interest to the Mercury individual. The Mercury individual may also take an intellectual interest in the Eighth House individual's psychic and occult experiences. The Eighth House individual may employ the Mercury individual's ideas and methodologies in business enterprises and corporate affairs. The natives may become mutually interested in life after death, telepathy, and psychic communication. There can be telepathic exchanges between them, and mutual involvement in investigations or efforts to solve mysteries.

If Mercury is badly afflicted in the comparison, there can be differences of opinion on how to handle joint finances, corporate affairs, insurances, inheritances, or alimony, or on the management of mutual property. There can be disagreements about occult interests or sex, with one of the natives taking the role of a skeptic.

A's Mercury in B's Ninth House

One of the best comparative combinations for a sharing of philosophical and intellectual pursuits, this combination is particularly suited to teacher–student relationships. The natives will generally stimulate each other's interest in religion, philosophy, higher education, foreign cultures, and travel. (This comparative combination is common among traveling companions.) The natives can learn a great deal from each other and expand each other's consciousness. The sharing of scientific, philosophic, and spiritual interests can deepen the relationship and make it more durable. The natives are likely to spend much time in philosophical discussion. The Mercury individual can help the Ninth House individual become aware of practical details concerning the usefulness of personal philosophic, cultural, and educational ideas. The Ninth House individual can help the Mercury gain a broader, more comprehensive understanding of religious, philosophic, cultural, and educational ideas.

If Mercury is badly afflicted in the comparison, there can be disagreements regarding religion, philosophy, law, and educational methods.

A's Mercury in B's Tenth House

The ideas and communications of the Mercury individual are likely to influence the professional affairs of the Tenth House individual. Whether this influence is constructive or negative, however, depends on how well Mercury is aspected in A's horoscope and in the comparison. The Mercury individual can come up with useful and practical ideas for making the Tenth House individual's career efforts more effective and successful in terms of both prestige and money. The Tenth House individual can help gain official and public recognition and support the Mercury individual's ideas, plans, and educational background. In general, this is a good combination for all types of business and professional partnerships. It is especially favorable for partnerships in writing, journalism, teaching, publishing, travel, transportation, communications media, scientific research, education, and related areas. The natives can be involved in political strategy, planning, publicity, and advertising. If Mercury is seriously afflicted in A's horoscope and in the comparison, there may be disagreements over policy decisions, professional recognition, and administrative procedures.

A's Mercury in B's Eleventh House

This comparative combination often indicates a friendship based on shared intellectual interests, especially the scientific, the occult, or the humanitarian. The natives are likely to participate together in group and organizational activities of an intellectual, scientific, or humanitarian nature, and they are likely to engage in much discussion about mutual friends. They will usually stimulate each other to original, creative thinking, and they are able to communicate with each other in a detached and unbiased way, unless Mercury is badly afflicted in the comparison. If Mercury is seriously afflicted in A's horoscope and in the comparison, there could be insincerity in the relationship, with the natives saying one thing and doing another or giving each other well-meaning but impractical advice. This is an excellent combination for friendships involving literary and educational pursuits. In marriage and romantic relationships, this combination can help to establish permanence by providing a basis of friendship which is not entirely dependent on emotional and sexual factors.

A's Mercury in B's Twelfth House

The Mercury individual can help the Twelfth House individual gain insight into the mechanisms and habit patterns of his or her subconscious mind. The natives can stimulate each other's creative imagination. There can be a mutual intellectual interest in subjects such as art, music, psychology, mysticism, and occult approaches to religion. The Twelfth House individual can bring out the intuitive perceptions of the Mercury individual, who, in turn, can help the Twelfth House individual to understand and make practical use of imagination and intuitive insights. The natives will stimulate each other's interest in areas of psychic awareness.

If Mercury is afflicted in the comparison, there may be difficulties in communication caused by confusion, deception, or mental aberrations caused by the subconscious mind. The natives may encourage each other to engage in deceptive, impractical, useless, and often morose, neurotic fantasies. These can take the form of escapist tendencies, which can be detrimental to both natives. On the positive side, the natives can help each other to draw upon inner, intuitive resources to solve problems and be more creative.

COMPARATIVE CONJUNCTIONS

The comparative conjunctions of one person's Mercury to planets, angles, and nodes in another's horoscope will be major factors in determining the nature of the mental relationship between the natives and the kind of communication that will occur between them. These comparative conjunctions indicate areas of expression in which the natives can relate to each other in a rational, scientific, practical way, and this leads to intellectual and tangible achievements for both parties. The affairs ruled by the planet making the comparative conjunction with Mercury will provide a basis for much conversation and communication. The Mercury individual may play the role of either teacher or student in respect to these matters. In either case, they will arouse the Mercury individual's curiosity.

These comparative conjunctions are usually a positive influence, unless Mercury is afflicted, since rational communication is almost always a positive force in resolving differences.

A's Mercury Conjunct B's Sun

See A's Sun Conjunct B's Mercury.

A's Mercury Conjunct B's Moon

See A's Moon Conjunct B's Mercury.

A's Mercury Conjunct B's Mercury (A's ☿ ☌ B's ☿)

This comparative conjunction indicates that the natives will have similar mental viewpoints and that there will be an ease in communication between them. There will be mutual intellectual interests in the things ruled by the sign and house in which the conjunction is found. The natives can overcome problems and disagreements through good communication and clear, rational thinking. In business and professional relationships, they can cooperate effectively in fields such as writing, publishing, reporting, communications media, and education.

If the conjunction is afflicted by other comparative aspects, there could be mental competition and intellectual disagreement between the natives. In work situations, too much idle conversation or meaningless comings and goings can interfere with the natives' efficiency. In general, there can be a mutual interest in intellectual subjects and scientific investigation.

A's Mercury Conjunct B's Venus (A's ☿ ☌ B's ♀)

These natives are usually able to communicate well about personal emotional issues. They can share an interest in literary, artistic, musical, and cultural affairs. The Mercury individual can help the Venus individual to gain mental insight into his or her own feelings and emotional and esthetic reactions, while the Venus individual can help the Mercury individual add grace and refinement to speech, writing, and other communications. The natives will make study and intellectual endeavors more enjoyable for each other. This is a good combination for business partnerships related to art, music, entertainment, and luxury items. In marital relationships, a sharing of esthetic, literary, scientific, and cultural interests can provide a basis for lasting compatibility. The natives will be sympathetic and understanding toward each other. They can also enjoy many mutual friends and social activities.

A's Mercury Conjunct B's Mars (A's ☿ ☌ B's ♂)

Much of the effect of this combination depends on how Mercury and Mars are aspected by other planets in the comparison and in the natal charts of both natives. If these aspects are good, this comparative conjunction can lead to mutual mental stimulation and constructive action. The ideas and know-how of the Mercury individual can make the work and actions of the Mars individual more efficient and effective. The Mars individual can help the Mercury individual to put ideas into action. This can be a good comparative aspect for cooperation in business enterprises where skill, efficiency, and hard work are required. If both natives are willing to exercise patience, consideration, and tact, they can learn many useful, practical things from each other and be an effective team. However, the tendency of the Mercury individual to cogitate about decisions can frustrate the Mars individual's desire for immediate action.

If Mercury and Mars are afflicted, the natives will not see eye to eye on many issues, and will often engage in heated arguments. The Mars individual, in such cases, is apt to regard the Mercury individual as nit-picking and overly critical, while the Mercury individual may regard the Mars individual as overbearing, bossy, brash, too impulsive, and inconsiderate.

A's Mercury Conjunct B's Jupiter (A's ☿ ☌ B's ♃)

These natives will share many educational, intellectual, cultural, philosophical, and religious interests. The Mercury individual can help the Jupiter individual to formulate cultural, philosophical, and religious ideas and beliefs in a more rational and scientific way, while the Jupiter individual can help the Mercury individual develop a more positive, optimistic mental outlook. The Jupiter individual can also help the Mercury individual promote and gain social acceptance for his or her ideas. This combination aids good will, constructive communication, and mutual helpfulness in all relationships. It is especially beneficial in teacher–student and parent–child relationships. The natives will generally have a sense of honor and fair play toward each other, unless other factors in the comparison strongly contradict this. They will make excellent traveling companions.

If this comparative conjunction is badly afflicted, there could be insincerity, hypocrisy, or differences of opinion regarding religion, philosophy, and education. In such cases, the Mercury individual is likely to regard the Jupiter individual as too impractical, superstitious, or unscientific, while the Jupiter individual may regard the Mercury individual as narrow in outlook, nit-picking, overly critical, too concerned with details, and lacking in intuitive wisdom.

Generally speaking, this is one of the most favorable of all comparative aspects: it helps the natives to communicate with mutual consideration and gives them common spiritual, cultural, and intellectual interests. It provides a broad basis for mutual compatibility which goes beyond mere emotional and sexual attraction and contributes to durability in romantic and marital relationships.

A's Mercury Conjunct B's Saturn (A's ☿ ☌ B's ♄)

This is a good comparative combination for business and professional relationships if both individuals are mature. There can be a strong mutual sense of purpose and responsibility. The Saturn individual is likely to make heavy demands on the Mercury individual in terms of discipline and concentration. If the individuals are mentally polarized, there can be a mutual interest in business, scientific, or mathematical interests. This combination occurs frequently in business, professional, and employer–employee relationships. It is good for cooperation in areas requiring discipline, hard work, attention to detail, accuracy, and precision. This can be an excellent comparative aspect for teacher–student relationships, provided the teacher is reasonably open-minded and the student is mature enough to accept discipline.

If Mercury and Saturn are afflicted in either horoscope or in the comparison, difficulties in communication can arise. The Saturn individual can have a negative, wet-blanket attitude toward the ideas of the Mercury individual. The Mercury individual is likely to regard the Saturn individual as negative, too conservative, slow, ignorant, prejudiced, or biased. The natives may be mistrustful of each other, suspecting ulterior motives, especially in financial matters or things pertaining to prestige and advancement. The Saturn individual will tend to demand mental discipline from the Mercury individual and expect more work and concentration.

This aspect does not indicate romance, but it can lead to a greater sense of mutual responsibility in a marital relationship, and it gives the natives the ability to face mutual responsibilities in a practical way.

A's Mercury Conjunct B's Uranus (A's ☿ ☌ B's ♅)

This comparative conjunction indicates exciting, unusual mutual stimulation in many realms of mental interest. The original ideas, intuitive flashes, and unusual experiences of the Uranus individual will stimulate and enliven the Mercury individual mentally. The Uranus individual will help the Mercury individual to become more open-minded and unbiased in his or her mental attitudes and opinions. The Mercury individual can help the Uranus individual to formulate and express intuitive perceptions and put them to practical use. The natives will tend to stimulate intuitive, mental insights in each other and will engage in brainstorming sessions together. They will share intellectual interests, especially in such areas as science, electronics, astrology, occultism, parapsychology, education, political reform, or humanitarian work.

If Mercury and Uranus are badly afflicted in the natal horoscopes and in the comparison, there may be intellectual disagreements, or the natives may encourage each other in impractical, eccentric ideas. The many stimulating intellectual exchanges which occur with this combination usually form the basis of a lasting friendship.

The natives are often involved in group and organizational activities of a humanitarian, scientific, or occult nature, and enjoy associating with many friends. This combination is also indicative of mental telepathy between the natives.

A's Mercury Conjunct B's Neptune (A's ☿ ☌ B's ♆)

This combination indicates a telepathic link between the natives, at least on a subconscious, subliminal level. If Mercury and Neptune are afflicted in the individual horoscopes and in the comparison, there may be deliberate or unintentional deceptiveness, especially on the part of the Neptune individual. The natives may share an interest in art, music, literature, religion, mysticism, occultism, psychic phenomena, astrology, and other related subjects. The Mercury individual can help the Neptune individual gain intellectual insight into his or her subconscious, psychological mechanisms and emotional conditionings based on past experiences. The Neptune individual can help the Mercury individual to utilize intuitive faculties to find solutions to problems. This aspect occurs frequently between patient and psychiatrist or psychological therapist. The natives' activities may include spiritual healing, involvement in occult groups or societies, or other psychic activities.

When Mercury and Neptune are badly afflicted, the natives may encourage each other in self-deception and in self-destructive habits such as drinking and drug abuse.

A's Mercury Conjunct B's Pluto (A's ☿ ☌ B's ♀)

As with the Mercury–Uranus and Mercury–Neptune comparative combinations, there can be a mutual interest in occult, astrological, psychic, and parapsychological subjects. There can also be a psychic, telepathic link between the natives. They are likely to share an interest in reincarnation and life after death. The Pluto individual is likely to be the dominating influence in the relationship. The natives may become involved in investigating mysteries—scientific, occult, political, or social. They can have a profound transforming effect on each other's basic concepts, beliefs, and level of awareness. This can be an effective combination for cooperation in corporate enterprises, especially those related to scientific research, engineering, energy, insurance, taxes, or the affairs of the dead.

When this combination works negatively, the natives are likely to be mistrustful of each other and engage in mutual spying, secret investigations, and tale-bearing behind each other's backs. The Pluto individual may attempt to use or mentally dominate or overpower the Mercury person. Sometimes, there could be attempts at psychic control or domination, by the Pluto individual, usually on an unconscious level. This will not be manifested strongly unless Pluto is powerful and afflicted in the Pluto individual's chart. The Mercury individual will be irritated by such attempts at domination. On the positive side, the natives can encourage each other in mental and spiritual self-improvement and work out methods of improving the efficiency of techniques for work. They can help each other gain a much more profound scientific and spiritual understanding of life.

A's Mercury Conjunct B's North Node Opposition B's South Node (A's ☿ ☌ B's ☊ ☍ B's ☋)

These natives can help each other gain insights into prevailing cultural ideas, attitudes, trends, and fads. Through insight into these factors, the Nodes individual can help the Mercury individual gain popular acceptance for personal ideas and mental expressions of all types. The Mercury individual can help the Nodes individual to analyze and understand popular trends and can originate ideas about how to benefit from such trends. On the negative side, the natives may encourage each other to blindly follow prevailing ideas and beliefs. This is a favorable combination for those who work together in advertising, publicity, or politics.

A's Mercury Conjunct B's South Node Opposition B's North Node (A's ☿ ☌ B's ☋ ☍ B's ☊)

This comparative combination indicates an association based upon individualistic and less popular ideas and activities. The Nodes individual is negative or unreceptive at times toward the Mercury individual's ideas, but can also give the Mercury individual a deeper understanding of the social forces which shape cultural history.

A's Mercury Conjunct B's Ascendant Opposition B's Descendant (A's ☿ ☌ B's Asc. ☍ B's Desc.)

Basically the same as "A's Mercury in B's First House," this combination, however, indicates greater intensity and immediacy of interaction. The basic spiritual awareness and intuitive perceptions of the Ascendant/Descendant individual will influence the thinking and mental attitudes of the Mercury individual. The ideas, mental attitudes, and communications of the Mercury individual are likely, in turn, to influence the self-image and basic attitude and actions of the Ascendant/Descendant individual. This is a good combination for teacher–student and parent–child relationships.

A's Mercury Conjunct B's Midheaven Opposition B's Nadir (A's ☿ ☌ B's M.C. ☍ B's Nadir)

This is a good comparative combination for business and professional relationships. The ideas and knowledge of the Mercury individual can help the Midheaven/Nadir individual's status and professional advancement. The Mercury individual is likely to set up communication lines important for the career advancement of the Midheaven/Nadir individual and introduce him or her to people who will be valuable professional contacts. The Mercury individual can act as an agent for the Midheaven/Nadir individual. The Midheaven/Nadir individual can in turn help the Mercury individual gain recognition for his or her ideas and support for the implementation of these ideas from people of power and importance. This is a favorable combination for teacher–student relationships that involve professional training or apprenticeship. The natives may be mutually involved in business, professional, or political planning and strategy.

A's Mercury Conjunct B's Descendant Opposition B's Ascendant (A's ☿ ☌ B's Desc. ☍ B's Asc.)

The Mercury individual is likely to give the Descendant/Ascendant individual considerable psychological feedback about how he or she appears to others. This can be either constructive or destructive, depending upon how Mercury is aspected both in the horoscope of the Mercury individual and in the comparison. The Descendant/Ascendant individual will introduce the Mercury individual to new social contacts and acquaintances. The natives can share an interest in mutual friends, group activities, and a variety of subjects of intellectual interest, with a special emphasis on things relating to psychology. This sharing will provide a basis for compatibility which goes beyond mere emotional and sexual attraction. This combination will greatly aid the ability to communicate in a marital relationship and will provide a means of discussing and finding solutions to whatever problems may exist in the relationship.

A's Mercury Conjunct B's Nadir Opposition B's Midheaven (A's ☿ ☌ B's Nadir ☍ B's M.C.)

The Mercury individual can help the Nadir/Midheaven individual to understand many personal deep-rooted emotional attitudes based upon past experience and family upbringing. The Nadir/Midheaven individual can provide the Mercury individual with a home or base of operations for intellectual activities. The natives are likely to spend time talking about family affairs and family background. They can involve themselves in all types of intellectual activities, especially those carried on in the home, such as collecting a library, group educational studies, scientific projects, or skilled crafts.

COMPARATIVE SEXTILES

Comparative sextiles of Mercury indicate opportunities for the natives to communicate logically and harmoniously about the affairs ruled by the planet in one horoscope which Mercury in the other horoscope sextiles. In these areas, there will be a flow of ideas, practical information, and know-how, and a friendly intellectual exchange. This intellectual exchange will also concern the affairs ruled by Mercury and the other planet in their respective horoscopes. These comparative sextiles aid mutual thinking, planning, and skilled work. For this reason, they are especially helpful in teacher–student, employer–employee, and all types of professional relationships, as well as in mutual group and organizational endeavors.

A's Mercury Sextile B's Sun

See A's Sun Sextile B's Mercury.

A's Mercury Sextile B's Moon

See A's Moon Sextile B's Mercury.

A's Mercury Sextile B's Mercury (A's ☿ ✳ B's ☿)

This comparative sextile indicates mutual intellectual interests and the ability to resolve problems through clear thinking and communication. The natives can cooperate effectively in fields such as science, writing, teaching, medicine, communications media, publishing, and other pursuits requiring intellectual ability. They can help each other achieve goals and objectives through stimulating each other's mental processes and conveying useful information. Good communication and sharing of knowledge and know-how will make work easier. There can be mutual interest in health, diet, clothing, hygiene, and medical technology, especially if Virgo is involved.

A's Mercury Sextile B's Venus (A's ☿ ✳ B's ♀)

These natives will usually relate to and communicate with each other in a kind and considerate way. They can share literary, esthetic, and social activities and interests. The esthetic perceptions of the Venus individual will be of intellectual interest to the Mercury individual, and the ideas of the Mercury individual will provide esthetic inspiration for the Venus individual. The natives will enjoy mutual friends, and their intellectual and social activities will involve these friends. The natives are also likely to stimulate each other's interest in psychology and human relationships. In a romantic relationship or marriage, the natives' ability to communicate about emotional, psychological concerns will help them to work out whatever differences and difficulties may arise. This is a favorable comparative aspect for business partnerships related to art, literature, fine clothes, or luxury items. The natives enjoy showing each other fine art objects of beauty and craftsmanship.

A's Mercury Sextile B's Mars (A's ☿ ⚹ B's ♂)

Natives with this comparative sextile will intellectually stimulate and energize each other. The Mars individual can help the Mercury individual to put his or her ideas into action. The Mercury individual can help the Mars individual to more efficient and organized action. This is a favorable combination for cooperation in scientific and engineering endeavors or in corporate business enterprises. The natives can also work together effectively in political and promotional endeavors. The Mercury individual can reason with the Mars individual and keep him or her from being overly impulsive. This is an excellent aspect for employer–employee, co-worker, and all types of professional relationships. The natives tend to bring out each other's inventive and resourceful qualities.

A's Mercury Sextile B's Jupiter (A's ☿ ⚹ B's ♃)

This comparative combination indicates friendships based upon mutual intellectual and philosophical interests. The natives are often involved together in group and organizational activities of a scientific, educational, philosophical, philanthropic, religious, or humanitarian nature. Often, they become acquainted through going to school together or through religious or philosophical organizations. They can make good traveling companions. The Jupiter individual will bring out moral and ethical qualities in the Mercury individual, while the latter can help the Jupiter individual to be more detailed and practical in pursuing humanitarian and philosophical goals and ideas. This is one of the best combinations for parent–child and teacher–student relationships, as well as for all types of family relationships. There will be an ease of communication between the natives that will smooth any difficulties that may arise. The natives will be honest, considerate, and straightforward with each other. This combination will bring out a sense of humor in both natives.

A's Mercury Sextile B's Saturn (A's ☿ ✳ B's ♄)

An excellent comparative combination for associations where clear, precise, disciplined thinking and working are required, it is therefore helpful in teacher–student, employer–employee, co-worker, and all types of business and professional relationships. The natives may also be associated through political, professional, or fraternal organizations. The Saturn individual can help the Mercury individual to achieve constructive mental discipline, experience, and care and exactness in work. The Mercury individual can devise creative, ingenious ideas for making the work of the Saturn individual more efficient and effective. The natives will help each other to be more resourceful and efficient. They will encourage each other's interest in serious professional education and training, especially along the lines of mathematics, science, engineering, business, or medicine. How strongly the natives will respond to these mutual influences depends largely upon how strong these planets are in both natal horoscopes. In marriage and family relationships, this comparative aspect will encourage the acceptance of mutual responsibility, a willingness to work together, and the ability to communicate sensibly about problems and serious issues.

A's Mercury Sextile B's Uranus (A's ☿ ✳ B's ♅)

This is one of the best comparative aspects for exciting, intellectual friendships. The natives will spark each other's intuitive mental creativity. Shared interests can include scientific endeavors, humanitarian causes, occultism, astrology, literature, education, group and organizational activities, and mutual friendships. The natives will do much traveling together, investigating things of intellectual interest and excitement. They may enjoy an intuitive, telepathic communication, if other factors in their natal horoscopes and in the comparison bear this out. The Uranus individual can help the Mercury individual gain a greater understanding and appreciation of the intuitive and occult side of life, and the Mercury individual can, in turn, help the Uranus individual to communicate his or her intuitive perceptions in a rational way and put them to practical use and expression.

Because of the triple-Aquarius/Eleventh House significance of this combination, there will be much mutual involvement in group and organizational activities, including a mutual interest in humanitarian causes and work, scientific discoveries, occult organizations, and efforts at expansion of consciousness. These activities will usually involve many mutual friends. This tends to be a very group-conscious comparative aspect.

A's Mercury Sextile B's Neptune (A's ☿ ✳ B's ♆)

This comparative aspect can indicate a psychic, telepathic link between the natives. The Neptune individual can bring out the Mercury individual's intuitive, imaginative capacities, while the Mercury individual can help the Neptune individual to utilize imagination and intuitive inspiration in a practical and communicable way. The Mercury individual can also help the Neptune individual to gain psychological insight into his or her subconscous mind and emotional conditionings based on past experiences.

The natives may share an interest in poetry, literary art forms, theater, and other creatively imaginative expressions that combine communication with creative, artistic imagination. There is also the possibility of mutual involvement in groups and organizations of a secretive, occult, or mystical nature, if other tendencies in the comparison and in the natal horoscopes confirm this. There is also the possibility of collaboration in writing or teaching, or in use of the communications media with respect to mystical, psychic, or occult subjects. The natives can develop a mutual interest in religion and mystical philosophy and may become traveling companions in pursuit of such goals.

A's Mercury Sextile B's Pluto (A's ☿ ✳ B's ♀)

The natives will tend to bring out each other's mental resourcefulness and interest in scientifically understanding Nature's invisible occult energies. To reap the full benefit of the possibilities of this comparative combination, the individuals must be at an advanced level of consciousness. The Pluto person can help the Mercury individual to deepen perceptions of the unseen occult realms of reality, thus awakening an interest in the metaphysical aspects of life. The Mercury individual can help the Pluto individual to verbalize and communicate these levels of perception and, in some cases, to put them to scientific use. The natives may develop a mutual interest in life after death, reincarnation, mind projection in time and space, and other occult phenomena and practices. In other cases, they can share an interest in deep scientific subjects such as atomic physics, higher dimensions, or genetic codes. Naturally, both natives must be at an advanced level for this to occur. In more ordinary cases, there can be occasional psychic, telepathic exchanges or an interest in corporate business, taxes, insurance, the affairs of the dead, physical or financial self-improvement, or group and organizational finances. In any event, these natives can help each other to see beneath surface appearances.

A's Mercury Sextile B's North Node Trine B's South Node
(A's ☿ ✳ B's ☊ △ B's ☋)

Natives with this comparative combination can help each other to gain insight into prevailing social trends, customs, fads, and fashions. The Mercury individual can devise ideas as to how these conditions can be utilized or adjusted to the best advantage, and the Nodes individual can help the Mercury individual communicate with the public more effectively. The natives can help each other come to a better understanding of their cultural conditioning.

A's Mercury Sextile B's South Node Trine B's North Node
(A's ☿ ✳ B's ☋ △ B's ☊)

This comparative combination has basically the same significance as "A's Mercury Sextile B's North Node Trine B's South Node," except that these natives will be intellectually conservative, independent, and critical regarding social trends and popular beliefs.

A's Mercury Sextile B's Ascendant Trine B's Descendant
(A's ☿ ✳ B's Asc. △ B's Desc.)

This comparative combination indicates good communication between the natives regarding planning and cooperative action. The Ascendant/ Descendant individual can help the Mercury individual to put ideas into action, while the Mercury individual can help the Ascendant/Descendant individual to plan and organize actions. Their ability to communicate can help smooth out possible difficulties in the relationship. The natives are able to think and plan together and to communicate with their mutual friends.

A's Mercury Sextile B's Midheaven Trine B's Nadir
(A's ☿ ✳ B's M.C. △ B's Nadir)

The ideas and planning ability of the Mercury individual can help the Midheaven/Nadir individual to organize career and domestic affairs. The Midheaven/Nadir individual can help the Mercury individual implement ideas by providing a base of operations for them and by helping to gain recognition and official support for the Mercury individual's ideas.

A's Mercury Sextile B's Descendant Trine B's Ascendant
(A's ☿ ✳ B's Desc. △ B's Asc.)

The significance of this comparative combination is basically that of "A's Mercury Sextile B's Ascendant Trine B's Descendant," except that these natives will be more intellectually concerned with their relationship and with psychological affairs and less with personal self-expression.

A's Mercury Sextile B's Nadir Trine B's Midheaven
(A's ☿ ✳ B's Nadir △ B's M.C.)

This comparative combination has basically the same significance as "A's Mercury Sextile B's Midheaven Trine B's Nadir," except that these natives will be more intellectually concerned with family and domestic affairs, and more intuitive in their approach to professional matters.

COMPARATIVE SQUARES

Comparative squares of Mercury indicate that the natives must exercise patience and discipline if they are to understand and get along with each other. These comparative squares often indicate difficulties in communication or fundamental differences of opinion between the natives regarding important issues. These difficulties are especially likely to arise in professional or domestic affairs, although they can and do touch upon many areas of life, according to the house and sign positions and rulerships of Mercury and the planet making the square. Emotionally based habit patterns, aggressiveness, or crystallized, rigid viewpoints can stand in the way of the natives' ability to hear and understand each other. If both natives are sufficiently intelligent and mature, comparative squares can lead to concrete, practical accomplishments and incorporation of constructive qualities into the relationship. (This is due to the Mars–Saturn–Capricorn nature of the square aspect.) These squares can also be conducive to the exchange of ideas that have practical value.

A's Mercury Square B's Sun

See A's Sun Square B's Mercury.

A's Mercury Square B's Moon

See A's Moon Square B's Mercury.

A's Mercury Square B's Mercury (A's ☿ □ B's ☿)

Difficulties in communication and differing intellectual viewpoints, both of which can cause misunderstanding and conflict are indicated by this comparative square. The natives are likely to disagree on things related to dress, personal hygiene, health, and the handling of work and professional responsibilities. They can have difficulty cooperating in the areas of study, work, communication, writing, and transportation.

A's Mercury Square B's Venus (A's ☿ □ B's ♀)

This comparative aspect can cause difficulties in communicating about emotional issues, especially in romantic and marital relationships. In some cases, it merely indicates disagreements in esthetic, cultural, and social values. The Venus individual may feel that the Mercury individual is too wrapped up in his or her ideas and in constant intellectual discussion to recognize or respond to the Venus individual's feelings and emotional and esthetic values. The Mercury individual may regard the Venus individual as overly sentimental and impractical. The natives may rationalize and overanalyze their emotional reactions to each other, and thus block real understanding and sensitivity to each other's feelings. On the other hand, emotional reactions and sentimentality can stand in the way of clear-headed thinking and planning, and excessive expenditures of time and money on frivolous social activities and luxuries can result. The natives may tend to talk excessively instead of getting their work done.

A's Mercury Square B's Mars (A's ☿ □ B's ♂)

A difficult comparative combination, this often results in arguments and heated disagreements. The natives are prone to regard threats to their points of view as threats to their egos when dealing with each other. This emotional stance makes it difficult for them to communicate in a calm, rational way and to find workable solutions to problems. The Mercury individual is likely to regard the Mars individual as too brash and impulsive, while the Mars individual is likely to regard the Mercury person as all talk and no action, vacillating, and indecisive. The natives need to exercise patience to avoid becoming irritated and annoyed with each other. The Mercury individual can be annoyed by the tendency of the Mars individual to do things without first informing him or her. The natives can have a tendency to yell and shout at each other and generally lose their tempers in heated verbal exchange. When they attempt to repress this, however, they can feel nervous and ill at ease.

A's Mercury Square B's Jupiter (A's ☿ □ B's ♃)

The Mercury individual can regard the Jupiter individual as vague and impractical, while the Jupiter individual may regard the Mercury person as overly concerned with details and lacking in wisdom and broad philosophical outlook. The natives sometimes encourage each other to overindulge in grandiose, unrealistic, impractical thinking, dreaming, and wool-gathering. There can be differences of opinion and belief regarding religion, philosophy, education, work methodologies, and methods of communication. The subconscious, emotional conditionings of the Jupiter individual can be a source of annoyance to the Mercury individual, who has a more practical outlook. Much depends on how strong these planets are in the natal horoscopes. There can be differences of opinion in the handling of domestic and family affairs or in the carrying out of work and service. The natives often have a tendency to engage in long-winded, verbose discussions which go around in circles and fail to reach a decisive conclusion. They may also engage in much meaningless, nonproductive traveling about together. Confusion in co-ordinating schedules and appointments is typical of this combination.

A's Mercury Square B's Saturn (A's ☿ □ B's ♄)

The Mercury individual is likely to regard the Saturn individual as too conservative, opinionated, dull, unsympathetic, stupid, negative, or uninspired. The Saturn individual is likely to react negatively and unsympathetically to the ideas and communications of the Mercury individual and make heavy demands on the Mercury individual in terms of mental discipline and work. These combinations produce difficulties in nearly all types of relationships. The natives can tend to make each other more negative and depressed. Sometimes, jealousy and resentment enter into the picture. Usually these natives avoid each other, unless they are forced into association by unavoidable circumstances or responsibilities. This tends to be a difficult combination for employer–employee relationships; there is usually dissatisfaction on the part of one or both parties. Some kind of blockage or restriction of communication can accompany this comparative aspect and make it difficult for the natives to understand or sympathize with each other.

A's Mercury Square B's Uranus (A's ☿ □ B's ♅)

This comparative combination can produce interesting, but not necessarily stable or predictable, mental interactions. The Mercury individual is likely to regard the Uranus individual as eccentric and unreliable. The Uranus individual may, in turn, consider the Mercury individual to be overly concerned with detail or lacking in intuitive insight. In some cases, the natives will encourage each other in unrealistic and impractical ways of thinking. They tend to take too much for granted and jump to conclusions in communicating with each other, and misinterpretations often result. The natives tend to be impatient toward each other, and this creates friction in planning and communication. There can be different preferences where friends and group associations and activities are concerned; the natives may not enjoy the same company and activities. There can be major intellectual differences of opinion. The Uranus individual may often change his or her mind, thus upsetting the plans of the Mercury individual and, in general, the erratic, unpredictable behavior of the Uranus individual can make the Mercury person feel nervous and ill at ease. In general, these natives will tend to get on each other's nerves.

A's Mercury Square B's Neptune (A's ☿ □ B's ♆)

The Neptune individual will seem impractical, vague, moody, and indecisive to the Mercury individual, while the latter can seem uninspired, prosaic, overly intellectual, and lacking in sensitivity and intuition to the Neptune person. The natives have a difficult time communicating on the same wavelength. The Mercury individual is likely to regard the Neptune individual as unreliable. In some cases, the natives will have an undermining effect upon each other, encouraging each other to dreaming, laziness, and unrealistic thinking. The Neptune individual may be evasive, untruthful, deceptive, and indecisive toward the Mercury individual. The Mercury individual can have a difficult time relating to the Neptune person's neurotic emotional patterns, habits, and subconscious conditionings. The Mercury person may fail to appreciate the esthetic and intuitive perceptions and talents of the Neptune individual. These natives are not likely to deal with each other in a reliable or truthful way.

A's Mercury Square B's Pluto (A's ☿ □ B's ♀)

The Pluto individual may try to dominate the thinking of the Mercury individual psychically or mentally, and the Mercury individual is likely to regard the Pluto individual as overbearing or dictatorial. The Pluto individual will in turn regard the Mercury individual as superficial and lacking in depth of perception. The natives are likely to suspect each other's motives or try to pry into each other's secrets. This is not a favorable combination for cooperation in business, professional, or scientific relationships. The natives may expand each other's level of awareness, but they will not always see eye to eye on important issues. There can be disagreements over occult practices and beliefs, joint finances, wills and inheritances, corporate financial affairs, alimony, taxes, or insurance. The natives are likely to get into arguments and debates over these matters, as well as over scientific or philosophical ideas and beliefs.

A's Mercury Square B's North Node Square
B's South Node (A's ☿ □ B's ☊ □ B's ☋)

These natives are not likely to agree in their ideas about and their opinions and perceptions of prevailing social trends, fads, and attitudes. They can differ on how to adjust to or take advantage of these trends, and on political matters.

A's Mercury Square B's South Node Square B's North Node

See A's Mercury Square B's North Node Square B's South Node.

A's Mercury Square B's Ascendant Square
B's Descendant (A's ☿ □ B's Asc. □ B's Desc.)

Because these natives may have difficulty understanding each other, they may be unable to cooperate mentally in marriage or partnerships. The Ascendant/Descendant individual may regard the Mercury individual as vacillating or indecisive, while the Mercury individual may consider the Ascendant/Descendant individual to be too impulsive in action.

A's Mercury Square B's Midheaven Square B's Nadir
(A's ☿ □ B's M.C. □ B's Nadir)

These individuals are likely to think differently about the planning and handling of professional and domestic affairs. This is not a favorable comparative combination for family, domestic, and professional relationships. There are likely to be major political differences of opinion. The Midheaven/Nadir individual may regard the Mercury individual as vacillating, indecisive, or unreliable where important professional or domestic responsibilities are concerned. The Mercury individual may disagree with the Midheaven/Nadir native's ideas about the handling of domestic and professional affairs.

A's Mercury Square B's Descendant Square B's Ascendant

See A's Mercury Square B's Ascendant Square B's Descendant.

A's Mercury Square B's Nadir Square B's Midheaven

See A's Mercury Square B's Midheaven Square B's Nadir.

COMPARATIVE TRINES

Comparative trines of Mercury indicate the areas of interpersonal communication in which the natives will have a natural and intuitive ability to communicate with each other and to understand each other's intellectual viewpoints. This ability to communicate will help the natives solve interpersonal problems whenever they arise. In the affairs ruled by Mercury and by the trining planet in the comparison, there will be a harmonious creative and philosophical rapport in decision-making, planning, and understanding. The natives can communicate easily about these affairs and may engage in travel or study together for purposes of gaining knowledge about them. Comparative trines are also favorable for cooperation in writing or other mentally creative projects.

A's Mercury Trine B's Sun

See A's Sun Trine B's Mercury.

A's Mercury Trine B's Moon

See A's Moon Trine B's Mercury.

A's Mercury Trine B's Mercury (A's ☿ △ B's ☿)

This comparative trine indicates practical and intellectual communications between the natives. They can cooperate effectively in work and study and in matters related to diet, dress, and personal hygiene. The natives will share an intellectual interest in the things ruled by the Element or Triplicity in which Mercury is found. They can work together effectively in research, writing, travel, transportation, education, publishing, and the news and communications media.

A's Mercury Trine B's Venus (A's ☿ △ B's ♀)

This comparative combination indicates compatible ideas in the areas of art, literature, social activities, and cultural pursuits. There is mutual consideration and gentleness in communication. The natives usually enjoy their mutual friends and engage in many social activities. This is a favorable combination for cooperation in teaching children and for working together in literature, art, music, and entertainment. It also favors business partnerships, especially in such businesses as writing, publishing, communications, music, advertising, fine clothing, or luxury items. In romantic and marital relationships, the natives are able to communicate about their feelings and emotional reactions and so resolve whatever emotional difficulties may exist in the relationship. The natives will bring out each other's refined tastes and esthetic, cultural interests. They can also make congenial traveling companions. They tend to stimulate each other's sense of humor and fun-loving qualities.

A's Mercury Trine B's Mars (A's ☿ △ B's ♂)

The Mars individual can help the Mercury individual to put ideas into action, while the latter can help the Mars to plan actions more effectively. The natives can cooperate well in projects requiring skill and hard work, such as engineering, business, or scientific enterprises. This is a favorable combination for cooperation in business, manufacturing, or construction. The natives can have a sense of friendly mental competition and can be fond of games such as chess that involve strategy and skill. There may be a mutual interest in politics and a fondness for debate. This is a favorable combination for planning in corporate enterprises, especially those related to engineering, insurance, taxes, sports, travel, transportation, newspapers, periodicals, writing, or publishing. The natives can help each other put ideas to constructive use and direct energy into actualizing worthwhile ideas. They will encourage each other's enthusiasm, enterprising ambition, and resourcefulness.

A's Mercury Trine B's Jupiter (A's ☿ △ B's ♃)

The natives share many intellectual, spiritual, and philosophical interests. The Jupiter individual can help to develop wisdom and broaden the spiritual and philosophical outlook of the Mercury individual. The Mercury individual can help the Jupiter individual to fill in some of the practical details in his or her broad philosophical outlines. This is an excellent combination for cooperation in communications work, publishing, writing, traveling, education, religion, law, or philosophy. It is probably the best comparative aspect for traveling companions to share. It is also excellent for teacher–student and parent–child relationships. By itself, it does not produce romantic and sexual attraction, but in a romantic or marital relationship, it can improve communication and provide a rich basis for shared cultural values and thus increase the durability of the relationship. The natives tend to foster optimism and a constructive mental outlook in each other by encouraging each other to positive thinking.

A's Mercury Trine B's Saturn (A's ☿ △ B's ♄)

This comparative combination is excellent for all business and professional relationships. The natives will improve each other's capacity for hard-headed, practical thinking, especially in such areas as science, mathematics, engineering, accounting, business, writing, organizational activities, law, medicine, or politics. The wisdom, discipline, and experience of the Saturn individual can improve the mental productivity, ability, and skill of the Mercury individual, and the Saturn individual usually nurtures greater mental maturity in the Mercury native. The ideas and intellectual insights of the Mercury individual can help the Saturn individual to work more efficiently and successfully. The natives can assist each other in planning and handling serious legal business and scientific and political endeavors and projects. This combination is often found in enduring friendships. It signifies cooperation in serious group and organizational activities. It is favorable for employer–employee and teacher–student relationships. Relationships with this comparative trine require discipline and hard work, but they produce worthwhile, lasting practical results. The combination works best if the Saturn individual is the older or more experienced of the two natives and is thus able to assume a natural teacher's role.

A's Mercury Trine B's Uranus (A's ☿ △ B's ♅)

Because this comparative combination indicates a rapid exchange of ideas between the natives, they will tend to spark each other's creative, original thinking and intuitive mental processes. The Uranus individual will broaden the mental outlook of the Mercury individual and help the Mercury individual develop original thinking, and the Mercury individual can help the Uranus individual find practical application for his or her original ideas. The natives will have many friends and group activities in common. They will also share an interest in scientific, humanitarian, astrological, or occult subjects. They can cooperate in such areas as writing, the communications media, advertising, and scientific work of all kinds. This is also a favorable combination for business and professional cooperation in such areas as electronics, communications, scientific research, writing, or publishing. The natives can communicate on a telepathic level. They are apt to go on sudden, unexpected journeys in search of knowledge or excitement.

A's Mercury Trine B's Neptune (A's ☿ △ B's ♆)

This combination indicates a telepathic, psychic link between the natives. This may be on a subconscious level; in some cases, however, the natives may be consciously able to read each other's thoughts and feelings. There can also be a mutual interest in religion, philosophy, foreign cultures, mysticism, and psychic phenomena. The Mercury individual can help the Neptune individual to understand and gain insight into emotional habit patterns based on past experiences and subconscious psychological mechanisms. The Neptune individual will tend to make the Mercury individual aware of the intuitive, imaginative side of life. The Mercury individual can help the Neptune individual to communicate these new perceptions and find a practical outlet for their expression. In romantic, marital, and family relationships, this combination will make for a greater degree of sympathetic emotional understanding or intuitive perception of each other's moods. This is a good combination for cooperation in writing of a poetic or imaginative nature.

A's Mercury Trine B's Pluto (A's ☿ △ B's ♀)

These natives may develop a mutual interest in occult subjects, reincarnation, life after death, or advanced aspects of science such as atomic physics, the theory of relativity, higher mathematics, or the fourth dimension. However, both natives must be advanced for these tendencies to be manifest. In general, they can help each other solve mysteries and discover secrets. In some cases, there is a telepathic link between them. The Mercury individual can help the Pluto individual to verbalize or set down in writing some of his or her deeper perceptions about nature and the subtler levels of existence. The Pluto individual can deepen the perception and understanding of the Mercury individual, profoundly affecting mental and philosophical outlook. This is a favorable comparative aspect for cooperation in corporate business enterprises related to technology, writing, publishing, travel, research, secret investigations, insurance, and taxes.

A's Mercury Trine B's North Node Sextile B's South Node

See A's Mercury Sextile B's South Node Trine B's North Node.

A's Mercury Trine B's South Node Sextile B's North Node

See A's Mercury Sextile B's North Node Trine B's South Node.

A's Mercury Trine B's Ascendant Sextile B's Descendant

See A's Mercury Sextile B's Descendant Trine B's Ascendant.

A's Mercury Trine B's Midheaven Sextile B's Nadir

See A's Mercury Sextile B's Nadir Trine B's Midheaven.

A's Mercury Trine B's Descendant Sextile B's Ascendant

See A's Mercury Sextile B's Ascendant Trine B's Descendant.

A's Mercury Trine B's Nadir Sextile B's Midheaven

See A's Mercury Sextile B's Midheaven Trine B's Nadir.

COMPARATIVE OPPOSITIONS

Comparative oppositions of Mercury indicate that the natives, particularly the Mercury native, must be willing to see the other person's point of view fairly and impartially if the relationship is to work. These combinations indicate a need for willingness to communicate and listen to work out differences and effectively coordinate mutual actions and comings and goings. If both natives are mature and sufficiently open-minded and willing to compromise in planning and decision-making, differences can be worked out satisfactorily. With patience and mutual consideration, the natives can learn a great deal from each other and fill out deficiencies in their own natures by including other points of view. Much will depend on the general flexibility of their temperaments. Adaptable people can adjust to these comparative aspects more easily than people who have rigid personalities.

A's Mercury Opposition B's Sun

See A's Sun Opposition B's Mercury.

A's Mercury Opposition B's Moon

See A's Moon Opposition B's Mercury.

A's Mercury Opposition B's Mercury (A's ☿ ☍ B's ☿)

This comparative opposition indicates relationship problems arising from differences in intellectual viewpoints and difficulties in communication. The natives can have difficulty in cooperating in matters related to writing, study, communications media, transportation, work, health, or planning. Confusion can arise over keeping appointments or properly understanding and keeping agreements. Lack of proper communication in work can cause inefficiency and wasted effort. The natives are apt to disagree in matters of dress, personal hygiene, diet, or work habits.

A's Mercury Opposition B's Venus (A's ☿ ☍ B's ♀)

The Mercury native in this comparative combination must endeavor to be sensitive to the feelings of the Venus individual, while the latter must make an honest effort to understand rationally the ideas and communications of the Mercury native. There may be differences of opinion regarding art, music, social activities, and friends which will need adjustment and compromise. There can also be a mutual sharing of interest in these areas. The Venus individual often sees the Mercury individual as too intellectual, dry, and unemotional. The Venus individual can seem too emotional, lazy, and sentimental to the Mercury individual. There can be differences of opinion over the handling of finances, work, or business affairs. The Mercury individual may resent the tendency of the Venus individual to spend money on what the Mercury person considers to be unnecessary luxuries. In work situations, the natives may spend too much time talking and neglect their work and practical responsibilities.

A's Mercury Opposition B's Mars (A's ☿ ☍ B's ♂)

The natives have a tendency to lose patience with each other and get into arguments. The Mercury individual is likely to regard the Mars individual as too impulsive and aggressive, while the Mars individual is likely to view the other as all talk and no action. The Mars individual is likely to make the Mercury individual irritable and nervous. This is not a good combination for business partnerships, group and organizational associations, or work and professional relationships. There can be disagreements and disputes over the handling of communications, letters, documents, driving and transportation, advertising, publicity, joint finances, corporate financial affairs, inheritances, or alimony. If the natives are to get along, they must work hard at exercising patience and consideration in speech and communication. Sometimes the natives are opponents in debates and lawsuits. If both natives are sufficiently mature, their association can lead to productive and well-thought-out action.

A's Mercury Opposition B's Jupiter (A's ☿ ☍ B's ♃)

These natives are apt to engage in many long-winded, inconclusive discussions and philosophical meanderings. The Mercury individual may regard the Jupiter individual as too general and impractical in philosophical outlook, while the Jupiter individual is likely to regard the Mercury individual as overly concerned with details and lacking in overall wisdom and comprehensive understanding. The natives can have differences of opinion regarding education, religion, philosophy, writing, and communication. In some cases, the natives spend much time wandering around together on short and long journeys. Confusion can arise in the relationship over keeping appointments and adhering to agreed-upon schedules. The natives may also promise each other more than they are actually willing or able to deliver. However, with patience and open-mindedness, the natives can learn a great deal from each other and can cooperate in areas of writing, philosophy, education, or humanitarian group activity.

A's Mercury Opposition B's Saturn (A's ☿ ☍ B's ♄)

This comparative combination indicates that the natives could be unfriendly or suspicious toward each other. The Saturn individual is likely to be negative and unsympathetic toward the ideas and communications of the Mercury individual and see the Mercury individual as superficial and unreliable. The Saturn individual can also make heavy demands on the Mercury individual in terms of mental discipline and work. The Saturn individual may be a burden on the Mercury individual or a restrictive influence on freedom and mental independence. Much depends on the relative ages and overall horoscopes of the natives involved in the relationships. The natives may have difficulties with each other over binding contracts, lawsuits, or other legal difficulties. This is not a good combination for business, professional, medical, or educational relationships. The natives can increase each other's tendency toward a pessimistic and negative mental outlook. However, if both natives are sufficiently mature and disciplined, their association can produce practical accomplishments through hard work.

A's Mercury Opposition B's Uranus (A's ☿ ☍ B's ♅)

These natives will stimulate each other mentally with many unusual, interesting ideas, but their association may be lacking in the discipline, common sense, and follow-through necessary to bring these ideas into useful, practical expression. The natives can also increase each other's tendency to excitability and nervousness. They have a tendency to scatter and diffuse each other's mental concentration and sense of purpose. They will have many mutual friends, but these also are likely to contribute to the same tendency. There can be a mutual interest in science, occult subjects, education, group activities, and social reforms; however, the natives can encourage each other in impractical attitudes with regard to these things. On the positive side, they can broaden each other's mental outlook and bring about a more unbiased and comprehensive understanding of life. They can also introduce each other to many interesting new ideas and acquaintances. There can be telepathic rapport in some cases.

A's Mercury Opposition B's Neptune (A's ☿ ☍ B's ♆)

This combination makes for mental confusion and deception in the relationship. The natives may not be really honest with each other about their real motives and intentions. They are not on the same wavelength in their communication, and so have a difficult time understanding each other. They are apt to get appointments and schedules mixed up. The Neptune individual is likely to be vague, elusive, deceptive, and confusing toward the Mercury individual. The Mercury individual may seem too mental and lacking in empathy, imagination, and intuitive perception to the Neptune individual. The subconscious emotional habit patterns, past conditionings, and neurotic tendencies of the Neptune individual can confuse and exasperate the Mercury individual. The Neptune individual may see the Mercury individual as superficial and overly concerned with details. There can be differences of opinion regarding religion, philosophy, mysticism, and practical-material versus subjective-intuitive values in life. If both natives are willing to be honest and work at the relationship, the Neptune individual can help the Mercury individual to be more intuitively aware and the Mercury individual can help the Neptune individual to be more practical.

A's Mercury Opposition B's Pluto (A's ☿ ☍ B's ♇)

These natives are apt to be suspicious of each other and mistrust each other's motives. The Pluto individual may consciously or subconsciously try to psychically dominate or control the thinking of the Mercury individual. The Mercury individual may seem superficial and lacking in sustained purpose and will power to the other. There can be disagreements concerning the handling of joint finances, corporate finances, inheritances, alimony, insurances, or taxes. The Mercury individual may consider the Pluto individual as overly secretive or, when he or she does speak, too blunt and lacking in tact.

A's Mercury Opposition B's North Node Conjunct B's South Node

See A's Mercury Conjunct B's South Node Opposition B's North Node.

A's Mercury Opposition B's South Node Conjunct B's North Node

See A's Mercury Conjunct B's North Node Opposition B's South Node.

A's Mercury Opposition B's Ascendant Conjunct B's Descendant

See A's Mercury Conjunct B's Descendant Opposition B's Ascendant.

A's Mercury Opposition B's Midheaven Conjunct B's Nadir

See A's Mercury Conjunct B's Nadir Opposition B's Midheaven.

A's Mercury Opposition B's Descendant Conjunct B's Ascendant

See A's Mercury Conjunct B's Ascendant Opposition B's Descendant.

A's Mercury Opposition B's Nadir Conjunct B's Midheaven

See A's Mercury Conjunct B's Midheaven Opposition B's Nadir.

X
Venus

Comparative influences of Venus are important indicators of how two people interact where financial, business, marital, social, romantic, and esthetic values are concerned. These influences are also important factors in determining how two people will relate emotionally when they are involved in close personal interactions and to what extent two individuals will enjoy each other's company.

COMPARATIVE HOUSE PLACEMENTS

Comparative house placements of Venus indicate the affairs of life where there will be a sharing of musical, artistic, social, and romantic interests.

In romantic and marital relationships, the comparative house placement of Venus is highly important in determining the extent to which the relationship will be successful. Venus, as ruler of Taurus, indicates, by its house position in a comparison, the extent of cooperation in financial and business affairs, the way these affairs are handled, and the nature of shared business interests. Venus is considered a beneficent planet, and it brings harmony into the affairs ruled by the house in which it falls in the comparison. These affairs bring the natives an empathy and understanding that can reach the level of intuitive rapport.

If Venus is afflicted, there could be disharmony with respect to these affairs, caused by the lack of emotional compatibility.

A's Venus in B's First House

These natives tend to identify with each other emotionally. The Venus individual can help the First House individual to develop a more harmonious manner of personal self-expression. The First House individual can, in turn, help the Venus individual to be more self-confident and direct in social activities and creative artistic endeavors. If the First House individual tends to be shy and retiring, the love and attention of the Venus individual can help to draw him or her out. They share social, artistic, and musical interests.

The First House partakes of the nature of Aries and Mars. Consequently, the Venus individual may regard the First House individual as too aggressive and self-centered, especially if Venus is afflicted in the comparison. The Venus individual is apt to look to the First House individual for luxuries and pleasures and could become a financial responsibility for the First House individual.

This can be a favorable comparative placement for business partnerships related to art and luxury items. If the natives are of similar age and opposite sex, there can be a strong romantic attraction that could lead to marriage.

A's Venus in B's Second House

This is a common comparative placement in business partnerships dealing with financial affairs or pleasure-oriented services, or with items that represent beauty, refinement, and luxury. The natives can together acquire art and objects of material value and beauty. The Second House individual can provide the Venus individual with wealth or material possessions. By the same token, the Venus individual can help the Second House individual acquire wealth or material possessions of beauty and refinement and assist in the social aspects of these activities. In a marriage relationship, one or both parties may be motivated by considerations of money or material possessions. If the Venus is afflicted in the comparison, the natives may encourage each other to make unwise expenditures on unnecessarily luxurious or expensive living habits.

A's Venus in B's Third House

The natives will share an interest in poetry, literature, and other forms of art that are communicated through the media. This comparative position of Venus helps make communications harmonious. The natives will use tact, diplomacy, and consideration in their speech, and this enables them to work out misunderstandings and interpersonal difficulties. The Third House individual can help the Venus individual to become more intellectually aware. The Venus individual can help the Third House individual to be more socially aware, especially in communications. The natives will send each other affectionate greetings and remembrances. They are apt to take short pleasure trips together and in general enjoy each other's company. Their social activities are likely to include brothers, sisters, or neighbors, and there will be many comings and goings. They will share interesting books, articles, art histories, television, and much social telephone conversation. If Venus is afflicted, there could be much idle, meaningless chitchat and social gossip.

A's Venus in B's Fourth House

These natives will enjoy family gatherings, social times at home, and eating meals together. The Venus individual will decorate and beautify the home of the Fourth House individual. The Fourth House individual will provide a place for the Venus individual to express creative, artistic, and social talents. The Venus individual will encourage the Fourth House individual to make the home a place of parties and other social gatherings. The art of cooking will be an important part of this relationship. The natives will spend much money to make the home a place of beauty and charm. In some cases, the home will be used as a place for business partnership activities or for some kind of artistic or social business endeavors.

This combination helps bring harmony into the family life. It is a favorable combination for marriage, especially if a woman's Venus falls into a man's Fourth House. Those having this combination will have a peaceful, harmonious home life in their later years, unless Venus is afflicted. In romantic relationships, the natives will usually prefer the home atmosphere to going out for dining, entertainment, or social activities.

If Venus is afflicted in the Fourth House in a comparison, there can be emotional difficulties as a result of moodiness or supersensitivity. Too much social life could disrupt the home atmosphere.

A's Venus in B's Fifth House

This is one of the strongest comparative combinations for romantic and sexual attraction. The natives will engage in many pleasure-oriented activities—they will enjoy parties, theater, music, and eating out. This can be a good combination for parent–child relationships and for raising children because of the sensitivity, gentleness, and genuine love that is present. Marriage will be for love rather than money or status.

The Venus individual can bring the Fifth House individual much pleasure and romantic fulfillment. The Venus individual will appreciate the social, artistic, and romantic inclinations of the Fifth House individual. Together, they will enjoy all forms of artistic, creative self-expression. Business partnerships with this comparative combination will be related to entertainment, art, music, or luxury items used for pleasure.

A's Venus in B's Sixth House

This comparative combination often indicates social friendships established at work. These business and work associations are apt to relate to health, food, art, music, entertainment, or public relations. The natives can work together harmoniously in a business or professional situation. They can share an interest in cooking, arts, and crafts.

The Venus individual will seek to improve the harmony and beauty of the Sixth House individual's working environment. The Venus individual will have a beneficial effect on the Sixth House individual through pleasing personal mannerisms and gentleness. Music could be used as a means of healing and relaxation. If Venus is afflicted, the natives may try to gain sympathy through hypochondria. Too much socializing could interfere with efficiency and work.

A's Venus in B's Seventh House

A strong romantic attraction, often leading to marriage, can be indicated by this comparative combination. The natives enjoy each other's company and interact harmoniously, unless Venus is afflicted. They are usually considerate of each other's feelings and want to make each other happy. There is a mutual enjoyment of social activities in art, music, or public relations. Business partnerships with this comparative combination will often relate to art, music, entertainment, or public relations, as well as luxury items.

This is an especially strong comparative position for Venus, because of her rulership of the Seventh House; consequently, mutual interests in love, affection, interpersonal harmony, and all things of beauty and refinement will be strongly emphasized. If Venus is afflicted, emotional tensions, misunderstandings, quarrels, and accusations of selfishness can arise.

A's Venus in B's Eighth House

Frequently found in business partnerships and corporate relationships, this comparative combination often indicates financial gain through marriage or business associations for one or both parties. Legacies and inheritances can often influence the relationship and can mean financial gain for one or both natives. In marriage, financial considerations are sometimes a significant motivation. If Venus is afflicted, this can stand in the way of a genuine love relationship. This combination can produce a strong sexual attraction and resultant passionate emotions. There can be strong emotional ties based on a psychic, intuitive link between the natives.

The Venus individual can help the Eighth House individual exercise diplomacy in business affairs, and the Eighth House individual can help the Venus individual gain the financial support necessary for artistic and social expressions.

If Venus is afflicted, jealousy and possessiveness can become a serious problem in the relationship. If Venus is well-aspected, this can be a favorable influence for businesses related to art, music, entertainment, luxury items, banking, taxes, insurance, and financial investments.

A's Venus in B's Ninth House

The natives can have a mutual love of philosophy, religion, and higher education. Often, they meet through universities, schools, churches, or other social organizations, or through business, travel, or matters related to entertainment, art, music, banking, luxury items, foreigners or foreign trade. The natives share a fondness for travel for pleasure, as well as for education. They will have common interests in art history, classical art, music, and the art of foreign cultures.

The Venus individual can help the Ninth House individual in handling the financial, social, and artistic aspects of educational, cultural, and religious activities. The Ninth House individual can help to expand the Venus individual's social, artistic, and business scope through educational, business, and cultural activities.

In a marriage or romantic relationship, one or both persons may try to convert the other to his or her religious or philosophical viewpoints in order to establish greater harmony and compatibility in the relationship.

A's Venus in B's Tenth House

This comparative combination brings professional and business partnerships. Often these are related to the things ruled by Venus, such as banking, luxury items, art, music, and entertainment. In romantic and marital relationships, material status can be an important motivation for one or both natives. The charm and diplomacy of the Venus individual can help advance the career of the Tenth House individual. The Tenth House individual can, in turn, help the Venus individual gain greater social status and recognition for his or her creative, artistic talents.

The natives' relationship is often involved with public relations in a business sense, or with the social aspects of business dealings or political affairs. These could involve diplomatic secrecy and romantic intrigues. If Venus is afflicted, money can be wasted on luxurious entertaining and material luxuries that represent status.

A's Venus in B's Eleventh House

This combination is favorable for cooperation in group activities and social affairs. The natives' mutual friends will bring them pleasure. Their mutual business interests are likely to involve friends and group associates, and they will involve their friends in much social activity. There will be a sharing of humanitarian, occult, and scientific intellectual ideas and pursuits. In romantic and marital relationships, the natives have compatible goals and objectives, and they will be good friends, as well as romantic partners. One or both natives will tend to resent possessiveness on the part of the other.

The Eleventh House individual can expand the social and artistic scope of the Venus individual by introducing new friends and group and organizational contacts. The Eleventh House individual also stimulates original ideas in the Venus individual. The Venus individual can, in turn, help the Eleventh House individual to introduce social and artistic flair into friendships and organizational activities.

If Venus is afflicted in the comparison, the natives can be unreliable with each other, breaking promises and commitments. The desire for personal freedom without accounting for actions can break down the effectiveness of marriages and close relationships.

A's Venus in B's Twelfth House

Because this combination indicates a close psychic and emotional link between the natives, they will be sympathetic and compassionate toward each other. This can be manifested as a psychic awareness of each other's moods and feelings. They can share a sensitive appreciation of music, art, and religion, as well as a mystical and intuitive psychic awareness.

COMPARATIVE CONJUNCTIONS

Comparative conjunctions of Venus indicate active, dynamic social, emotional, and financial relationships, especially with respect to the affairs of the planet Venus is conjuncting. Their interactions in these affairs can create a close emotional identification between the natives and can lead to considerable social exchange, diplomacy, and mutual creativity in art or financial affairs.

A's Venus Conjunct B's Sun

See A's Sun Conjunct B's Venus.

A's Venus Conjunct B's Moon

See A's Moon Conjunct B's Venus.

A's Venus Conjunct B's Mercury

See A's Mercury Conjunct B's Venus.

A's Venus Conjunct B's Venus (A's ♀ ☌ B's ♀)

This comparative combination often produces romantic attractions. The natives will be emotionally sympathetic and understanding toward each other. They will have similar tastes in regard to art, music, and social conduct. It is a good combination for business partnerships, especially if they relate to art, music, entertainment, finance, public relations, or luxury items.

A's Venus Conjunct B's Mars (A's ♀ ☌ B's ♂)

This is perhaps the strongest single comparative aspect for sexual attraction. Whether or not this leads to more sensitive, romantic feelings or to lasting relationships that could lead to marriage depends on the rest of the natal horoscopes and on the comparison. If Venus and Mars are afflicted, sexual jealousy and possessiveness can be a problem. There will be much passion and excitement in the relationship if the natives are of the opposite sex and appropriate ages. (This does not necessarily apply to homosexual relationships, as Uranus and Neptune would be involved in affliction with Venus.)

This combination can be important in associations of a corporate or financial nature relating to such things as banking, insurance, taxes, accounting, inheritances, marketing of luxury products, or public relations. The Venus individual can help the Mars individual to be more sensitive, diplomatic, and cooperative in pursuing personal desires. The Mars individual can help the Venus individual to be more dynamic in action in pursuing social and artistic goals.

A's Venus Conjunct B's Jupiter (A's ♀ ☌ B's ♃)

Relations in otherwise difficult associations can be smoothed by this comparative aspect. There will be a strong mutual appreciation of religious, educational, esthetic, and social values. The natives will be sympathetic, generous, and benevolent toward each other, displaying an inner refinement. This comparative aspect favors lasting compatibility in marriage and romantic relationships. It is conducive to mutual optimism and cheerfulness. The natives' home life will tend to be cheerful, peaceful, and harmonious.

The natives will tend to bring each other social popularity and financial prosperity. The Venus individual can help the Jupiter individual incorporate social and esthetic activities into religious, educational, and cultural activities. The Jupiter individual can, in turn, help the Venus individual to incorporate cultural, educational, and philosophical insights into artistic and social activities. In business relationships, this comparative combination is a favorable influence on legal affairs related to public relations associated with the business.

If Venus and Jupiter are seriously afflicted, the natives can encourage each other to excessive self-indulgence and self-destructive escapist habits.

A's Venus Conjunct B's Saturn (A's ♀ ☌ B's ♄)

Because this comparative combination indicates mutual concern with professional or financial affairs, it works best in business and professional relationships that require discipline and good management. Of itself, this comparative aspect is not conducive to sexual attraction. However, if Saturn and Venus are well-aspected in the natal horoscopes as well as in the comparison, the natives can enjoy lasting friendship and steadfast loyalty. When this comparative conjunction occurs in a marriage, friendship, or business relationship, it favors the durability of the association. If it is afflicted by other planets, ulterior motives of status or financial gain can sour the relationship.

The Saturn individual may be cold and unresponsive, stingy, or mean where the Venus individual is concerned. The Venus individual may be interested in the Saturn individual as a means of gaining material status or professional advancement. The Saturn individual could be lecherous or calculating toward the Venus individual, especially in romantic relationships where there is a considerable age difference. Where genuine affection exists on the part of the Saturn individual, it can be of a parental nature and have the effect of disciplining and restraining the Venus individual. The Saturn person, in such a case, would be concerned for the long-range security and safety of the Venus individual. In all relationships, the Venus individual can brighten the disposition of the Saturn individual, and the Saturn individual can help stabilize the emotions of the Venus individual.

A's Venus Conjunct B's Uranus (A's ♀ ☌ B's ♅)

This comparative combination creates sudden and exciting romantic attractions. It is second only to the Venus/Mars conjunction in the potential it provides for strong sexual attraction between the natives. This is largely due to Uranus' exaltation in Scorpio. The natives will have a romantic fascination for each other. If there are favorable aspects from other planets to this comparative conjunction, this attraction could lead to a lasting relationship. Otherwise, it will be a short-lived infatuation, ending as suddenly as it began.

The natives will share an interest in unusual forms of art, music, entertainment, scientific, or occult subjects. They will enjoy the same friends and group activities. An interest in mysticism and psychic phenomena can be an important part of the relationship.

The Uranus individual can bring excitement and adventure into the life of the Venus individual. The Venus individual will be companionable and willing to participate in the unusual activities of the Uranus individual.

This is a good combination for partnerships involving unusual business and professional ideas that employ advanced technology in the fields of art, entertainment, or finance.

A's Venus Conjunct B's Neptune (A's ♀ ☌ B's ♆)

A subtle magnetic attraction between the natives is indicated by this comparative aspect. They can experience a psychic, telepathic, and emotional link. The double-Pisces connotation of this combination indicates sympathetic, sensitive, emotional understanding and rapport. The intuitive sensitivity of the Neptune individual can help the Venus individual express a more spiritual type of affection and love. The Venus individual can help the Neptune individual express creative and intuitive ideas in a more practical and outgoing way and to be less shy and retiring. This is an excellent combination for mutual appreciation of music and art and creative work involving such endeavors.

A's Venus Conjunct B's Pluto (A's ♀ ☌ B's ♀)

A strong, intense, romantic, sexual attraction is indicated by this comparative combination. If it is afflicted, the Pluto individual may be jealous and possessive toward the Venus individual and attempt to emotionally mold, control, or remake the Venus individual. In romantic or marital relationships, this affliction could mean excessive or abnormal sexual demands. If the comparative conjunction is well-aspected, the relationship can have a regenerating effect on both natives.

The Pluto individual can help the Venus individual to be financially resourceful. However, if the comparative conjunction is afflicted, the Pluto individual could try to manipulate the Venus individual financially.

It is a good combination for cooperation in corporate business affairs—banking, insurance, art, music, entertainment, tax accounting, or inheritances. There can be a mutual appreciation of spiritual and artistic values.

A's Venus Conjunct B's North Node Opposition
B's South Node (A's ♀ ☌ B's ☊ ☍ B's ☋)

The Nodes individual's social awareness of prevailing cultural attitudes and trends can help the Venus individual to gain greater popular acceptance. The grace and charm of the Venus individual can help the Nodes individual to capitalize on his or her awareness of cultural trends. The natives can cooperate effectively in public relations and business promotion. If this comparative combination is afflicted, the natives may encourage each other to blindly follow popular social trends and fads, regardless of their social or business merit.

A's Venus Conjunct B's South Node Opposition
B's North Node (A's ♀ ☌ B's ☋ ☍ B's ☊)

This comparative combination indicates a mutual critical awareness of prevailing social fads and popular beliefs. The Venus individual will draw out the Nodes individual and help him or her to be less reclusive and antisocial. The Nodes individual will tend to restrain and caution the Venus individual in social activities, and prevent the Venus individual from blindly following social trends and beliefs. If the conjunction is afflicted, the Nodes individual can be cold, unsympathetic, and discouraging toward the Venus individual, and the Venus individual will regard the Nodes individual as withdrawn and antisocial.

A's Venus Conjunct B's Ascendant Opposition
B's Descendant (A's ♀ ☌ B's Asc. ☍ B's Desc.)

In love relationships, this combination can create a strong romantic, sexual attraction. It often occurs in marriages. The natives will tend to identify with each other emotionally. The general effects of this combination will be similar to those of "A's Venus in B's First House," only more intense.

A's Venus Conjunct B's Midheaven Opposition
B's Nadir (A's ♀ ☌ B's M.C. ☍ B's Nadir)

The diplomacy of the Venus individual can further the career of the Midheaven/Nadir individual. In turn, the professional status and social position of the Midheaven/Nadir individual can provide status and social security for the Venus individual. There will be cooperation in the professions, business, finance, art, music, entertainment, or public relations. The general effects of this combination will be similar to those of "A's Venus in B's Tenth House," only more intense.

A's Venus Conjunct B's Descendant Opposition B's Ascendant (A's ♀ ☌ B's Desc. ☍ B's Asc.)

This comparative combination indicates a strong emotional romantic tie, often leading to marriage. The natives will share a strong social awareness and a high degree of cooperation in regard to their personal relationship. They will be gentle, considerate, and cooperative toward each other. The general effects of this combination will be much like those of "A's Venus in B's Seventh House," only stronger.

A's Venus Conjunct B's Nadir Opposition B's Midheaven (A's ♀ ☌ B's Nadir ☍ B's M.C.)

The natives will share a strong desire for cooperation, beauty, and harmony in the family life and home. They will have a sympathetic understanding of each other's deep-seated psychological habit patterns. The Venus individual will beautify the home environment of the Midheaven/Nadir individual. The Midheaven/Nadir individual will provide a home or base of operations for the social and artistic activities of the Venus individual. The general effects of this combination will be much the same as those of "A's Venus in B's Fourth House."

COMPARATIVE SEXTILES

Comparative sextiles of Venus indicate opportunities for harmonious social cooperation in business, social, artistic, romantic, and marital relationships. Because of the intellectual nature of the sextile aspect, the natives can communicate intelligently about their personal feelings and about social, business, and romantic relationships. They will involve each other in new and exciting social and business friendships and related group activities. They will encourage each other to develop friendly social relations with brothers, sisters, and neighbors. The natives will share many short journeys and communications in the pursuit of social and business activities.

A's Venus Sextile B's Sun

See A's Sun Sextile B's Venus.

A's Venus Sextile B's Moon

See A's Moon Sextile B's Venus.

A's Venus Sextile B's Mercury

See A's Mercury Sextile B's Venus.

A's Venus Sextile B's Venus (A's ♀ ✳ B's ♀)

This is a favorable comparative combination for cooperation in matters related to social group activities and for harmonious communication with brothers, sisters, and neighbors. There can be many comings and goings in the mutual pursuit of pleasure.

The natives will be able to communicate with each other intelligently about their emotional feelings and responses. They will enjoy social activities with mutual friends. Often, they are romantically attracted to each other and share similar esthetic and social values.

A's Venus Sextile B's Mars (A's ♀ ✳ B's ♂)

If the natives are of similar age and opposite sex, there will be opportunities for sexual and romantic involvement. Often, they meet through friends or group activities. The energy and action orientation of the Mars individual can help the Venus individual overcome inertia. The Venus individual can help the Mars individual to make his or her actions and self-expression more harmonious and socially acceptable and to tone down tendencies to anger and rash impulsiveness. The diplomatic, social abilities of the Venus individual can help the Mars individual to achieve financial gain and professional advancement and to use energies more constructively.

A's Venus Sextile B's Jupiter (A's ♀ ✳ B's ♃)

This comparative combination indicates a harmonious cultural and social interchange between the natives. They will share an interest in philosophy, religion, higher education, business, law, religious, or histori-cal art. There can be mutual activity in religious and cultural group organizations. They will share many social and business friends who, in turn, will expand and benefit their lives.

The natives will encourage each other in expressions of sympathy, compassion, and understanding toward those who are in need. They can be an effective team in charitable, religious, or organizational work. In marriage and romantic relationships, the sharing of religious, cultural, and educational values provides a basis of lasting compatibility that goes beyond emotional, sexual attraction.

A's Venus Sextile B's Saturn (A's ♀ ⚹ B's ♄)

This can be an effective comparative combination for cooperation in business and professional matters, especially where organizational and diplomatic skills are required. It is an excellent combination for profes-sional, business, and legal partnerships of all kinds. It can also be effective in serious creative, artistic work. The Saturn individual can help the Venus individual to organize and find practical expression for his or her creative, artistic, and social talents. The Venus individual will pro-vide social charm and diplomacy that will help promote the business and professional objectives of the Saturn individual.

In marriage or romantic relationships, this comparative combination increases the mutual sense of responsibility, loyalty, and steadfastness. It does not, of itself, indicate romantic attraction, but it does give stability when other factors in the horoscope indicate romantic attraction.

A's Venus Sextile B's Uranus (A's ♀ ⚹ B's ♅)

An unusual and exciting friendship is indicated for these natives. If they are of opposite sex and similar age, this comparison is a strong factor in favor of romantic attraction. There will be a mutual appreciation of art, music, science, or occult subjects.

The Venus individual will appreciate and participate in the unusual creative activities of the Uranus individual. The Uranus individual will facilitate the social, artistic, and business activities of the Venus indi-vidual by introducing new and unusual ideas, friends, and groups.

The natives often meet through friends or group activities. Many friends and groups will be shared and enjoyed. They will inspire each other to express more sparkle and enthusiasm in personal mannerisms and social interaction. They will draw out and encourage each other's original creative talents. In romantic and marital relationships, there will be sexual attraction and a sharing of intellectual friendships.

A's Venus Sextile B's Neptune (A's ♀ ✳ B's ♆)

This comparative aspect indicates a sensitive, psychic, emotional rapport between the natives that will show itself in their understanding and appreciation of each other's attitudes toward mutual friends, neighbors, brothers and sisters, religion, philosophy, mysticism, art, music, or entertainment. They will encourage each other to express sympathy and compassion toward those in need. In romantic and marital relationships, there will be a subtle mystique or magnetic fascination. There will be mutual sensitivity and tenderness, unless this is contradicted by other factors in either the natal horoscopes or in the comparison. This comparative aspect is helpful in creative partnerships relating to the fine arts, hospitals, institutions, or psychology.

A's Venus Sextile B's Pluto (A's ♀ ✳ B's ♇)

Because this comparative combination is helpful in romantic, marital, and business relationships, natives will influence each other to be resourceful and creative in improving the status quo of both their business and personal affairs. The Pluto individual can help the Venus individual to regenerate social and emotional attitudes. The Venus individual can help the Pluto individual further his or her purposes by exercising charm and diplomatic ability.

In romantic and marital relationships, this comparative combination indicates strong sexual attraction. It is favorable for business relationships related to banking, corporate financial affairs, tax accounting, insurance, inheritances, art, entertainment, or luxury items. There can be financial gain through marriage or partnerships.

A's Venus Sextile B's North Node Trine B's South Node (A's ♀ ✳ B's ☊ △ B's ☋)

This comparative combination indicates an ability on the part of both natives to take advantage of current social trends, popular beliefs, and fads, which can benefit them socially or financially. The Nodes individual contributes awareness of such trends and fads, and the Venus individual provides the charm and diplomatic ability to utilize and capitalize on this awareness. The net result is an opportunity for mutual social growth and financial expansion. Whether or not the natives can take advantage of this opportunity depends on their understanding of the cyclic nature of these trends, as revealed by A's South Node.

A's Venus Sextile B's South Node Trine B's North Node
(A's ♀ ✶ B's ☋ △ B's ☊)

This comparative combination has much the same effect as "A's Venus Sextile B's North Node Trine B's South Node," except that these natives will display more individuality in departing from current popular beliefs and trends. They will rely on a longer-range perspective on current trends and fads in planning their business and social activities.

A's Venus Sextile B's Ascendant Trine B's Descendant
(A's ♀ ✶ B's Asc. △ B's Desc.)

Indicating mutual harmony and friendship and general emotional and social compatibility, this comparative combination is favorable for marriages, romantic relationships, and business partnerships. There is sexual attraction if this combination is combined with other comparative influences of a similar nature. The natives can help each other in the diplomatic, public relations aspects of social and business affairs.

A's Venus Sextile B's Midheaven Trine B's Nadir
(A's ♀ ✶ B's M.C. △ B's Nadir)

The natives relate harmoniously with regard to social and financial affairs, career planning and domestic and family harmony. The social, artistic, and diplomatic abilities of the Venus individual will help advance the career of the Midheaven/Nadir individual. The Venus individual will bring harmony, beauty, and opulence into the home and family life of the Midheaven/Nadir individual. The Midheaven/Nadir individual can provide professional and domestic security for the artistic and social expression of the Venus individual. This is an excellent combination for business partnerships dealing in art, entertainment, and luxury items. The artistic commodities these natives deal with often represent status and wealth.

A's Venus Sextile B's Descendant Trine B's Ascendant
(A's ♀ ✶ B's Desc. △ B's Asc.)

This comparative combination has basically the same meaning as "A's Venus Sextile B's Ascendant Trine B's Descendant," except that these natives will be intellectually concerned with their relationship, as well as with public relations and social affairs. This difference is subtle, not readily apparent.

A's Venus Sextile B's Nadir Trine B's Midheaven
(A's ♀ ✶ B's Nadir △ B's M.C.)

This comparative combination has much the same meaning as "A's Venus Sextile B's Midheaven Trine B's Nadir." However, these natives will take a more intellectual approach to planning domestic and family affairs, and a more direct intuitive, creative approach to professional and career activities.

COMPARATIVE SQUARES

Comparative squares of Venus usually indicate interpersonal difficulties of an emotional or financial nature. In some cases, one or both parties will be unnecessarily extravagant in expenditures, bringing about waste and financial loss. Often, the Venus individual feels that the other native is lacking in consideration, taste, refinement, or proper manners. There can be unrequited love or other factors that cause difficulties, especially in a romantic or marital relationship. The natives do not agree in their musical, cultural, or artistic tastes.

A's Venus Square B's Sun

See A's Sun Square B's Venus.

A's Venus Square B's Moon

See A's Moon Square B's Venus.

A's Venus Square B's Mercury

See A's Mercury Square B's Venus.

A's Venus Square B's Venus (A's ♀ □ B's ♀)

The natives' temperaments are often incompatible where social manners, artistic tastes, and emotional needs are concerned. They are apt to encourage each other in self-indulgent habits and unwise expenditures, and they tend to be overly sentimental and lacking in sincerity.

A's Venus Square B's Mars (A's ♀ □ B's ♂)

This comparative combination often produces strong sexual attractions; however, there is usually a lack of real emotional compatibility and mutual consideration. The relationship can be entered into by one or both parties merely for sexual gratification, without real concern for the other party as a person.

In romantic and marital relationships, sexual jealousy and possessiveness can be a problem. The natives tend to influence each other to be impulsive in both emotional expressions and financial expenditures. This is not a good combination for a business partnership where prudence and thrift are important.

The Venus native is likely to see the Mars individual as impulsive, brash, ill-mannered, or inconsiderate. The Mars native may consider the Venus individual to be soft, lazy, self-indulgent, and emotionally supersensitive. This is a very difficult comparative aspect, especially for close personal relationships.

A's Venus Square B's Jupiter (A's ♀ □ B's ♃)

Since this comparative aspect is not overly harmonious, natives can be insincere and hypocritical toward each other. They may pretend to express sweetness and light, while, in reality, they are avoiding unpleasantness or seeking personal, social, or financial gain. They can encourage each other in nonproductive self-indulgent habits or financial extravagance. There can be differences in cultural, esthetic, religious, or educational habits and tastes. The Venus individual may regard the Jupiter individual as overly concerned with religion, philosophy, and cultural institutions. The Jupiter individual may regard the Venus individual as superficial, self-indulgent, and hedonistic.

This is not a good combination for realistic thinking in business affairs. The natives will encourage each other to ignore practical reality. There can be a "let George do it" attitude, which leads to ineffectiveness in getting the job done.

A's Venus Square B's Saturn (A's ♀ □ B's ♄)

Usually this comparative combination leads to a difficult, cold, unfriendly relationship. In most cases, the natives will not be voluntarily attracted to each other. However, in some cases, such as family and parent–child relationships, student–teacher relationships, or business relationships, there is no choice in the matter. This is not a good combination for marital and romantic relationships. When these occur, there is usually some ulterior financial or status motive involved, either on the part of the natives themselves or their families.

The Venus individual usually regards the Saturn individual as harsh, burdensome, cold, unsympathetic, and negative. The Saturn individual often sees the Venus individual as lazy, superficial, self-indulgent, and lacking in serious purpose and discipline.

A's Venus Square B's Uranus (A's ♀ □ B's ♅)

This comparative combination leads to sudden, exciting, but unstable and nonenduring romantic infatuations. It is often found in homosexual relationships or unlikely or unsuitable romantic attachments. Often, the natives confuse romance and friendship. In some cases, there is a magnetic attraction; however, as a rule, the life-styles of the natives will be so different as to make lasting compatibility impossible. It is not favorable for business or corporate financial relationships, because the natives are apt to promise more than they can deliver. Unexpected or unforeseen factors can upset the natives' plans. There is also the danger of get-rich-quick schemes or unreliability in business dealings. If the natives are sincere friends, the counsel they give each other can be lacking in wisdom and experience, and often leads to disappointment and loss.

The Venus individual is likely to regard the Uranus individual as eccentric, inconstant, unstable, and unreliable. The Uranus individual may regard the Venus person as overly possessive, emotionally hypersensitive, or too concerned with material values.

A's Venus Square B's Neptune (A's ♀ □ B's ♆)

Often found in homosexual or unsuitable romantic relationships, this comparative combination can lead to peculiar illusory romantic attractions. In some cases, the attraction is one-sided or deceptive, and insincerity can enter the picture. This comparative combination does not favor business or financial dealings; the natives will lack practicality and discipline. They can excuse each other's shortcomings to the point of encouraging character defects, and encourage each other in the use of alcohol or drugs, or in dissipating self-destructive habits. They can indulge in maudlin sentimentality and mutual commiseration that serves no useful purpose.

The Venus individual is likely to regard the Neptune individual as difficult to understand, elusive, deceptive, unreliable, or impractical. The Neptune individual may consider the Venus individual lacking in spiritual sensitivity and awareness. Like the Venus/Uranus comparative square, the natives can give each other faulty and impractical advice, even though their intentions are good.

A's Venus Square B's Pluto (A's ♀ □ B's ♇)

This comparative combination indicates strong sexual attractions. Its effects are similar to those of the "Venus Square Mars" comparative combination. The motivation behind the attraction is often sexual desire rather than genuine romantic feeling. Sexual jealousy and possessiveness can be a problem to these natives. The Pluto individual is likely to try to control and dominate the Venus individual emotionally and, in some cases, try to take financial advantage of him or her. The Venus individual may regard the Pluto individual as jealous, aggressive, dictatorial, and sexually demanding. The Pluto individual may regard the Venus individual as superficial, frivolous, and self-indulgent.

This is not a good combination for business enterprises or corporate relationships. There can be disagreements and conflicts over joint finances, alimony, inheritances, taxes, insurance, or corporate financial affairs.

A's Venus Square B's North Node Square B's South Node
(A's ♀ □ B's ☊ □ B's ☋)

Because this comparative combination indicates major differences of life-style with respect to personal, social adjustment to the prevailing social fads, trends, and attitudes, natives will not agree on social conduct or on the handling of financial or business affairs. Because of the significant differences in life-style indicated by this combination, it does not give emotional compatibility.

A's Venus Square B's South Node Square B's North Node

See A's Venus Square B's North Node Square B's South Node.

A's Venus Square B's Ascendant Square B's Descendant
(A's ♀ □ B's Asc. □ B's Desc.)

This comparative combination is not favorable for marital and romantic relationships. The personal habits and social mannerisms of the Ascendant/Descendant individual are likely to be unattractive to the social sensibilities of the Venus individual. The Venus individual may seem like a "prima donna" to the Ascendant/Descendant individual. The natives may not share esthetic, business, and social values. Impulsive, emotional behavior on the part of one or both may cause problems in the relationship.

A's Venus Square B's Midheaven Square B's Nadir
(A's ♀ □ B's M.C. □ B's Nadir)

This comparative combination is difficult in family relationships, as well as in business and professional associations. There can be differences of opinion about the handling of family finances and social conduct connected with business dealings and professional affairs. This is not a good combination for business partnerships if they are involved with public relations, finance, music, art, or entertainment.

The Venus individual may regard the Midheaven/Nadir individual as exploitative and demanding. The Midheaven/Nadir individual may regard the Venus individual as lazy, hedonistic, and lacking in a sense of responsibility.

A's Venus Square B's Descendant Square B's Ascendant

See A's Venus Square B's Ascendant Square B's Descendant.

A's Venus Square B's Nadir Square B's Midheaven

See A's Venus Square B's Midheaven Square B's Nadir.

COMPARATIVE TRINES

Comparative trines of Venus indicate harmonious social and, at times, romantic relationships between the natives. They are highly favorable influences for romantic and marital relationships and parent–child relationships. Genuine love and affection are expressed. The Venus individual brings a sense of beauty, harmony, and social grace into the affairs ruled by the planet trining Venus in the comparison.

Comparative trines of Venus are favorable for mutual business, pleasure, and travel. They favor harmonious sharing of cultural, educational, religious, and social activities and art forms. The natives will share an interest in and enjoyment of social activities, art, music, or the cultural aspects of the arts.

A's Venus Trine B's Sun

See A's Sun Trine B's Venus.

A's Venus Trine B's Moon

See A's Moon Trine B's Venus.

A's Venus Trine B's Mercury

See A's Mercury Trine B's Venus.

A's Venus Trine B's Venus (A's ♀ △ B's ♀)

This is a favorable indication for romantic, marital, and business relationships. The natives enjoy each other's company in social activities and artistic pursuits, and they appreciate the same cultural art forms. There will be an intuitive, emotional rapport between them regarding feelings, moods, and social attitudes. They will have a calming, emotionally soothing effect on each other.

A's Venus Trine B's Mars (A's ♀ △ B's ♂)

This is perhaps the best comparative aspect for sexual compatibility. If the natives are of the opposite sex and appropriate ages, there is likely to be a strong romantic attraction between them. This comparative combination is conducive to emotional and social compatibility. It is favorable for business partnerships involving construction, corporate financial affairs, banking, insurance, tax accounting, luxury items, art, music, or entertainment.

The natives will enjoy each other's company in social activities, romantic relationships, games, sports, and travel. They will have compatible tastes with respect to cultural art forms and social beliefs regarding romance and sexual mores. The Venus individual can help the Mars individual to be more diplomatic and harmonious in personal action and self-expression. The Mars individual can help the Venus individual to put creative artistic ideas into expression. The Mars individual will stir the Venus individual into action and help the Venus individual overcome shyness and inertia.

A's Venus Trine B's Jupiter (A's ♀ △ B's ♃)

Mutual interests in social and cultural art forms and religious, educational, and philosophical pursuits related to the arts and social affairs are characteristic of this comparative aspect. The natives will stimulate each other's interest and participation in religious and charitable activities and pursuits, especially when these are combined with social functions. They will be considerate, gentle, and generous toward each other and share an intuitive, emotional rapport.

The Venus individual can help the Jupiter individual to make religious, philosophical, cultural, or educational interests more personally meaningful and effective. The Jupiter individual can help the Venus individual to express social and esthetic talents in a way that is effective and meaningful in the larger cultural context.

This is an excellent comparative combination for harmony in romantic and marital relationships. It is a good comparative combination for long-range compatibility and marriage because of its combination of shared cultural, religious, and philosophical values and personal, emotional considerations.

A's Venus Trine B's Saturn (A's ♀ △ B's ♄)

In this comparative combination there tends to be a strong sense of personal friendship and loyalty. Although this combination, by itself, does not indicate sexual, romantic attraction, it can increase the stability and durability of a relationship when romantic attraction is indicated by other factors in the comparison. This is a good combination for parent–child relationships, especially when the parent is the Saturn individual. There will be mutual love and respect combined with reasonable discipline and moral guidance.

The Saturn individual can help the Venus individual find emotional, financial, and social security. The Venus individual can draw out the Saturn individual, providing love, warmth, beauty, grace, and sociability.

This combination is favorable for business, legal, and professional partnerships and relationships, especially if they involve public relations, finance, banking, entertainment, arts, or luxury items. Because Venus and Saturn are both related to the sign Libra, there will be a sense of mutual respect and just dealing. The natives can count on each other's loyalty and cooperation.

A's Venus Trine B's Uranus (A's ♀ △ B's ♅)

This comparative combination indicates strong, dramatic romantic and sexual attractions. The natives stimulate each other's sense of fun, romance, and excitement. There can be an intuitive, emotional link between them. They enjoy the same friends and the same group and organizational activities. There can be a mutual interest in unusual forms of art, music, or entertainment.

This is a good combination for business relationships and partnerships involving art, music, and entertainment as they are related to the electronic media. The natives will bring new social contacts, experiences, and friendships into each other's lives, creating a sense of excitement and adventure. There can be love at first sight. Although by itself this combination does not necessarily promise an enduring relationship, if such a relationship is indicated by other factors, this combination will keep it from becoming humdrum, routine, or boring.

Through diplomatic skills the Venus individual can help promote the unusual ideas and talents of the Uranus individual. The Uranus individual brings new creative insights, change, and excitement to the Venus individual, and, in some cases, an interest in the occult or astrological implications of art, music, and social relationships.

A's Venus Trine B's Neptune (A's ♀ △ B's ♆)

Natives of this comparative combination enjoy a sensitive, emotional, intuitive, spiritual rapport. They attract each other with a subtle romantic magnetism. Often, the relationship is highly idealistic and romantic. There is a strong mutual appreciation of the spiritual, cultural, historic aspects of the fine arts. The natives bring out each other's refined, artistic, social tastes. Romantic and marital relationships are often characterized by tenderness and intuitive emotional sensitivity. Many of the finer qualities of the sign Pisces are brought out in the relationship because of the double-Pisces connotation of the Venus–Neptune comparative trine.

The Neptune person can bring a sense of mystery, intuitive appreciation, awe, and spirituality to the Venus individual. The Venus individual can bring beauty, charm, personal warmth, and affection to the Neptune individual.

There is sensitive, warm rapport in parent–child relationships. The natives will be congenial traveling companions on pleasure trips, pilgrimages, and cultural or educational journeys.

This is a good combination for partnerships in business related to the fine arts and luxury items. However, some good comparative Saturn and Mercury aspects should be present to provide the needed organization, discipline, and practical business sense.

A's Venus Trine B's Pluto (A's ♀ △ B's ♀)

If the natives are of opposite sex and similar age, this comparative aspect indicates intense romantic and sexual attractions. The aspect can be a good combination for business relationships relating to corporate finance, banking, insurance, tax accounting, inheritance, art, music, or entertainment.

The Venus individual can help the Pluto individual to be more sensitive and diplomatic in social and business relationships. The Pluto individual can help the Venus individual become more spiritually aware and make positive efforts at self-improvement and regeneration. The Pluto individual can bring an occult level of awareness to the artistic and social appreciations of the Venus individual, and the Venus individual can, in turn, help the other to use his or her occult abilities in a harmonious, creative, productive way.

A's Venus Trine B's North Node Sextile B's South Node

See A's Venus Sextile B's South Node Trine B's North Node.

A's Venus Trine B's South Node Sextile B's North Node

See A's Venus Sextile B's North Node Trine B's South Node.

A's Venus Trine B's Ascendant Sextile B's Descendant

See A's Venus Sextile B's Descendant Trine B's Ascendant.

A's Venus Trine B's Midheaven Sextile B's Nadir

See A's Venus Sextile B's Nadir Trine B's Midheaven.

A's Venus Trine B's Descendant Sextile B's Ascendant

See A's Venus Sextile B's Ascendant Trine B's Descendant.

A's Venus Trine B's Nadir Sextile B's Midheaven

See A's Venus Sextile B's Midheaven Trine B's Nadir.

COMPARATIVE OPPOSITIONS

The opposition aspect has a Seventh House/Libra connotation. Venus is natural ruler of the Seventh House and Libra is the natural Seventh House sign. Therefore, comparative oppositions of Venus have a special importance in marital relationships and all partnerships.

Comparative oppositions of Venus are frequently found in romantic and marital relationships. They usually indicate a sexual or emotional attraction of some kind. To succeed in relationships with comparative oppositions of Venus, natives must have a strong sense of mutual consideration, cooperation, and willingness to compromise. Here is where the natives must learn the lesson of love and consider the interests and well-being of the other individual. To the extent that both natives are capable of doing this, the relationship can succeed.

A's Venus Opposition B's Sun

See A's Sun Opposition B's Venus.

A's Venus Opposition B's Moon

See A's Moon Opposition B's Venus.

A's Venus Opposition B's Mercury

See A's Mercury Opposition B's Venus.

A's Venus Opposition B's Venus (A's ♀ ☍ B's ♀)

These natives will tend to mirror each other's moods and feelings. Often, they are romantically attracted, but a delicate mutual emotional balance must be maintained. They must cultivate a sensitive awareness of each other's moods, feelings, tastes, and social reactions if they are to succeed in a close relationship. There can be an interest in the same social and artistic pursuits.

A's Venus Opposition B's Mars (A's ♀ ☍ B's ♂)

This comparative combination indicates intense sexual, romantic attractions. Unless there are other harmonizing factors in the comparison, however, this sexual attraction is no guarantee of stable, harmonious, or enduring relationships. There can be problems with jealousy and possessiveness. The natives must exercise consideration and diplomacy if they are to remain friends. The Mars individual must avoid being overly aggressive and inconsiderate, and the Venus individual must avoid being supersensitive and easily hurt.

It is necessary for the individuals to work in harmony with respect to financial affairs and mutual property. If this is not done, one or both parties will feel that they are being used, and resentment and conflict will result.

The Venus individual can find the Mars individual exciting and sexually stimulating. However, the Venus individual will resent any aggressiveness, crudeness, or domineering tendencies on the part of the Mars individual. The Mars individual finds the Venus individual sexually desirable, attractive, and beautiful, but may tend to dislike what he or she considers petty emotional supersensitivity in the person.

This description applies most accurately to a relationship in which the man's Mars is in opposition to the woman's Venus. If the reverse is the case, the woman may try to assume the dominant masculine role, especially if Venus is in an Air or Fire sign (Gemini, Libra, Aquarius, Aries, Leo, or Sagittarius).

A's Venus Opposition B's Jupiter (A's ♀ ☍ B's ♃)

Although this comparative combination indicates congenial social and romantic relationships, there is the danger of polite hypocrisy, with the natives pretending friendliness and affection to avoid unpleasantness or to gain social, financial, or cultural advancement and status. When the relationship is sincere, the natives can enjoy the same religious, philosophical, educational, artistic, or social interests and activities.

This comparison benefits romantic and marital relationships by improving the spiritual and cultural basis of compatibility. The natives will enjoy each other's company while traveling or pursuing educational, religious, or charitable interests and activity.

The Venus individual will find the Jupiter individual culturally interesting and knowledgeable, and the Jupiter individual is likely to regard the Venus individual as charming and socially diplomatic. If other afflictions enter into this combination, and if the natives lack personal discipline and moral fiber, they can indulge each other's destructive habits and financial extravagance.

A's Venus Opposition B's Saturn (A's ♀ ☍ B's ♄)

This comparative combination indicates cold, emotionally distant relationships. The natives are not voluntarily attracted to each other, although circumstances may force them into an association. In some cases, the association is based on ulterior motives, such as gaining money and status, rather than on genuine friendship and affection.

The Venus individual is likely to regard the Saturn individual as cold, harsh, unfeeling, insensitive, and disciplinarian. The Saturn individual may regard the Venus individual as lazy, superficial, and irresponsible.

This combination is not good for parent–child relationships because of the emotional distance and lack of understanding which it engenders. In social relationships, this combination tends to make for stiff, formal interactions. It is more suited to business and professional partnerships, providing both natives are mature enough to act in an honest, responsible way.

A's Venus Opposition B's Uranus (A's ♀ ☍ B's ♅)

As a rule, this comparative combination indicates strong, sudden romantic and sexual infatuations which are not stable or lasting, unless other comparative aspects indicate stability.

The Uranus individual can bring change, excitement, and adventure into the life of the Venus individual. The Venus individual can bring affection, love, and companionship to the Uranus individual. The natives may become mutually involved in group and organizational activities and friendships. Often, they first meet through mutual friends or groups. There can be mutual interest and excitement over occult, scientific, humanitarian, or corporate business endeavors. In business relationships, the natives can become involved in dealing with unusual products or services, occult subjects, electronic technology, or new inventions. However, the overall comparison must show dependability, integrity, and common sense for these to succeed or endure. This combination can indicate homosexual relationships or peculiar abnormal attractions.

A's Venus Opposition B's Neptune (A's ♀ ☍ B's ♆)

This comparative combination indicates alluring, but not necessarily reliable or stable, romantic and sexual attractions. In some cases, the natives can be deceptive toward each other emotionally. The relationship is apt to be highly romantic, but not necessarily practical. Romantic attractions can sometimes be one-sided, leading to emotional hurts and disappointments, or one party can use the other for sexual gratification.

The Venus individual is apt to regard the Neptune individual as peculiar, unreliable, and deceptive. The Neptune individual may regard the Venus as spiritually unaware or lacking in imagination.

There can be a mutual appreciation of fine arts, music, or religious mysticism. Since both these planets are linked to Pisces, they are not necessarily incompatible, even though this is technically an adverse comparative aspect. However, other factors in the comparison must be favorable for a relationship to be lasting and practical, especially if it involves areas of serious responsibility encountered in business and marriage. If the natives are weak or immature, they can encourage each other to indulge in hedonistic and disappointing, self-destructive habits and extravagances.

A's Venus Opposition B's Pluto (A's ♀ ☍ B's ♀)

Strong romantic, sexual attractions similar to those of "A's Venus Opposition B's Mars" are indicated by this comparative combination. The Venus individual may regard the Pluto individual as domineering, controlling, possessive, and jealous. The Pluto individual is apt to regard the Venus individual as superficial or someone to be molded, dominated, or controlled. Much will depend on the relative strength of Pluto in the horoscopes. On the positive side, a love relationship with this combination can have a deep spiritual, regenerative quality, which can bring out profound creative abilities in both natives. Mutual respect and consideration are essential if these higher possibilities are to be realized. The natives can have a mutual interest in the metaphysical aspects of art, music, and social affairs. There can also be mutual involvement with corporate financial affairs, inheritance, tax accounting, banking, or business. In the case of divorces with this comparative aspect, there is likely to be a conflict over alimony and the dividing up of property.

A's Venus Opposition B's North Node Conjunct B's South Node

See A's Venus Conjunct B's South Node Opposition B's North Node.

A's Venus Opposition B's South Node Conjunct B's North Node

See A's Venus Conjunct B's North Node Opposition B's South Node.

A's Venus Opposition B's Ascendant Conjunct B's Descendant

See A's Venus Conjunct B's Descendant Opposition B's Ascendant.

A's Venus Opposition B's Midheaven Conjunct B's Nadir

See A's Venus Conjunct B's Nadir Opposition B's Midheaven.

A's Venus Opposition B's Descendant Conjunct B's Ascendant

See A's Venus Conjunct B's Ascendant Opposition B's Descendant.

A's Venus Opposition B's Nadir Conjunct B's Midheaven

See A's Venus Conjunct B's Midheaven Opposition B's Nadir.

XI
Mars

Comparative house placements and aspects of Mars indicate the way in which the natives influence each other through the desires that activate their actions. They show the way in which the natives will initiate actions that relate to the other individual in the relationship. These actions can be related to sexual desire, competition in sports or other physical activities, and professional and financial ambitions. When these comparative influences of Mars are adverse, there can be quarrels and disagreements.

COMPARATIVE HOUSE PLACEMENTS

Comparative house placements of Mars show how the desires that motivate the actions of the Mars individual will directly affect the practical affairs of the other individual.

The affairs ruled by the comparative house placement of Mars can be a source of competition or vying for power. If Mars is afflicted, they can be a source of conflict and resentment. When Mars is favorably aspected in the comparison, however, they will be an area of positive action and constructive accomplishment. The Mars individual will tend to activate and motivate the other native to action through the things ruled by the house in which Mars is placed in the comparison, especially in the areas of personal, physical expression, career ambitions, or joint finances.

A's Mars in B's First House

The Mars individual will have an energizing influence on the First House individual and will spur the First House individual into action. The First House individual can also spur the Mars individual into action, because of the natural Aries–Mars connotation of the First House. Whether this interaction is constructive or leads to conflict will depend on the maturity of the natives, as well as on the comparative aspects of Mars.

At times, the natives will compete with each other. They can encourage each other to greater professional or political ambition and activity. This comparative combination can indicate sexual attraction if the natives are of similar age and opposite sex.

A's Mars in B's Second House

This comparative combination produces energetic interaction in business and financial affairs. If Mars is well-aspected in the comparison, the natives can be enterprising, effective, energetic business partners. They can work effectively in corporate financial affairs that deal with insurance, taxes, building, or engineering industries. If Mars is afflicted in the comparison, the natives are apt to have disagreements over financial expenditures, property, and ownership. This applies to all types of relationships, business or otherwise.

The Second House individual may regard the Mars individual as overly aggressive, impulsive, demanding, and extravagant in financial affairs. The Mars individual may regard the Second House individual as niggardly and overly conservative in financial affairs.

A's Mars in B's Third House

This comparative combination indicates rapid and energetic mental communication. If Mars is well-aspected, the natives will inspire each other to greater effort in writing, scientific investigation, engineering, planning, and design, or political discussion. If Mars is afflicted in the comparison, there can be arguments and heated disagreements regarding these affairs. The natives should be careful to avoid arguments if Mars is afflicted in the comparison, especially while traveling, as accidents could result. The natives are apt to engage in criticism and mutual accusation. There is likely to be much short-distance travel and communication involving corporate affairs and professional activities. This can be a good combination for partnerships involving advertising, writing, communications media, or political campaigning.

The Third House individual is apt to regard the Mars individual as lacking in diplomacy and much too impulsive in speech and communication. The Mars individual may regard the Third House individual as prone to excessive talk without action and unnecessary mental gymnastics.

The natives should carefully consider all contractual agreements between themselves so as to avoid conflict later. This comparative combination is apt to involve brothers, sisters, and neighbors in intellectual activities and debates.

A's Mars in B's Fourth House

Natives with this comparative combination are likely to be active together in home and family life. If Mars is well-aspected, they are apt to get each other involved in "do-it-yourself" home improvement projects, family business enterprises, or family sports. If Mars is afflicted, domestic discord and emotional problems will arise from the natives' inability to be considerate of each other in family and domestic affairs.

This can be a difficult comparative placement for marital and family relationships, because Mars is accidentally debilitated in the Fourth House.

The Fourth House individual is likely to become upset with the inconsiderateness, aggressiveness, and emotional insensitivity of the Mars individual, especially where family and domestic affairs are concerned. The Fourth House individual sees the Mars person as a threat to inner emotional security and peace of mind. The Mars individual is likely to regard the Fourth House individual as lazy and emotionally tied down to family affairs. On the positive side, the Mars individual can help the Fourth House individual to mobilize domestic affairs and bring about needed changes.

A's Mars in B's Fifth House

If the natives are of opposite sex and appropriate ages, this comparative placement produces strong romantic attractions of a sexual nature.

In romantic relationships, the Fifth House individual can view the Mars individual as sexually demanding and socially unrefined. The Mars individual is apt to be impulsive in pleasure-oriented activities and in advances toward the Fifth House individual. If the natives are immature and Mars is afflicted in the comparison, this could lead to dangerous or personally damaging consequences for one or both of them.

The natives may become mutually involved in competitive games, especially of a physical nature. If Mars is afflicted, these could lead to physical injury. Parents overseeing their children should bear this in mind. In business and corporate relationships, the Mars individual can be impulsive and aggressive in influencing the Fifth House individual to take speculative risks. If Mars is afflicted or if the natives are very impulsive, this can lead to serious financial losses.

A's Mars in B's Sixth House

This comparative combination makes for an energetic relationship in work, service, and employment. In employer–employee, co-worker, and family relationships, one or both parties will make heavy demands for work and productivity. If Mars is afflicted, this can lead to resentment, with one or both natives feeling pressured into a heavy work load. Under these circumstances, there can be danger of industrial accidents, occupational hazards, and illness due to overwork or unsanitary conditions. On the positive side, the natives can encourage each other and cooperate in useful productive work. The Mars individual is likely to prod the Sixth House individual to greater action to increase productivity, or vice versa. The Mars individual should discipline him- or herself to exercise patience and caution in work relationships, so as to avoid the aggravation of mistakes, work spoilage, and accidents. The Sixth House individual can invent better or more effective ways of getting the job done.

This comparative combination often occurs in doctor–patient and therapist–patient relationships, where one native is instrumental in healing the other.

A's Mars in B's Seventh House

Dynamic, action-oriented partnerships are characteristic of this comparative combination. Much depends on how Mars is aspected by the other planets and on the overall maturity of the natives. The individuals are in danger of behaving too aggressively and impulsively toward each other, and thus arousing hostility and resentment.

The Mars native can activate the Seventh House individual to greater activity in self-expression, whether in a partnership or competition. The Seventh House individual can help the Mars individual to be more diplomatic in pursuit of his or her personal desires. If Mars is well-aspected, the natives can be partners in business, professional, and corporate affairs that lead to productive, practical accomplishments.

This combination can indicate sexual attraction between natives of appropriate age and opposite sex. However, this sexual attraction is no guarantee that the relationship will endure, unless other factors in the comparison can provide loyalty, harmony, and stability. In a marital relationship, mutual consideration and a democratic attitude are necessary. Any attempt on the part of either native to order the other around will cause a breakdown in the relationship.

If Mars is afflicted, this comparative combination can result in divorce and/or a lawsuit between the natives. In extreme cases, the natives can become open enemies, or even be involved in physical confrontations. In any event, this comparative combination engenders competition between them.

A's Mars in B's Eighth House

This comparative combination often produces dynamic business, corporate, scientific, or occult relationships.

The natives are apt to be mutually involved in corporate affairs related to insurance, tax accounting, engineering, construction, or scientific research. In many cases, such dealings involve secrecy. The natives may be involved in military strategy, secret investigation, police work, or occult investigation. If Mars is afflicted, plotting and intrigue can be part of the relationship. The natives can expose each other to danger; in extreme cases, this could result in death for one or both. This is a dynamic combination because of the natural Scorpio connotation of the Eighth House. The natives will encourage each other in efforts at self-regeneration and improvement. They will tend to strengthen each other's determination and resolve to "do and dare" and to follow through on projects and purposes.

A's Mars in B's Ninth House

A dynamic mutual interaction involving philosophy, religion, publishing, law, or travel is indicated by this comparative combination.

The natives will encourage each other to become crusaders for religious, cultural, or educational causes. In some cases, one native will try to force the other to subscribe to particular religious, philosophical, educational, moral, or cultural beliefs. If Mars is afflicted, this can lead to annoyance and resentment in the person who is the target of the proselytizing. There can be conflict, argument, and disagreement over religious views, legal affairs, philosophy, or education.

The natives are often inclined to travel together for excitement and adventure or as a result of military assignments, corporate business or professional advancement and expansion. If Mars is afflicted, they can cause each other danger while on long journeys, due to rash, impulsive acts.

The Mars individual can regard the Ninth House individual as philosophically impractical or locked in an ivory-tower existence. The Ninth House individual may regard the Mars individual as lacking in spiritual insight and refinement, narrow-minded, and overly aggressive in support of his or her own point of view.

In general, this comparative combination can indicate mutual activity in initiating religious or educational projects. The natives will encourage each other to put religious and spiritual ideals into action.

A's Mars in B's Tenth House

This comparative combination indicates strong interactions between the natives in their professional affairs. In some cases, they will compete for higher positions or professional honors. There can be mutual interests in fields such as engineering, construction, insurance, or corporate finance. The Mars individual is apt to be attracted to the Tenth House individual for the purpose of gaining professional advancement and status. The Tenth House individual may admire the energy and ambition of the Mars native, while regarding that person as rash and impulsive, and, in some cases, as a threat to his security, position, and status.

These individuals could work well together in political campaigns, commercial promotions, or industrial labor organizing, particularly in such fields as steel work, machinery, construction, insurance, mortuary work, physical sports, or any field requiring physical exertion and aggressive ambition. If Mars is afflicted in the comparison, the natives are apt to be in competition with each other. If Mars is well-aspected, the natives will be on the same team.

A's Mars in B's Eleventh House

In this comparative combination there is dynamic interaction between the individuals and their friends; this includes mutual participation in group and organizational activities. The natives will encourage each other to action to accomplish goals and objectives. These goals and objectives often relate to political reform, humanitarian causes, scientific research, technological invention, or occult work. If Mars is afflicted in the comparison, the natives may cultivate their friendship for selfish or ulterior reasons and mutual suspicion and conflict will result.

The Mars individual may try to dominate group and organizational activity, and thus arouse resentment in the Eleventh House individual, and the Eleventh House individual will see the Mars person as autocratic, selfishly ambitious, and undemocratic. The Mars individual will in turn regard the Eleventh House individual as eccentric and intellectually impractical. However, on the positive side, the Eleventh House individual can supply the other with creative, original ideas and organizational discipline which the Mars native can translate into action. The natives can accomplish much work together that is creative and productive of worthwhile goals that will benefit humanity in some way.

A's Mars in B's Twelfth House

This comparative combination indicates that the natives will be involved together in behind-the-scenes and possibly secret activities.

The Mars individual is likely to stir up the subconscious mind of the Twelfth House individual. If Mars is afflicted in the comparison, this can take the form of the activation of painful subconscious memories and lead to undesirable emotional reactions between the natives. The Twelfth House individual may regard the Mars individual as crude, overbearing, and emotionally insensitive. The Mars individual is likely to regard the Twelfth House native as impractical, lost in a private dream world, weak, self-indulgent, and indecisive. If Mars is heavily afflicted in the comparison, one or both persons may practice psychological cruelty. In extreme cases, they can be secret enemies.

On the positive side, the natives can accomplish much that has practical value in a quiet, unobtrusive manner, thereby circumventing opposition and conflicts. They can work together in valuable charitable service, often in connection with religious institutions, hospitals, or asylums. When Mars is well-aspected, they can cooperate effectively in occult or psychic work.

COMPARATIVE CONJUNCTIONS

Comparative conjunctions of Mars indicate direct and dynamic interaction between the natives that can run the entire gamut from constructive mutual cooperation to open quarrels and conflicts. Its form will depend on the overall nature of the comparison, the individual characteristics of the natives themselves, and other comparative aspects made to the planets in Mars comparative conjunctions.

Because of the First House–Aries nature of the conjunction aspect, these comparative aspects will be major factors in determining the nature of relationship. Comparative conjunctions of Mars show how the desires that motivate the Mars individual's actions affect the affairs of the other native. They also indicate in what affairs the natives will combine their actions.

A's Mars Conjunct B's Sun

See A's Sun Conjunct B's Mars.

A's Mars Conjunct B's Moon

See A's Moon Conjunct B's Mars.

A's Mars Conjunct B's Mercury

See A's Mercury Conjunct B's Mars.

A's Mars Conjunct B's Venus

See A's Venus Conjunct B's Mars.

A's Mars Conjunct B's Mars (A's ♂ ☌ B's ♂)

This comparative combination indicates engagement in strong mutual action. The natives are apt to react to each other aggressively and impulsively. Much depends on how this comparative conjunction is aspected in the natal horoscopes, and on other comparative aspects. Both natives usually have a strong sense of competition, which can show itself in many ways, depending on the signs, houses, and other aspects involved. If the natives lack maturity, they may goad each other into impulsive, unwise, and even dangerous acts.

On the positive side, the natives can increase each other's resolve for constructive action and self-improvement. They can cooperate in professional and corporate business affairs. Their mutual action often takes the form of activities that involve muscular exertion; for example, sports, heavy construction, or heavy mechanical work. The natives often begin new enterprises at the same time; this is related to the two-year cycle of Mars. Sexual attraction can be indicated.

A's Mars Conjunct B's Jupiter (A's ♂ ☌ B's ♃)

Because this comparative conjunction indicates dynamic, enthusiastic cooperation in business, professional, corporate, religious, educational, legal, political, or social enterprises, it can lead to dynamic action that transforms idealism and religious philosophy into constructive action. The Mars individual can energize the social ideals and purposes of the Jupiter individual. The Jupiter individual can guide the energy of the Mars native into useful, constructive channels. The wisdom and moral judgment of the Jupiter person can help the Mars individual to avoid unwise and impulsive acts. The Mars individual can help the Jupiter individual to be more active and effective in implementing his social, business, educational, and cultural goals and projects.

The natives often enjoy sports, exploration, and outdoor activities. This is a favorable combination for people who work together in political campaigns or business promotion, for family relationships, and for constructive action in the home.

A's Mars Conjunct B's Saturn (A's ♂ ☌ B's ♄)

In this comparative combination the Saturn individual will restrain the impulsiveness of the Mars individual and endeavor to channel the energy of the Mars individual into disciplined, purposeful work, especially along career and status lines. The Mars individual can help the Saturn individual to overcome unnecessary fear and inertia. The Mars individual is likely to lash out in anger because of what he or she feels are unreasonable restraints imposed by the Saturn native. The Saturn individual is likely to regard the Mars person as overly impulsive, unwise, inconsiderate, and a threat to position, status, and security.

This is not necessarily a negative combination, even though it involves two malefic planets. Saturn and Mars have a natural affinity through the sign Capricorn, where Mars is exalted and Saturn rules.

If the conjunction is favorably aspected and the natives are mature, they can be an effective team in professional and political endeavors, especially in fields such as engineering, politics, military affairs, business, and corporate finance.

The natives are apt to make heavy demands on each other in terms of effort and discipline. Their mutual concerns will be of a serious nature. If the individuals lack maturity and Mars is afflicted in the comparison, there can be mutual conflict, jealousy, and resentment. In rare cases, the natives may become involved in lawsuits over business and financial affairs.

A's Mars Conjunct B's Uranus (A's ♂ ☌ B's ♅)

This comparative combination indicates dynamic, interesting, but potentially explosive relationships. If the natives are of the opposite sex and appropriate ages, this combination can indicate sexual attraction. There is the danger that the natives will encourage each other's rash, impulsive acts. The Mars individual may regard the Uranus as eccentric and unpredictable, but interesting and exciting as a companion. The Uranus individual is likely to regard the Mars as energetic, but impulsive and overbearing.

If this comparative conjunction is afflicted, the natives can have an irritating effect on each other, which could lead to sudden, unexpected, uncontrolled outbursts of anger. Any attempt to order each other around is bound to cause disharmony. Both natives will be strongly independent and they will not yield to each other.

If the conjunction is well-aspected, the natives can share an interest in occult, scientific, or engineering activities. There can be mutual activity with the same friends, groups, and organizations. This can be a good combination for cooperation in professional endeavors that require daring, resourcefulness, and ingenuity, especially in such fields as electronics, engineering, or scientific research. In some cases, the natives will have a mutual interest in social reforms or revolutionary movements. Often, they will share the desire to drastically change or reform some aspect of the existing power structure. The strength of these tendencies will depend on the power of Mars and Uranus in the natal horoscopes.

A's Mars Conjunct B's Neptune (A's ♂ ☌ B's ♆)

In this comparative combination a strong, but subtle, emotional interaction between the natives is indicated. If the conjunction is afflicted, there is danger of dishonesty and deceit. In business dealings and corporate affairs, the Mars individual is likely to regard the Neptune individual as deceptive, unreliable, and, at times, dishonest. At best, he or she views the Neptune native as an inactive, impractical dreamer. The Neptune individual may regard the Mars individual as crude, aggressive, impulsive, autocratic, and lacking in sensitivity and imagination. On the positive side, the Neptune individual's intuitive and imaginative abilities can help the Mars person to plan actions more effectively, and the Mars individual can help the Neptune individual to put creative, intuitive insights into action. The natives often enjoy dancing and the physical expression of emotional feeling that dancing makes possible. This can be a good combination for activities that demand secrecy and work behind the scenes, occult work, for example, or work related to hospitals and institutions. The natives may encourage each other to adopt extreme and, in some cases, fanatical religious, philosophical, or educational viewpoints.

Conflict can arise from one or both natives taking action without consulting the other. This often causes problems in family relationships. There can also be a tendency for the natives to get each other involved in unwise or dangerous occult practices, such as seances or the selfish use of magic. At times, the Mars individual could stimulate distortions in the subconscious mind of the Neptune native.

A's Mars Conjunct B's Pluto (A's ♂ ☌ B's ♇)

This comparative combination indicates strong, dynamic mutual action. If it is well-aspected, the natives will be energetic and effective in corporate business enterprises, professional affairs, physical work, or occult endeavors. These could involve police work, military affairs, engi-

neering, science, or construction. The natives are likely to become mutually involved in secret intrigues and strategies. They are apt to compete
with each other in career ambitions, strategy, and feats of physical
strength. Any attempt by either to coerce or order the other around will
meet with resistance and resentment. If the natives are to have a harmonious relationship, they must respect each other's freedom of choice
and action.

The Pluto individual is apt to try to reform or remake the Mars native
in some way. The Pluto individual will try influencing the Mars individual to be discreet and less obvious. The Mars individual will try to
influence the Pluto toward more overt outward action. The Mars individual is likely to get the Pluto native to spend money unwisely or
impulsively.

If the natives are of similar age and opposite sex, this combination can
indicate a strong sexual attraction and mutual excitement. They can
help each other in their efforts at self-regeneration, physical and spiritual.
They will increase each other's determination and resolve to follow
through with intended actions, even in the face of great obstacles and
severe consequences. If the natives are immature and this comparative
conjunction is afflicted by other comparative aspects, there can be the
danger of daring or driving each other to dangerous, ill-considered actions.

A's Mars Conjunct B's North Node Opposition
B's South Node (A's ♂ ☌ B's ☊ ☍ B's ☋)

This comparative combination indicates dynamic interaction with respect to prevailing popular trends and social beliefs. The Mars individual can motivate the Nodes individual to take action to exploit
prevailing social trends and fads for financial gain and career and status
advancement. The Nodes individual can help the Mars individual to be
more effective in his or her activities by taking into consideration the
prevailing social attitudes.

There can be a mutual interest in popular forms of sports and physical
activity. The natives can share an allegiance to their particular social
class or nationality.

A's Mars Conjunct B's South Node Opposition
B's North Node (A's ♂ ☌ B's ☋ ☍ B's ☊)

The Nodes individual in this comparative combination will be a
restraining influence on the Mars individual, keeping him or her from

blindly following prevailing social fads and activities, or encouraging the Mars individual to have the courage of personal convictions, which may differ from popularly held views. The Mars individual will help the Nodes native to put individualistic beliefs into action and to defend them when necessary. If the comparative combination is afflicted, the natives may be cold, indifferent, and resentful toward each other. The Nodes individual can regard the Mars individual as impulsive and inconsiderate. The Mars individual may regard the Nodes person as old-fashioned, negative, and stodgy and may resent the restraints the Nodes individual attempts to impose.

A's Mars Conjunct B's Ascendant Opposition B's Descendant (A's ♂ ☌ B's Asc. ☍ B's Desc.)

Similar to "A's Mars in B's First House," this comparative combination is stronger and more immediate in its implications. The natives will have a direct and immediate effect on one another through their actions and means of personal self-expression. They will motivate each other to action in a direct and personal way.

This combination can indicate sexual attraction if the natives are of opposite sex and appropriate age. There can be mutual involvement in professional and business enterprises and, if this comparative combination is afflicted, a strong sense of competition with each other in professional and financial affairs. There can be danger of mutual conflict and a tendency to motivate each other to rash, impulsive action.

A's Mars Conjunct B's Midheaven Opposition B's Nadir (A's ♂ ☌ B's M.C. ☍ B's Nadir)

This comparative combination indicates strong career interaction and possible competition. The effect will be similar to "A's Mars in B's Tenth House," but stronger and more immediate. Mutual professional concerns are likely to involve political affairs, corporate finance, military, police affairs, engineering, or construction. The natives can have important and immediate effects on each other's reputation and status.

A's Mars Conjunct B's Descendant Opposition B's Ascendant (A's ♂ ☌ B's Desc. ☍ B's Asc.)

Basically, this comparative combination has the same meaning as "A's Mars in B's Seventh House," but its effects are stronger and more immediate.

The Mars individual is likely to motivate the Descendant/Ascendant individual to impulsive, dynamic mutual action. The Descendant/Ascendant individual could introduce the Mars individual to new social situations and make him or her more aware of the social reaction to his or her actions. This comparative combination can indicate sexual attraction, if the natives are of opposite sex and appropriate ages. This attraction, however, does not guarantee that the natives will get along harmoniously over a long period of time: this is a common comparative aspect in situations of marital discord and divorce. If this comparative combination is well-aspected, it can be favorable for business, professional, and financial partnerships that require ambition and energetic action. If it is afflicted, the natives can be rivals or open enemies. They may get involved in lawsuits and, in extreme cases, physical combat.

A's Mars Conjunct B's Nadir Opposition B's Midheaven (A's ♂ ☌ B's Nadir ☍ B's M.C.)

The indication of this comparative combination is dynamic mutual action in the home. Its general significance is the same as "A's Mars in B's Fourth House," but its effects are stronger and more immediate.

If this comparative combination is afflicted, there can be quarrels over domestic and family affairs. It is not a good indicator for family relationships, unless it is well-aspected. In that case, it can be good for business and professional relationships dealing with real estate, construction, farming, or mining.

The Nadir/Midheaven individual is likely to regard the Mars individual as inconsiderate of emotional feelings and family harmony. The Mars individual can regard the Nadir/Midheaven individual as emotionally supersensitive, indolent, and set in his or her ways.

COMPARATIVE SEXTILES

Comparative sextiles of Mars indicate opportunities for intelligent cooperation in action. The Mars individual can help the other native to put his or her ideas into action. There is likely to be a great deal of communication and short trips in connection with business, corporate, or professional affairs. Comparative sextiles of Mars help the natives in cooperative action with mutual friends and organizations. The efficiency and effectiveness of the Mars individual's efforts are often enhanced by valuable information and insights provided by the other native.

A's Mars Sextile B's Sun

See A's Sun Sextile B's Mars.

A's Mars Sextile B's Moon

See A's Moon Sextile B's Mars.

A's Mars Sextile B's Mercury

See A's Mercury Sextile B's Mars.

A's Mars Sextile B's Venus

See A's Venus Sextile B's Mars.

A's Mars Sextile B's Mars (A's ♂ ✶ B's ♂)

This comparative combination is favorable for intelligent, mutual cooperation in action. The natives can act effectively together where communication, travel, and vehicles and their maintenance are concerned. They can work effectively in group activities, mutual friendships, neighborhood affairs, and things relating to brothers and sisters. The intellectual nature of the sextile aspect helps the natives to plan their mutual actions intelligently, avoiding wasted time and effort. This can be a favorable comparative combination for cooperation in joint finances and in mutual professional affairs that are related to engineering, construction, machinery, or police or military affairs. The natives can spur each other to greater effort through a sense of friendly competition. They will enjoy physical work together, sports, and other activities requiring muscular exertion.

A's Mars Sextile B's Jupiter (A's ♂ ✶ B's ♃)

Favorable for intelligent action in religious, educational, social, and charitable group activities, this comparative combination also helps family relationships, especially between brothers and sisters.

The natives help increase each other's enthusiasm and impetus to constructive action. The Mars individual can help the Jupiter individual to implement religious, educational, social, legal, or philosophical goals. The Jupiter individual helps the Mars individual to find constructive outlets for the expression of energy through action.

The natives may become traveling companions for adventure or in the course of professional, business, or corporate endeavors. They will encourage each other to uphold their shared goals and principles, and they can become crusaders for worthwhile causes. There can be a mutual interest in furthering religious, educational, political, or legal reforms. They can be constructive and intelligent in service-oriented or behind-the-scenes work designed to help those less fortunate than themselves. Such work may relate to hospitals, colleges, schools, or institutions.

A's Mars Sextile B's Saturn (A's ♂ ✳ B's ♄)

This comparative combination indicates mutual constructive effort and discipline in professional, financial, corporate, or administrative affairs.

The Saturn individual can help the Mars to use more discipline, organization, and caution in carrying out actions and ambitions. The Mars individual can help the Saturn individual to be more courageous and energetic in implementing plans and goals and in overcoming fear and negativity.

The natives can cooperate effectively in group and organizational activities which have a serious purpose. These activities are often linked to a profession. The natives can cooperate in administrative work related to public relations and communications. This is a good combination for work relating to engineering, construction, machinery, mining, or metal industries. There can be effective cooperation in political work, military affairs, or police matters.

This is not a favorable comparative aspect for romantic attraction; however, if other factors in the comparison indicate a romantic or marital relationship, this combination helps the natives to exercise the necessary discipline and determination to endure difficulties and trying times together.

A's Mars Sextile B's Uranus (A's ♂ ✳ B's ♅)

Unusual, energetic, and resourceful cooperation is possible between these natives. The Uranus individual can help the Mars individual through intuitive, creative, resourceful, and intellectual insights. The

Mars individual can help the Uranus person to put these insights into practice and bring them into practical manifestation. Together they can arrive at unusual ideas and methods for accomplishing group and organizational, professional, or corporate goals and purposes. This is an excellent combination for cooperation in fields such as engineering, electronics, scientific research, invention, economics, or administration. The natives are apt to share an interest in aviation, automobiles, communications, or the electronic media. If they are inclined toward occult interests, they can work together effectively in these areas.

Because of the intellectual nature of this sextile aspect, the natives will help each other to plan actions which will be carried out in a decisive manner at the right time and in the right way. They boost each other's energy and determination to accomplish what they set out to do.

A's Mars Sextile B's Neptune (A's ♂ ✳ B's ♆)

This comparative sextile indicates an ability to act together in intelligent, intuitively directed ways. The psychic sensitivity and intuitive ability of the Neptune individual can help make the activities of the Mars individual more effective. The Mars individual can help the other to put his or her intuitive insights and creative, artistic abilities into action. The Mars individual can also help the Neptune individual to implement improvement in the home and domestic affairs. There can be a mutual interest in mystical philosophies, programs of spiritual self-improvement through yoga, meditation, and metaphysics, or in reincarnation and life after death. This comparative combination improves the ability to sense and communicate about each other's moods and feelings. If the natives are inclined toward mysticism or the occult, they can cooperate effectively in the use of psychic abilities and the pursuit of occult interests.

The natives will enjoy sharing artistic, physical expressions such as dancing. This is a good comparative combination for professional, corporate, and business dealings requiring secrecy and intuitive strategy. If the natives are of opposite sex and appropriate age, there can be a subtle sexual attraction.

A's Mars Sextile B's Pluto (A's ♂ ✳ B's ♇)

Energetic, purposeful cooperation in self-improvement, physical exercise, business, technology, engineering, or professional, corporate, or financial affairs is characteristic of this comparative sextile. Because of the double-Eighth House connotation of this aspect, the natives can share an interest in life after death and reincarnation. If the natives are inclined toward occult and spiritual interests, they further each other's drive for self-improvement and the unfoldment of spiritual faculties. Because of the intellectual nature of the sextile, this comparative combination retains the Mars–Pluto capacity for powerful, dynamic, decisive action with the added advantage of intelligent planning. This is a favorable combination for cooperation in military, police, governmental, industrial, or administrative affairs. The natives can cooperate effectively with friends, brothers, sisters and neighbors.

The Pluto individual can give the Mars individual penetrating and intuitive insights into how to make his or her actions more effective. The Mars individual can help the Pluto individual to be more effective on the physical level of action. This comparative sextile can indicate sexual attraction if the natives are of opposite sex and appropriate age.

A's Mars Sextile B's North Node Trine B's South Node
(A's ♂ ✶ B's ☊ △ B's ☋)

These natives have an ability to cooperate in action where popular, social fads and attitudes are concerned, and in businesses relating to these trends and fads. The Nodes individual can provide the Mars individual with valuable insights into these popular trends, and the Mars individual can help the Nodes individual to put these insights into action in a manner that will be beneficial to the personal, political, or professional affairs of the Nodes individual.

A's Mars Sextile B's South Node Trine B's North Node
(A's ♂ ✶ B's ☋ △ B's ☊)

This comparative combination has basically the same meaning as "A's Mars Sextile B's North Node Trine B's South Node." These natives, however, will be more individualistic and more likely to depart from prevailing social trends and attitudes. The natives can employ their intellectual abilities in gaining personal profit by refusing to blindly follow these trends and fads.

A's Mars Sextile B's Ascendant Trine B's Descendant
(A's ♂ ✶ B's Asc. △ B's Desc.)

Effective and harmonious mutual action is favored by this comparative combination. It indicates sexual attraction between natives of the opposite sex and appropriate age. In marital relationships, the individuals can coordinate their actions effectively and will respond instantly to each other's needs. This is a favorable comparative combination for mutual efforts in physical and mental self-improvement. The natives can work together effectively in business, financial, and professional partnerships.

A's Mars Sextile B's Midheaven Trine B's Nadir
(A's ♂ ✳ B's M.C. △ B's Nadir)

This comparative combination favors effective cooperation in business, professional, corporate, and domestic affairs. It is also a good combination for mutual initiative and constructive effort in improving the home through do-it-yourself projects. The Midheaven/Nadir individual can provide the Mars individual with professional opportunities, increased status, and a base of operations. The Mars individual can encourage the Midheaven/Nadir individual to show more initiative and spur him or her to get things done in home and professional affairs.

A's Mars Sextile B's Descendant Trine B's Ascendant
(A's ♂ ✳ B's Desc. △ B's Asc.)

This has basically the same meaning as "A's Mars Sextile B's Ascendant Trine B's Descendant." However, these natives will take a more intellectual approach to their relationship.

A's Mars Sextile B's Nadir Trine B's Midheaven
(A's ♂ ✳ B's Nadir △ B's M.C.)

This comparative combination has basically the same significance as "A's Mars Sextile B's Midheaven Trine B's Nadir," except that these natives will take a more intellectual approach to family and domestic activities.

COMPARATIVE SQUARES

Comparative squares of Mars indicate that the natives will have difficulty in getting along harmoniously. There is likely to be conflict and disagreement over professional, domestic, and family affairs. The natives are often rivals or competitors in seeking status and career advancement.

The Mars individual can be somewhat abrupt, impulsive, inconsiderate, aggressive, and selfish, thereby arousing resentment. These relationships can succeed only if the natives involved cultivate a considerate and democratic attitude toward each other.

A's Mars Square B's Sun

See A's Sun Square B's Mars.

A's Mars Square B's Moon

See A's Moon Square B's Mars.

A's Mars Square B's Mercury

See A's Mercury Square B's Mars.

A's Mars Square B's Venus

See A's Venus Square B's Mars.

A's Mars Square B's Mars (A's ♂ □ B's ♂)

Important differences are indicated in the natives' approaches to personal action, professional ambition, and business affairs. Any attempts to order each other around or coerce each other will result in conflict and resentment. The natives are apt to dare or goad each other to ill-considered, impulsive acts. Outbursts of temper and, in extreme cases, physical combat can occur with this combination. Romantic and marital relationships can be based on a desire for sexual gratification rather than on genuine love. This is not a good combination for professional or corporate business partnerships.

A's Mars Square B's Jupiter (A's ♂ □ B's ♃)

This comparative combination indicates relationships that could lead to rash, impulsive, and costly acts. The natives can encourage foolish and unrealistic opportunism in each other. Conflicts can arise over differences in religious, philosophical, ethical, legal, political, social, or educational outlook. The Mars individual is likely to regard the Jupiter individual as sanctimonious, lazy, inefficient, and self-indulgent. The Jupiter individual is likely to regard the Mars as impulsive, self-centered, and lacking in moral principles and in social and cultural refinement.

This is not a good combination for business, corporate, or professional partnerships. It is a difficult one for people who must work together in connection with hospitals, asylums, or religious or educational institutions. There is always the danger of becoming involved in lawsuits and of a breakdown of cooperation. Nor is this a good comparative combination for family and domestic relationships: the Mars individual will have a difficult time accepting and adjusting to the domestic habits and standards of the Jupiter individual.

A's Mars Square B's Saturn (A's ♂ □ B's ♄)

Difficulties in professional relationships of all kinds are indicated. The natives are likely to make unreasonable and inconsiderate demands on each other. The Saturn individual will try to exercise a restraining influence on the Mars individual, which he or she will resent. The Saturn individual will, in turn, resent the Mars individual's aggressive attempts to initiate what the Saturn considers rash and impulsive actions and will regard these actions as a threat to status and security.

In general, the natives are apt to use bad timing in dealing with each other. This is not a favorable comparative aspect for friendships or cooperation in organizational group endeavors. There can be conflict and, possibly, lawsuits over corporate funds, insurance, inheritances, and alimony. Marital or parent–child relationships with this comparative square are likely to experience difficulties.

A's Mars Square B's Uranus (A's ♂ □ B's ♅)

This comparative combination makes for volatile and unstable relationships. The natives are likely to encourage each other to ill-considered, impulsive acts. Things will not go as planned, especially in friendships, group endeavors, or professional or corporate affairs.

Difficulties can arise over engineering projects, electronic media, or scientific endeavors. The natives will not agree about the administration of corporate finances or business affairs. They will not see eye-to-eye on how to handle joint finances, corporate endeavors, or occult activities.

The Mars individual is likely to regard the Uranus individual as eccentric, unpredictable, and uncooperative. The latter will resent and rebel against the authoritative attitudes of the Mars individual. Attempts on the part of the natives to order each other around will lead to resentment and conflict. In general, they will be a threat to each other's authority and independence.

If the natives are immature, they can get each other involved in dangerous activities. Periodic explosive outbursts of temper characterize relationships with this comparative combination.

A's Mars Square B's Neptune (A's ♂ □ B's ♆)

This comparative combination is one of the most deceptive and treacherous combinations that can exist in a relationship, especially if it is afflicted by other planets in the comparison.

The Neptune individual is apt to be devious and deceptive, and these traits will arouse anger and resentment in the Mars individual. The Neptune individual will resent the coercive tactics of the Mars individual, but will employ evasive action as a way of getting around the Mars individual rather than retaliating directly. The Neptune native is likely to regard the Mars as crude, overbearing, and insensitive. If the natives lack maturity and moral fiber, they can lead each other into dangerous, self-destructive habits and indulgences such as alcoholism and drug abuse.

In a marital or romantic relationship, one or both natives may use sex as a means of manipulating the other for selfish, ulterior motives. This is not a good combination for professional or business relationships, since some form of deception is likely to be practiced. The Neptune individual is likely to annoy the Mars individual because of his or her inefficiency, confusion, and daydreaming. Nor is this a good combination for psychological understanding between the natives, especially in family and domestic relationships.

A's Mars Square B's Pluto (A's ♂ □ B's ♇)

For natives of this comparative square an intense and difficult relationship is indicated. They must avoid attempts to coerce or order each other around if they are to cooperate effectively. The Mars individual will resent attempts on the part of the Pluto individual to remake or reform him or her. The Pluto individual will resent what he or she considers to be unsophisticated, obvious, impulsive acts on the part of the other.

If the natives are immature, they can dare or goad each other into

dangerous or ill-considered actions, much as with the Mars–Square–
Uranus comparative combination. They will not agree about the handling of business, corporate, financial, administrative, or professional
affairs. This is a dangerous comparative combination for mutual involvement in police, military, or political affairs. In extreme cases, the
natives can involve each other in criminal activities or become enemies.

A's Mars Square B's North Node Square B's South Node
(A's ♂ ☐ B's ☋ ☐ B's ☊)

This comparative combination indicates an inability to cooperate and
adjust to prevailing social attitudes and beliefs. The Nodes individual is
likely to regard the Mars individual as crude and insensitive to appropriate social conduct and behavior. The Mars individual may think that the
Nodes native is overly concerned with trivial and unimportant social
niceties, activities, or fads and that these traits make that individual
ineffectual in really important actions. This is not a good combination
for cooperation in business or professional affairs related to popular
trends and fads.

A's Mars Square B's South Node Square B's North Node

See A's Mars Square B's North Node Square B's South Node.

A's Mars Square B's Ascendant Square B's Descendant
(A's ♂ ☐ B's Asc. ☐ B's Desc.)

The natives will have difficulty in getting along harmoniously in
marriage and other domestic or professional partnerships. The Ascen-
dant/Descendant individual is likely to consider the Mars individual as
selfish, inconsiderate, and domineering. The Mars individual may feel
impatient with the personal idiosyncrasies of the Ascendant/Descendant
person. Generally, the natives are annoyed and impatient with each
other.

A's Mars Square B's Midheaven Square B's Nadir
(A's ♂ ☐ B's M.C. ☐ B's Nadir)

This comparative combination is not good for cooperation in domestic,
business, or professional affairs. The natives are apt to disagree about

administrative procedures. The Midheaven/Nadir individual is likely to regard the Mars individual as a threat to his professional status and domestic security. The Mars individual may regard the Midheaven/Nadir individuals as overly conservative and unwilling to change.

A's Mars Square B's Descendant Square B's Ascendant

See A's Mars Square B's Ascendant Square B's Descendant.

A's Mars Square B's Nadir Square B's Midheaven

See A's Mars Square B's Midheaven Square B's Nadir.

COMPARATIVE TRINES

Comparative trines of Mars indicate that the natives can cooperate in creative and expansive action. These combinations can indicate sexual compatibility in romantic and marital relationships. The natives will encourage each other in the use of their will power, energy, and optimism. There will be mutual enjoyment of physical activity and adventure; this enjoyment could relate to romantic affairs, sports, dancing, hiking, or outdoor work. The natives can help each other to acquire education and understanding through performing practical tasks. There is mutual harmony in planning and executing action. These are favorable comparative aspects for professional, business, corporate, or engineering relationships.

A's Mars Trine B's Sun

See A's Sun Trine B's Mars.

A's Mars Trine B's Moon

See A's Moon Trine B's Mars.

A's Mars Trine B's Mercury

See A's Mercury Trine B's Mars.

A's Mars Trine B's Venus

See A's Venus Trine B's Mars.

A's Mars Trine B's Mars (A's ♂ △ B's ♂)

This comparative trine is favorable for mutual action and accomplishment in many areas. The natives spur each other's drive and initiative without ego confrontations. They will encourage each other's efforts at self-improvement through physical exercise, professional initiative, or business enterprise. This is a favorable combination for partnerships involving mechanical work, engineering, sports, building, corporate finance, administrative work, politics, or physical education. It can indicate sexual attraction if the natives are of opposite sex and appropriate age.

A's Mars Trine B's Jupiter (A's ♂ △ B's ♃)

This is an excellent comparative trine for partnerships involving business, legal, professional, educational, religious, or charitable work. The natives enjoy sharing outdoor activities, sports, and travel. This is a good combination for constructive, practical cooperation in family and domestic affairs. The natives can also work together effectively in corporate business enterprises relating to law, publishing, education, religion, hospitals, institutions, engineering, tax accounting, or handling affairs of the deceased. They will be effective in taking practical action to help those less fortunate than themselves—this can relate to religious, charitable, or educational institutions. There can be a mutual interest in political, religious, or economic reforms. Generally, these natives will encourage each other's efforts at physical, spiritual, or personal self-improvement. The Jupiter individual can help to channel the energy of the Mars individual into constructive action. The Mars individual will help the other to put educational, philosophical, or religious goals into action.

A's Mars Trine B's Saturn (A's ♂ △ B's ♄)

This comparative trine is excellent for mutual cooperation in business and professional affairs, especially in such fields as mechanics, engineering, heavy industry, politics, administration, or police or military affairs. The Saturn individual can help the Mars individual to be more effective in getting practical results. The Mars person can benefit from the Saturn's experience, discipline, caution, and good organization. The Mars individual can, in turn, help the Saturn individual to be more courageous and energetic, overcoming his or her fear and negativity. The natives encourage each other to take care of immediate work that requires patience and willingness and to handle the unpleasant tasks of life. This discipline saves time, trouble, and aggravation in the long run, especially where mechanical work, building, or tasks that require application and getting one's hands soiled are involved. In marital relationships, this combination helps the natives to have the mutual discipline required for getting through troubled times.

A's Mars Trine B's Uranus (A's ♂ △ B's ♅)

Dynamic and creative relationships in the fields of scientific research, the occult, astrology, business, corporate finance, and group or organizational endeavors are indicated. The natives will spur each other to greater accomplishment in new approaches to professional affairs or scientific, technological innovation. This is an excellent combination for those who need to break away from dull, monotonous routines. The natives can develop a mutual interest in occult sciences, and may become involved in occult groups and organizations.

The Uranus individual can give the Mars individual many intuitive, creative insights into how to make his or her efforts and actions effective. The Mars individual will inspire the Uranus individual with the energy and initiative to put insights to practical use. The natives will enjoy a dynamic friendship in which each can help the other to realize his or her goals and objectives. They will enjoy the same friends and the same group and organizational activities. There will be a mutual love of adventure and excitement, which can show itself in travel, efforts at political or social reform, inventiveness, games or sports. In romantic and marital relationships, this combination indicates sexual attraction because of the double-Scorpio connotation of Mars and Uranus.

A's Mars Trine B's Neptune (A's ♂ △ B's ♆)

Because this comparative trine indicates a mutual interest in occult and mystical pursuits, the natives will encourage each other to an increased capacity for psychic-intuitive awareness, especially in terms of increasing survival potential. They will have a sympathetic, emotional sensitivity to each other's desires and needs. The Neptune individual can have a calming and soothing influence when the Mars individual is upset. The Mars individual can help the Neptune overcome inertia associated with psychological problems. This is a good combination for cooperation in business and professional enterprises that require secrecy and careful strategy. The Neptune individual can have intuitive insights which can help make the efforts and actions of the Mars individual more effective. The Mars individual can help the Neptune individual to put dreams, visions, and intuitive perceptions into action.

This is a good comparative combination for those who work together in hospitals, religious institutions, or charitable work. It is also a good combination for dynamic cooperation in making the home and domestic environment a place conducive to inner growth and unfoldment.

A's Mars Trine B's Pluto (A's ♂ △ B's ♀)

This comparative trine indicates dynamic mutual action in many areas of expression. The natives cooperate in a way that is conducive to their mutual survival and self-preservation. They will encourage each other's determination and resolve in efforts at self-improvement. There can be a mutual interest in scientific and occult investigations. They can use their will power to overcome obstacles that stand in the way of success. This is a good combination for cooperation in professional, business, and corporate financial endeavors. The Pluto individual can help the Mars individual through penetrating, occult insights which help the Mars individual to make actions more meaningful and effective. The Mars individual can help the other to manifest inner, spiritual powers in a practical way. In marriage and romantic relationships, this comparative trine indicates sexual attraction.

A's Mars Trine B's North Node Sextile B's South Node

See A's Mars Sextile B's South Node Trine B's North Node.

A's Mars Trine B's South Node Sextile B's North Node

See A's Mars Sextile B's North Node Trine B's South Node.

A's Mars Trine B's Ascendant Sextile B's Descendant

See A's Mars Sextile B's Descendant Trine B's Ascendant.

A's Mars Trine B's Midheaven Sextile B's Nadir

See A's Mars Sextile B's Nadir Trine B's Midheaven.

A's Mars Trine B's Descendant Sextile B's Ascendant

See A's Mars Sextile B's Ascendant Trine B's Descendant.

A's Mars Trine B's Nadir Sextile B's Midheaven

See A's Mars Sextile B's Midheaven Trine B's Nadir.

COMPARATIVE OPPOSITIONS

Comparative oppositions of Mars indicate interpersonal conflicts arising out of self-centered attitudes and aggressive and inconsiderate actions. Mars, as ruler of Aries, is opposite Libra, sign of relationships. Aries and the First House, which Mars rules, deal with the instinct of self-preservation. Consequently, the impulsive desire principles of Mars as ruler of Aries can stand in the way of mutual cooperation and consideration. The opposition aspect, per se, relates to Libra and the Seventh House in the natural Zodiac. When Mars is involved in a comparative opposition, then, it represents a principle which is basically unfriendly to the principle of cooperation, which the opposition aspect demands. Since Mars rules the Eighth House of joint finances, conflict can arise over corporate moneys, division of property, inheritance, and alimony.

For relationships with comparative oppositions of Mars to succeed, the Mars individual must make a conscientious effort to consider the needs and wishes of the other party, and the other party must try to make allowances for the impulsiveness and egocentricity of the Mars individual. If the natives are unwilling to make this adjustment, conflict and mutual resentment are apt to be the result.

A's Mars Opposition B's Sun

See A's Sun Opposition B's Mars.

A's Mars Opposition B's Moon

See A's Moon Opposition B's Mars.

A's Mars Opposition B's Mercury

See A's Mercury Opposition B's Mars.

A's Mars Opposition B's Venus

See A's Venus Opposition B's Mars.

A's Mars Opposition B's Mars (A's ♂ ☍ B's ♂)

Both natives are apt to act in an impulsive, self-centered, aggressive way, and thus threaten each other's personal desires and drive for self-preservation. Any tendency toward coercive action on the part of either native will arouse opposition and resentment in the other.

The natives are generally prone to quarrel with each other, often from a strong sense of mutual competition. In extreme cases, actual physical confrontation can take place. The handling of business affairs, joint finances, corporate money, inheritance, or professional affairs can be a source of conflict and irritation. If both natives are mature, however, they can cooperate effectively in actions related to these affairs.

A's Mars Opposition B's Jupiter (A's ♂ ☍ B's ♃)

Relationships with this comparative combination require patience and moderation. The overoptimism of the Jupiter individual combined with the impulsiveness of the Mars individual can result in rash, ill-considered actions and expenditures. In some cases, the Jupiter individual exercises poor judgment by giving in to the selfish actions of the Mars individual, who may regard the Jupiter individual as pompous, inactive, hypocritical, and sanctimonious. The Jupiter individual is apt to regard the Mars individual as impulsive, rash, selfish, inconsiderate, and sometimes violent.

This is not a favorable comparative aspect for legal, professional, business, corporate, administrative, engineering, construction, or military relationships. There can be waste of money and resources because of a lack of proper coordination of effort. Neither is it a favorable combination for working harmoniously in religion, philosophy, higher education, or for compatibility in social or moral standards. There can be disagreements as to how to handle matters relating to hospitals or religious or educational institutions. There can also be conflict between the professional and domestic interests of the natives.

A's Mars Opposition B's Saturn (A's ♂ ☍ B's ♄)

This comparative combination indicates a lack of agreement as to how and when to act regarding personal, professional, or financial affairs. The natives will be out-of-phase with each other where timing is concerned. Attempts at control or domination on the part of either native will lead to resentment and conflict. The Saturn individual is likely to feel that his or her security and status is threatened by the Mars individual and to resent the aggressiveness and impulsiveness of the latter. The Mars individual will resent and feel frustrated by the restraining influence of the Saturn individual.

This is not a favorable combination for business, corporate, legal, professional, or industrial relationships. It is especially difficult in cases of employer–employee relationships. If the employer is the Saturn individual, he or she will make heavy work demands on the Mars individual. If the employer is the Mars individual, he or she will be impatient with the slow pace of the Saturn individual.

The natives can become involved in lawsuits over professional or financial affairs. In parent–child relationships, there is likely to be harshness and a lack of sympathy and understanding. In marital relationships, one or both partners may attempt to use the other for gaining money or status without showing real love or concern.

A's Mars Opposition B's Uranus (A's ♂ ☍ B's ♅)

This comparative combination indicates aggressive and impulsive interaction. If the natives are immature, they are likely to challenge, goad, or drive each other to rash, dangerous, impulsive acts.

The Mars individual may regard the Uranus individual as eccentric, unreliable, and uncooperative, and in turn, may be regarded as brutally forceful and lacking intelligence and refinement. Any attempt on the part of either individual to control or dominate the other will cause rebellion and conflict. The natives will be unwilling to sacrifice personal autonomy or freedom of action to make the relationship work.

This is not a favorable combination for cooperation in professional, administrative, organizational, group, occult, scientific, or technological activities. There can be conflict and disagreement over corporate business affairs, joint finances, inheritance, alimony, and mutual expenditures. This combination is often characterized by outbursts of anger which, in extreme cases, can bring about physical confrontation. This is a divorce-prone combination in marital relationships.

A's Mars Opposition B's Neptune (A's ♂ ☍ B's ♆)

This comparative combination indicates that the natives will experience psychological difficulties in adjusting to each other. The subconscious quirks and psychological difficulties of the Neptune individual are likely to aggravate and frustrate the desire of the Mars individual for decisive action. The Neptune individual will resent the other's crudeness, inconsiderateness, and lack of emotional sensitivity. The Mars individual will regard the Neptune individual as an impractical, self-indulgent, nonproductive dreamer, and may threaten the Neptune individual by arousing painful memories in his or her subconscious mind. This is not a favorable combination for cooperation in family and domestic affairs. The natives can get each other into difficulties through unwise occult or psychic activities. In some cases, they tend to encourage each other in self-destructive habits, such as alcoholism and drug abuse. There can be conflict over differences of religious, philosophical, or social outlook. The Neptune individual can be dishonest or deceptive in mutual business, financial, or professional affairs.

A's Mars Opposition B's Pluto (A's ♂ ☍ B's ♇)

Since this comparative combination makes for explosive and combative relationships, each native is apt to regard the other as a threat to personal self-preservation and individual interests. The natives should avoid ordering or coercing each other, as this will arouse resistance and resentment, much as with "A's Mars Opposition B's Mars" or "A's Mars Opposition B's Uranus." The Mars individual will resent and oppose any attempts on the part of the Pluto individual to remake or reform him. The Pluto individual is likely to consider the rash, impulsive acts of the Mars individual as unsophisticated, dangerous, or ineffectual.

There can be a strong sense of competition between the natives which, in extreme cases, can lead to enmity, even physical confrontation. As with the Mars–Uranus comparative square, the natives may challenge or goad each other to rash, impulsive acts. This is not a favorable combination for mutual involvement in occult work or psychic investigation. There can be conflict and disagreement over joint finances, alimony, inheritances, or corporate financial affairs. There can be major disagreements over the handling of professional or corporate affairs.

A's Mars Opposition B's North Node Conjunct B's South Node

See A's Mars Conjunct B's South Node Opposition B's North Node.

A's Mars Opposition B's South Node Conjunct B's North Node

See A's Mars Conjunct B's North Node Opposition B's South Node.

A's Mars Opposition B's Ascendant Conjunct B's Descendant

See A's Mars Conjunct B's Descendant Opposition B's Ascendant.

A's Mars Opposition B's Midheaven Conjunct B's Nadir

See A's Mars Conjunct B's Nadir Opposition B's Midheaven.

A's Mars Opposition B's Descendant Conjunct B's Ascendant

See A's Mars Conjunct B's Ascendant Opposition B's Descendant.

A's Mars Opposition B's Nadir Conjunct B's Midheaven

See A's Mars Conjunct B's Midheaven Opposition B's Nadir.

XII
Jupiter

Comparative influences of Jupiter indicate the ways in which the natives can help each other expand in spiritual, philosophical, educational, and social areas. They also indicate the ways in which the natives will show generosity and benevolence to each other.

If Jupiter is afflicted in the comparison, however, these influences can show the ways in which the natives encourage and abet each other's self-destructive, self-indulgent tendencies. In extreme cases, this affliction can lead to secret enmity or a form of hypocrisy and overindulgence.

Because of Jupiter's exaltation in Cancer, sign of the home, favorable comparative influences of Jupiter are excellent in family and marital relationships: they bring spiritual, cultural, educational, and ethical values into family life. In general, the natives help each other to integrate harmoniously into the larger social order.

When Jupiter is favorably aspected in the comparison, the good fortune the natives bring each other is often the reward of past good deeds. They can cooperate effectively in helping those less fortunate than themselves, often in connection with religious, educational, medical, cultural, and charitable institutions. The natives will help each other gain a philosophic understanding of life; they will instill in each other such virtues as patience, forgiveness, moral principles, and charity. Comparative influences of Jupiter are common among traveling companions.

COMPARATIVE HOUSE PLACEMENTS

The comparative house positions of Jupiter indicate the practical affairs of life which will be benefitted by Jupiter's expansive influences. The natives will share social, educational, cultural, religious, and philosophical values as they relate to these affairs. They will benefit each other and will cooperate in helping others where these affairs are concerned. These affairs will also be shared by the families of both natives. Often, mutual travel is involved.

A's Jupiter in B's First House

The Jupiter native will have a positive, beneficial effect on the self-image and self-expression of the First House individual. In general, the Jupiter individual can arouse the First House individual's interest in spiritual self-improvement. The Jupiter individual helps the First House individual gain greater self-confidence and a more positive outlook on life. The First House individual can, in turn, help the Jupiter individual to put social, domestic, philosophical, religious, cultural, and educational goals and purposes into action. The natives tend to increase each other's vitality and have a positive, healing effect on each other. They can learn a great deal from each other in the areas of spiritual, cultural, philosophical, educational, legal, or social knowlege, values, concepts and traditions. The natives enjoy traveling together and exploring faraway places and cultures.

The natives can cooperate effectively to make the home a better place, improving family relationships and helping others.

If Jupiter is heavily afflicted in the comparison, the Jupiter individual can be unwisely indulgent toward the First House individual, particularly in parent–child relationships. In such cases, the First House individual may feel that the Jupiter is trying to buy acceptance or is being sanctimonious and hypocritical.

A's Jupiter in B's Second House

This comparative combination is excellent for cooperation and mutual benefit in business and financial affairs. The Jupiter individual uses his or her wisdom, experience, and cultural knowledge to help the Second House individual to become more effective in business affairs. The Second House individual helps the other to obtain necessary money to pursue educational, spiritual, and philosophical goals. The Second House individual can provide financial security for the domestic and family affairs of the Jupiter individual, and the legal, educational, foreign, religious, and general cultural contacts of the Jupiter native can help the business affairs of the Second House individual. The Jupiter individual can influence the Second House individual to contribute money to educational, religious, or charitable purposes. This ultimately leads to greater prosperity for the Second House individual, as well as bringing the rewards of good action—like bread cast upon the water coming back as sponge cake. The Jupiter individual may also persuade the Second House individual to spend money on travel and other forms of cultural enrichment. The natives may travel for business or financial reasons. They could be involved together in raising funds for religious, charitable, or educational purposes.

If Jupiter is heavily afflicted in the comparison, the natives can influence each other to unwise expenditures, with financial loss and indebtedness as the result. There could be overexpansion in mutual business enterprises that often do not bring a suitable return on the investment.

A's Jupiter in B's Third House

An intellectual sharing of many spiritual, cultural, educational, and philosophical values is characteristic of this comparative combination. The Jupiter individual can help the Third House person achieve a more comprehensive spiritual and cultural, as well as a more optimistic and positive, way of thinking. The Third House individual can help the Jupiter individual to be more scientific, factual, and exact in philosophical endeavors.

The natives will spend much time discussing ideas and philosophies. There can be a mutual involvement in books, education, and short- and long-distance travel. This is a good combination for those mutually involved in teaching, lecturing, writing, and publishing. The Third House individual can help the Jupiter individual to find outlets for the promulgation of spiritual, educational, and cultural ideals and purposes through writing and other communications media.

This is a particularly good combination for brother or sister relationships and other family relationships.

If Jupiter is heavily afflicted in the comparison, the natives may become heavily involved in impractical, "pie-in-the-sky" thinking.

A's Jupiter in B's Fourth House

Natives enjoy a harmonious home and family relationship. If Jupiter is well-aspected, the natives will regard each other as part of the family, even in the absence of any blood or marital relationship.

The natives encourage each other to carry on community, religious, cultural, or educational functions in the home. The home will be used as a place of spiritual meditation and retreat. In some cases, the natives will take in outsiders who need their help. The Jupiter individual will bring educational, cultural, spiritual, and religious values into the family life. This is a good combination for business partnerships relating to real estate, building, farming, food, and domestic products.

If Jupiter is heavily afflicted in the comparison, there can be selfish, possessive love and overprotectiveness between the natives, especially if they belong to the same family. This is particularly true in a parent–child relationship.

A's Jupiter in B's Fifth House

This comparative combination is favorable for marital, romantic, parent–child, and teacher–student relationships. Because the Jupiter individual knows how to make the process of learning enjoyable for the Fifth House individual, this combination results in rapid learning in parent–child and teacher–student relationships. In romantic and marital relationships, the natives will gain pleasure through cultural, educational, religious, philosophical, and charitable activities. They will enjoy cultural or religious art and drama. This comparative combination promises an enduring romantic relationship because of the kindness and consideration the natives show for each other and because their cultural values are compatible. In marital relationships, this combination often produces a large family, especially if Jupiter is in a Water sign.

The natives enjoy vacations and travel together in the pursuit of pleasure. In business relationships, there can be gain through speculative investments, provided Jupiter is not afflicted. If Jupiter is afflicted in the comparison, the natives can lead each other into excessive self-indulgence in the pursuit of pleasure, and this could lead to dissipation of time, money, and health.

A's Jupiter in B's Sixth House

This is a favorable combination for employer–employee, co-worker, and doctor–patient relationships.

The Jupiter individual's kindness and consideration will make the working conditions of the Sixth House individual pleasant and enjoyable. The Jupiter individual can help the employment prospects of the Sixth House individual through education and training. The Jupiter individual can have a beneficial effect on the health of the Sixth House individual. In some cases, there can be a mutual interest in spiritual healing or the power of the mind to overcome illness.

This is an excellent combination for those who work together in hospitals, schools, and religious or charitable institutions. The natives will encourage each other's enthusiasm for helping those less fortunate than themselves. They can gain cultural, philosophical, religious, spiritual, and educational knowledge and wisdom through practical work in service. In some cases, the natives will travel together in connection with their work. This is a good combination for mutual help and service in the home and in family affairs.

A's Jupiter in B's Seventh House

This comparative combination indicates harmony and mutual consideration in marriage and partnerships. In a marriage relationship the natives will share compatible social, ethical, religious, educational, and cultural values, and these will provide a basis for harmony which extends beyond sexual and emotional considerations. In business and legal partnerships, the natives will deal with each other in an honest, ethical, and responsible way. This is an excellent combination for cooperation in public relations. The natives will know how to appeal to the ideals and beliefs of the prevailing social order. It is also a favorable combination for partnerships or associations relating to religion, law, higher education, or publishing.

The Jupiter individual will bring cultural, educational, religious, and spiritual values into the partnership. The Seventh House individual can help the Jupiter individual to expand his or her educational, philosophical, and religious goals and purposes through cooperative mutual action. If Jupiter is heavily afflicted in the comparison, difficulties can arise out of the tendency on the part of the natives toward hypocrisy or promising more than they can deliver.

A's Jupiter in B's Eighth House

Because this comparative combination is favorable for cooperation in corporate business enterprises, joint finance, and the financial affairs of religious, educational, or charitable institutions, the natives may be associated through fund-raising activities related to such institutions.

In marital relationships, this combination can bring wealth through marriage, as well as enabling the natives to handle joint funds harmoniously. One of the natives could benefit through gifts and legacies. Marriage partners with this combination will accumulate wealth and financial security in the latter part of their lives.

There can be a mutual interest in the aspects of religion related to life after death or reincarnation.

If Jupiter is afflicted in the comparison, the natives may enter into their association for ulterior motives of financial gain. In extreme cases, this leads to fraud or dishonesty in business dealings.

A's Jupiter in B's Ninth House

Jupiter's rulership of the natural Ninth House makes this a particularly strong combination. It favors mutual interest and activity in the fields of higher education, law, religion, publishing, philosophy, and travel. The natives will share the same point of view toward these affairs.

This is a good combination for marital and family relationships: the natives will incorporate spiritual and educational values in their domestic and family affairs. It is also an excellent combination for traveling companions, especially if the travel is related to exploration of foreign cultures, historical interests, religious pilgrimages, or educational pursuits.

The natives can develop a mutual interest in religious practices, meditation, spiritual teachers, and religious organizations. They can help each other with their intuitive, prophetic insights into the prevailing social order and its future trends.

A's Jupiter in B's Tenth House

This comparative combination is excellent for professional partnerships and political associations. The natives will help each other gain status, position, and public recognition. The educational, cultural, and religious contacts and background of the Jupiter individual can benefit the career advancement of the Tenth House individual. The Tenth House individual can in turn help the Jupiter individual gain official support for educational, religious, or philosophical goals and purposes. The Jupiter individual's insights into the cultural attitudes and trends of the prevailing social order can benefit the Tenth House individual.

This combination is excellent for professional partnerships or relationships involving religion, education, law, publishing, travel, or lecturing, and for mutual political advancement.

If Jupiter is heavily afflicted in the comparison, there could be a tendency to overexpand or use questionable, though expedient, measures in professional or political affairs. The natives could be unrealistic in their political, professional, and career expectations.

A's Jupiter in B's Eleventh House

This is a favorable combination for friendships and cooperation in group and organizational activities. The natives will have a mutual interest in humanitarian work and social reform, and can work together effectively in religious, educational, or charitable organizations. They enjoy the same friends and group activities, and share an interest in intellectual, scientific, or occult subjects, along with the educational activities relating to them.

The cultural, educational, and religious background and contacts of the Jupiter individual can help the Eleventh House individual to realize goals and objectives. The Eleventh House individual can, in turn, help the Jupiter individual to attain religious, educational, and philosophical goals through friendship and group activity.

If Jupiter is heavily afflicted in the comparison, the natives could be insecure or hypocritical both in their relationship and in their friendships with others, or they could make promises that they are unable to keep.

A's Jupiter in B's Twelfth House

A mutual interest in meditation, religious mysticism, and the development of intuitive powers can be indicated. The natives will be able to confide in each other and share their private lives and inner feelings.

This is a good combination for cooperation in work and service related to religious institutions and hospitals. The natives will become involved in helping those less fortunate than themselves.

The Jupiter individual can help the Twelfth House individual to understand and overcome subconscious emotional hangups based on past experiences and painful memories. The Twelfth House individual will share with the Jupiter individual an interest in uncovering deeper levels of intuitive wisdom belonging to the subconscious memory and, in some cases, to previous incarnations.

If Jupiter is heavily afflicted in the comparison, the natives may encourage each other in their psychological weaknesses and self-destructive subconscious habits.

COMPARATIVE CONJUNCTIONS

Comparative conjunctions of Jupiter indicate dynamic, positive, optimistic action in accomplishing shared cultural, religious, and educational goals and objectives.

These combinations have a beneficial and expansive effect on the lives of the natives. Greater knowledge, understanding, and social prestige often grow out of the relationship. Comparative conjunctions of Jupiter are especially helpful in family and domestic relationships. They are also beneficial in teacher–student relationships and in the association of people who work together for religious, educational, or charitable purposes.

The natives are able to share their inner, subjective, personal viewpoints and feelings with each other. There can be mutual interest in travel and exploration of foreign places and cultures.

A's Jupiter Conjunct B's Sun

See A's Sun Conjunct B's Jupiter.

A's Jupiter Conjunct B's Moon

See A's Moon Conjunct B's Jupiter.

A's Jupiter Conjunct B's Mercury

See A's Mercury Conjunct B's Jupiter.

A's Jupiter Conjunct B's Venus

See A's Venus Conjunct B's Jupiter.

A's Jupiter Conjunct B's Mars

See A's Mars Conjunct B's Jupiter.

A's Jupiter Conjunct B's Jupiter (A's ♃ ☌ B's ♃)

This comparative conjunction indicates a similar viewpoint toward religion, philosophy, higher education, culture, and travel. The natives will share an interest in religious and philosophical work. They will enjoy traveling together. This is an excellent combination for family and domestic relationships. The natives will bring social, religious, and cultural values into the family life. They can cooperate effectively in helping those less fortunate than themselves.

If the Jupiters are heavily afflicted by natal or comparative aspects, the natives are apt to encourage each other's indolence and unrealistic optimism.

A's Jupiter Conjunct B's Saturn (A's ♃ ☌ B's ♄)

Serious business and professional relationships characterize this comparative combination. The natives are usually involved together in political, business, legal, and professional affairs. This is a good comparative combination for group and organizational work. The social, educational, and cultural contacts of the Jupiter individual can help the Saturn individual in business, professional, and political affairs.

The Jupiter individual can help the Saturn individual overcome fear and negativity. The Saturn individual can help the Jupiter individual avoid unrealistic optimism and overexpansion.

This combination favors cooperation in administrative and public relations work, especially if it relates to educational or religious institutions, government, business administration, and professional organizations. This is also a good comparative combination for handling serious family responsibilities or for business dealings in real estate.

If the comparative conjunction is afflicted, the natives can cause each other difficulty through professional, legal, political, or business affairs. In extreme cases, this can result in lawsuits.

A's Jupiter Conjunct B's Uranus (A's ♃ ☌ B's ♅)

This comparative conjunction indicates unusual and mutually beneficial friendships. The natives will stimulate each other's intuitive qualities and encourage each other's efforts toward spiritual and mental self-improvement. The Uranus individual will give the Jupiter individual advanced ideas, scientific understanding, and intuitive insights into how to make personal humanitarian, scientific, educational, or spiritual efforts more effective. The Jupiter individual will help the Uranus person gain the acceptance and support of established religious and educational organizations and institutions. The natives instill in each other the enthusiasm necessary for accomplishing worthwhile scientific, philosophical, and humanitarian goals and endeavors. These are often carried out through humanitarian, scientific, or occult groups or organizations. The natives will stimulate each other's interest in advanced forms of occult or spiritual investigation and practice. This is an excellent aspect for mutual involvement in occult and astrological activities and organizations. It is also a good combination for creative innovation in the home. The home can be used as a place for entertaining mutual friends and pursuing group and organizational affairs.

If the comparative conjunction is afflicted, the Uranus individual may regard the Jupiter individual as much too traditional, conservative, narrow-minded, or sanctimonious. The Jupiter individual could, in turn, regard the other as eccentric, unpredictable, and much too revolutionary.

In general, the natives can bring about circumstances of sudden good fortune to each other, often through mutual friends.

A's Jupiter Conjunct B's Neptune (A's ♃ ☌ B's ♆)

This comparative combination is favorable for cooperation in religious mysticism or spiritual endeavors. The natives may become involved together in mystical cults or meditative practices. There is usually mutual interest in such things as investigating each other's previous incarnations or clairvoyant powers. In some cases, this involves an element of grandiose self-delusion, especially if the comparison is afflicted and the natives lack maturity.

If the comparative conjunction is afflicted, the natives can be carried away with flighty, unrealistic, emotional sentimentality and idealism. They can encourage each other's self-indulgent, self-destructive habits.

The natives will encourage each other's idealism and creative imagination. However, here also there is the danger of encouraging delusions of grandeur in each other. This combination can arouse a mutual interest in travel, religion, law, and education. They can work together in hospitals and religious institutions. In family relationships, there will be interest in using the home as a place of meditation or for the pursuit of religious activities.

The Jupiter individual is likely to regard the Neptune individual as intuitive and mystical in his or her approach to religion and philosophy, while the Neptune will regard the Jupiter individual as traditional and institutionally oriented in his religious and philosophical approach.

In general, the natives will show sympathy and understanding for each other. They will share their private feelings and aspirations.

A's Jupiter Conjunct B's Pluto (A's ♃ ☌ B's ♇)

This comparative conjunction is favorable for mutual occult and spiritual efforts at self-regeneration. The natives will actively encourage each other to pursue goals of higher education, religion, philosophy, and travel. There is apt to be a mutual interest in spiritual philosophies related to reincarnation and life after death.

The Jupiter individual can help the Pluto individual to express will and power constructively so as to benefit the larger social order and bring the Pluto individual personally the rewards of good action. The Pluto individual can help the Jupiter individual to put more energy and determination into efforts to improve the larger social order. The Pluto native, through occult knowledge, penetrating insights, and resourcefulness, can also help the Jupiter individual to raise his or her spiritual, philosophical understanding to a more occult or scientific level. Through such interactions, the natives can attain spiritual, religious, educational, or philosophical goals.

This can be a good combination for cooperation in corporate financial endeavors, especially if they relate to education, law, publishing, or charitable institutions. One or both natives can gain through inheritances, corporate financial affairs, grants, or government funding. This can be a good combination for the regeneration and improvement of family and domestic affairs, for parent–child relationships, and for teacher–student relationships. If the comparative conjunction is afflicted, the natives should beware of unwise financial speculation.

A's Jupiter Conjunct B's North Node Opposition B's South Node (A's ♃ ☌ B's ☊ ☍ B's ☋)

This comparative combination is favorable for mutual study of the prevailing cultural trends and popular beliefs, and for those natives working in public relations or businesses that appeal to current fads. The Nodes individual can help the Jupiter individual gain a better perception of current popular trends and social beliefs. The Jupiter individual can help the Nodes individual gain a long-range historical perspective on how these current trends and beliefs came into being and a prophetic insight into their future.

A's Jupiter Conjunct B's South Node Opposition B's North Node (A's ♃ ☌ B's ☋ ☍ B's ☊)

Both natives have a critical and conservative interest in prevailing popular trends and social beliefs. The natives are not likely to follow blindly those who try to exploit them for personal gain or profit.

The Jupiter individual's understanding of historical perspective on the motivating forces behind social change can help the Nodes individual to follow his or her own unique path. The Nodes individual will, in turn, encourage the Jupiter to be more independent and critical in analysis of current trends and of the larger social order.

A's Jupiter Conjunct B's Ascendant Opposition B's Descendant (A's ♃ ☌ B's Asc. ☍ B's Desc.)

This comparative combination has basically the same significance as "A's Jupiter in B's First House." The Jupiter individual encourages the Ascendant/Descendant individual's efforts at personal and spiritual self-improvement and helps that individual develop a more positive self-image and more socially constructive means of personal self-expression. The Ascendant/Descendant individual will give energy and active support to the Jupiter individual's efforts to aid or improve the larger social order. The natives will be natural friends and will enjoy each other's company.

A's Jupiter Conjunct B's Midheaven Opposition B's Nadir
(A's ♃ ☌ B's M.C. ☍ B's Nadir)

This comparative combination has basically the same significance as "A's Jupiter in B's Tenth House." The Jupiter individual helps to advance the career and status of the Midheaven/Nadir individual. If the Midheaven/Nadir individual occupies a position of power and authority in the world, he or she is likely to enlist the aid of people who have power and influence to help the Jupiter individual gain official support and recognition for his or her goals and purposes in aiding the larger social order. These could be directed toward religion, higher education, foreign relations, philosophy, or law. The Jupiter individual will, in turn, influence the Midheaven/Nadir person to acquire a sense of cultural responsibility and ethics in professional affairs and public life.

A's Jupiter Conjunct B's Descendant Opposition B's Ascendant
(A's ♃ ☌ B's Desc. ☍ B's Asc.)

Basically, this comparative combination has the same significance as "A's Jupiter in B's Seventh House." The Jupiter individual will bring cultural, educational, social, ethical, or religious values into the relationship. This comparative combination gives harmony in the marriage relationship and honest dealings in business relationships. The natives' association will be the means of their constructive involvement in the larger social order.

This is an excellent comparative combination for family and domestic relationships. Legal difficulties, should they arise, can be settled out of court in an amicable manner.

A's Jupiter Conjunct B's Nadir Opposition B's Midheaven
(A's ♃ ☌ B's Nadir ☍ B's M.C.)

Basically the same insignificance as "A's Jupiter in B's Fourth House," this comparative combination has a beneficial effect on family and domestic relationships. The Jupiter individual brings religious, educational, cultural, and ethical values into the family life and domestic affairs of the Nadir/Midheaven individual. The Nadir/Midheaven individual can, in turn, provide a home or base of operations for the religious, cultural, or educational pursuits of the Jupiter individual. There will be mutual kindness and an emotional sensitivity to each other's moods and feelings.

COMPARATIVE SEXTILES

Comparative sextiles of Jupiter indicate constructive interpersonal communication and friendly cooperation with regard to religious, philosophical, educational, and cultural goals and objectives. The natives may become involved together in organizational and group activities designed to improve and uplift the larger social order. This could take the form of humanitarian, educational, religious, or charitable work. The natives are able to communicate well regarding the affairs ruled by the planets in the comparative sextile. In general, these comparative combinations encourage benevolent cooperation.

A's Jupiter Sextile B's Sun

See A's Sun Sextile B's Jupiter.

A's Jupiter Sextile B's Moon

See A's Moon Sextile B's Jupiter.

A's Jupiter Sextile B's Mercury

See A's Mercury Sextile B's Jupiter.

A's Jupiter Sextile B's Venus

See A's Venus Sextile B's Jupiter.

A's Jupiter Sextile B's Mars

See A's Mars Sextile B's Jupiter.

A's Jupiter Sextile B's Jupiter (A's ♃ ✳ B's ♃)

This comparative sextile indicates intellectual compatibility in concepts and beliefs regarding philosophy, religion, higher education, law, and social ethics. The natives will cooperate effectively in groups and organizations of a humanitarian, religious, charitable, educational, or philosophical nature. This is also a good comparative sextile for those who work together in such areas as education, publishing, or communications media. It favors domestic harmony in family relationships. The natives will confide in each other about their inner emotional feelings and spiritual aspirations. There will be much traveling together, involving both long and short trips.

A's Jupiter Sextile B's Saturn (A's ♃ ✳ B's ♄)

This comparative combination is excellent for all business and professional relationships. The natives are apt to deal with each other in an honest, responsible, and ethical way. They will have a beneficial influence on each other's sense of timing and organization.

This combination favors mutual work in such fields as politics, administration, law, education, publishing, lecturing, travel, real estate, or public relations. Often, the individuals are involved in professional or fraternal organizations.

The Jupiter individual can help the Saturn individual to be more optimistic in pursuing business and professional goals. Through his or her educational or cultural background, the Jupiter individual can bring the Saturn individual valuable contacts. The Saturn individual can help the Jupiter to be more organized, efficient, and practical in pursuing religious, philosophical, cultural, or business goals and purposes. The Saturn individual can help the other overcome false optimism and unwise expansion, and the Jupiter individual can help the Saturn overcome pessimism and negative attitudes.

A's Jupiter Sextile B's Uranus (A's ♃ ✳ B's ♅)

This comparative sextile is excellent for friendship and for mutual involvement in religious, humanitarian, fraternal, charitable, educational, scientific, and occult groups and organizations.

The Uranus individual through sudden, intuitive insights and unique ways of doing things will help the Jupiter native to further religious, educational, or philosophical goals and purposes. The Jupiter individual will help gain acceptance and support for the Uranus individual's unique ideas and inventions in the larger social order and its established religious and educational institutions.

The natives will help bring out each other's intuitive qualities. They will share a sense of adventure in the exploration of unique occult, scientific, and philosophical ideas and experiences. They will have a mutual interest in the occult approach to religious philosophy and mysticism. There will be a mutual love of travel and the exploration of foreign places and cultures.

A's Jupiter Sextile B's Neptune (A's ♃ ✶ B's ♆)

Mutual interest in religious mysticism, psychic unfoldment, and the creative use of the imagination is indicated.

The Neptune individual can help the Jupiter individual to be more intuitive and inwardly creative in his or her approach to religion, philosophy, or higher education. The Jupiter individual can help the Neptune individual to use creative imagination and intuitive talents to aid the larger social order.

There will be mutual interest in making the home a place of peace, spiritual retreat, meditation, or religious or educational activity. The natives will enjoy travel, especially in search of spiritual and educational goals and cultural enrichment. This particularly applies to religious pilgrimages in search of spiritual instruction and upliftment. There will be much discussion and group activity related to mysticism, meditation, or religious or charitable pursuits. Both natives will be interested in helping those less fortunate than themselves.

A's Jupiter Sextile B's Pluto (A's ♃ ✶ B's ♀)

This comparative sextile is favorable for cooperation in spiritual, educational, and cultural self-improvement and enrichment. The Jupiter individual will help the Pluto individual to use his or her occult powers, psychic abilities, and resourcefulness in a way that is helpful to the larger social order. The Pluto individual will help the Jupiter individual to be more dynamic, resourceful, and focused in accomplishing worthwhile educational, religious, or cultural goals.

There will be a mutual interest in reincarnation, life after death, and the use of the power of the will for social, personal, and spiritual regeneration. The natives will work together effectively in improving conditions in hospitals and in educational and religious institutions. They can be mutually involved in occult, scientific, and religious groups and organizations—in some cases, of a secretive nature.

This is a good combination for corporate business enterprises involving insurance, tax accounting, law, education, publishing, travel, and handling of the goods of the dead. There will be an interest in aiding the education and spiritual development of children, and these values will be brought into the family life.

A's Jupiter Sextile B's North Node Trine B's South Node
(A's ♃ ✶ B's ☊ △ B's ☋)

Because this comparative combination brings mutual interest and cooperation in understanding and taking advantage of prevailing social trends and popular beliefs, natives will have compatible ideas regarding proper social and religious conduct. This is a good combination for people who are involved together in public relations and the promotion of religious, educational, charitable, business, or political organizations, groups, or purposes. There can be a mutual interest in molding public opinion or in studying the development of cultural attitudes.

A's Jupiter Sextile B's South Node Trine B's North Node
(A's ♃ ✶ B's ☋ △ B's ☊)

Basically, this comparative combination has the same significance as "A's Jupiter Sextile B's North Node Trine B's South Node." However, these natives will have a longer-range historical perspective on the development of cultural attitudes and popular beliefs. They are not likely to be interested in blindly following prevailing popular beliefs because of the intellectually discriminative nature of the sextile aspect and the conservative nature of the South Node.

A's Jupiter Sextile B's Ascendant Trine B's Descendant
(A's ♃ ✶ B's Asc. △ B's Desc.)

This comparative combination indicates compatibility in marriages, friendships, and business relationships through shared religious, philosophical, cultural, educational, and ethical beliefs, attitudes, and interests. It is favorable for teacher–student and parent–child relationships. It gives harmony in family and domestic relationships. The natives will share an enjoyment of travel and group and organizational activities related to cultural, religious, educational, or charitable work.

The Jupiter individual will help the Ascendant/Descendant individual to develop a more positive self-image, social adjustment, and means of self-expression. The Ascendant/Descendant individual can help the Jupiter individual to put religious, educational, cultural, or ethical goals and beliefs into practice.

A's Jupiter Sextile B's Midheaven Trine B's Nadir
(A's ♃ ✶ B's M.C. △ B's Nadir)

Cooperation in political, professional, domestic, and family affairs is favored. The cultural understanding and background of the Jupiter individual can help the Midheaven/Nadir individual in career advancement and status. The Midheaven/Nadir individual, by using status and influence and by providing a base of operations, can help the Jupiter to expand religious, cultural, or educational goals.

This is an excellent combination for harmony in family relationships; the Jupiter individual will incorporate educational, religious, and cultural values into the family life. It is also highly favorable for professional partnerships related to law, education, publishing, lecturing, politics, hospitals, or religious institutions.

A's Jupiter Sextile B's Descendant Trine B's Ascendant
(A's ♃ ✶ B's Desc. △ B's Asc.)

This comparative combination has basically the same meaning as "A's Jupiter Sextile B's Ascendant Trine B's Descendant." The natives will be concerned with gaining an intellectual understanding of the psychology of their relationship and of relationships in general.

A's Jupiter Sextile B's Nadir Trine B's Midheaven
(A's ♃ ✶ B's Nadir △ B's M.C.)

This comparative combination has basically the same meaning as "A's Jupiter Sextile B's Midheaven Trine B's Nadir." These natives, however, will be more intellectually oriented toward family and domestic affairs.

COMPARATIVE SQUARES

Comparative squares of Jupiter can indicate interpersonal difficulties arising from differences in religious, cultural, educational, family, or ethical values and background. The natives could influence each other to foolish optimism and overexpansion. There can be a tendency on the part of both to underestimate the magnitude and seriousness of professional and domestic tasks and responsibilities. The timing of mutual efforts in these areas can be out of phase or miscalculated.

The Jupiter individual can be hypocritical and take too much for granted in a relationship. The natives may encourage or excuse each other's weaknesses and self-indulgent or destructive habits, particularly in family, parent–child, romantic, or marital relationships. In some cases, the Jupiter individual gets a perverse enjoyment out of playing the role of martyr.

A's Jupiter Square B's Sun

See A's Sun Square B's Jupiter.

A's Jupiter Square B's Moon

See A's Moon Square B's Jupiter.

A's Jupiter Square B's Mercury

See A's Mercury Square B's Jupiter.

A's Jupiter Square B's Venus

See A's Venus Square B's Jupiter.

A's Jupiter Square B's Mars

See A's Mars Square B's Jupiter.

A's Jupiter Square B's Jupiter (A's ♃ □ B's ♃)

Difficulty arising from incompatible religious, educational, and philosophical viewpoints or cultural backgrounds is indicated. The natives are apt to encourage each other's self-destructive and self-indulgent tendencies, as with other Jupiter and Neptune afflictions. There can be a mutual indulgence in unrealistic, idealistic schemes and plans for a Utopian world. The natives can be fond of nonproductive, useless, time-

and money-wasting types of travel. In domestic and family relationships, the natives will have a "let-George-do-it" attitude, especially where everyday tasks are concerned.

A's Jupiter Square B's Saturn (A's ♃ □ B's ♄)

This comparative square is unfavorable for business, financial, and professional relationships. The natives' timing will be out of phase where these affairs are concerned. The natives can influence each other to expand or hold back at the wrong time.

The Jupiter individual is likely to regard the Saturn individual as selfish, materialistic, and overconcerned with worldly status. The Saturn individual is likely to regard the Jupiter as lacking in ambition, practicality, and common sense. The Jupiter individual may also view the Saturn individual as hard, cold, and unsympathetic, while the Saturn native is likely to regard the Jupiter as too soft and overindulgent toward human weaknesses.

In general, this is not a good combination for cooperation in organizational, professional, domestic, or business affairs. There can be disagreements over political, administrative, legal, business, educational, or religious matters. Conflict can arise from differences over the relative importance of professional versus domestic affairs. The natives will disagree on the correct way to handle public relations or business dealings. The natives' enjoyment of mutual travel may be thwarted by financial limitations or domestic and professional responsibilities.

A's Jupiter Square B's Uranus (A's ♃ □ B's ♅)

Because this comparative square indicates impulsive, extravagant mutual interactions, natives could influence each other to get involved in unwise, get-rich-quick schemes. There can be a mutual love of travel, adventure, and unusual experiences which can prove costly and dangerous.

The Jupiter individual is apt to regard the Uranus individual as eccentric, unreliable, and too revolutionary, and, in turn, may be regarded by the Jupiter individual as stodgy, hypocritical, and sanctimonious.

This is not a favorable comparative combination for mutual involvement in corporate financial affairs or occult practices. There is apt to be friction between the natives concerning group and organizational activities. They will have differing preferences where personal friends are concerned, and may even find each other's friends objectionable. In some cases, both natives will possess an impractical, unrealistic mutual social idealism. There could be a tendency for them to want to overthrow existing social institutions without having better alternatives.

A's Jupiter Square B's Neptune (A's ♃ □ B's ♆)

This comparative square indicates a tendency for the natives to get each other involved in impractical, emotionally oriented mystical religious practices, which can take the form of cults or various forms of guru worship. They are apt to encourage each other's shiftless and self-indulgent tendencies. There can be a mutual avoidance of discipline and necessary practical responsibilities. Both can neglect the practical handling of domestic and family responsibilities. They are apt to embark on meaningless religious pilgrimages or become vagabond travelers.

The Jupiter individual may regard the Neptune individual as spaced-out and immersed in a private dream world. The Neptune individual is likely to regard the Jupiter individual as too attached to traditional religious beliefs: institutionalized religious forms appeal to the Jupiter native, while the Neptune seeks an inner, mystical approach to religion.

A's Jupiter Square B's Pluto (A's ♃ □ B's ♇)

This is not a good comparative combination for mutual involvement in occult, mystical, legal, educational, or corporate affairs.

The Jupiter individual may resent the tendency of the Pluto individual to use what he or she considers unethical coercive tactics. The Jupiter individual may resent the Pluto individual's efforts at remaking or reforming him or her. The Pluto individual could, in turn, resent the attempts of the Jupiter individual at indoctrination into the Jupiter individual's own brand of religious or moral ethics. The Pluto individual may regard the Jupiter individual as self-indulgent, hypocritical, or sanctimonious. There will be differences of opinion in the handling of joint finances, joint resources, educational matters, religious philosophy, or occult practices. There can be conflict over inheritance or alimony.

If the natives have occult tendencies or an interest in magic, they could become involved in dangerous or questionable occult practices. Mutual travel could be dangerous and fraught with unforeseeable difficulties. This is not a good combination for mutual involvement in hospitals or religious or educational institutions. In some cases, the natives could become involved in unrealistic, grandiose schemes, as in the case of "Jupiter Square Neptune" and "Jupiter Square Uranus."

A's Jupiter Square B's North Node Square B's South Node
(A's ♃ □ B's ☊ □ B's ☋)

Natives will have different approaches to social conduct. They will have different values with respect to the prevailing social trends and popular beliefs. The Jupiter individual may regard the Nodes individual as superficial in blindly following current fads and popular beliefs. The Nodes individual may regard the social outlook of the Jupiter individual as stodgy and traditional.

A's Jupiter Square B's South Node Square B's North Node

See A's Jupiter Square B's North Node Square B's South Node.

A's Jupiter Square B's Ascendant Square B's Descendant
(A's ♃ □ B's Asc. □ B's Desc.)

Natives will be in disagreement regarding religious, ethical, educational, or cultural ideas and values. It is not a good combination for cooperation in professional, family, domestic, or marital affairs.

The Jupiter individual may regard the Ascendant/Descendant individual as impulsive and self-centered. The Ascendant/Descendant individual may regard the Jupiter individual as moralistic, stodgy, sanctimonious, and bigoted, or religiously fanatical.

There can be disagreement over the handling of affairs related to hospitals or religious or educational institutions. In some cases, the natives can be destructively overindulgent toward each other. They can make promises that they do not intend to keep, and, in some cases, insincere flattery can enter into the relationship as a means of avoiding unpleasantness or gaining private ulterior motives.

A's Jupiter Square B's Midheaven Square B's Nadir
(A's ♃ □ B's M.C. □ B's Nadir)

This is not a good combination for cooperation in professional, family, and domestic relationships. The natives are often unrealistic in their expectations. They lack sufficient discipline to carry out their business or career ambitions. This is not a good combination for employer–employee relationships.

The Jupiter individual may regard the Midheaven/Nadir individual as materialistic or interested only in self-advancement. The Midheaven/Nadir individual may regard the other as lazy, self-indulgent, impractical, and sanctimonious.

In romantic and marital relationships, difficulties can arise from differences in family, social, and cultural background. In some cases, the Jupiter individual will be overly indulgent toward the Midheaven/Nadir individual, particularly in family, marital, and parent–child relationships. This is not a good combination for employer–employee relationships.

A's Jupiter Square B's Descendant Square B's Ascendant

See A's Jupiter Square B's Ascendant Square B's Descendant.

A's Jupiter Square B's Nadir Square B's Midheaven

See A's Jupiter Square B's Midheaven Square B's Nadir.

COMPARATIVE TRINES

Comparative trines of Jupiter indicate an easy, harmonious, creative flow between the natives with respect to the affairs ruled by the planets involved in the comparative trines. (See *The Astrologer's Handbook,* Harper & Row, pp. 404–407.)

The natives will have a benevolent and philosophical attitude toward each other. There will be mutual interest in religion, philosophy, higher education, travel, artistic creativity, the performing arts, children and their education, and the pursuit of pleasure. These comparative trines are especially good in family, parent–child, and teacher–student relationships.

A's Jupiter Trine B's Sun

See A's Sun Trine B's Jupiter.

A's Jupiter Trine B's Moon

See A's Moon Trine B's Jupiter.

A's Jupiter Trine B's Mercury

See A's Mercury Trine B's Jupiter.

A's Jupiter Trine B's Venus

See A's Venus Trine B's Jupiter.

A's Jupiter Trine B's Mars

See A's Mars Trine B's Jupiter.

A's Jupiter Trine B's Jupiter (A's ♃ △ B's ♃)

Natives will have a strong mutual interest in religion, philosophy, education, travel, history, and foreign cultures. They will trust each other. They can work harmoniously together in religious, educational, or cultural institutions. There will be a mutual interest in bringing ethical, religious, cultural, and educational values into the home and family life.

A's Jupiter Trine B's Saturn (A's ♃ △ B's ♄)

This comparative combination indicates harmonious cooperation in business, politics, law, education, public relations, administrative work, or group and organizational activities. There will be a sense of responsibility to the larger social order and to the ethical standards of society. They will encourage each other to apply their religious and ethical principles in a practical and meaningful way.

The Jupiter individual is able to help the Saturn individual overcome pessimism and negativity. The Saturn individual will help the Jupiter individual to be practical and realistic in professional, organizational, and financial affairs.

This is an excellent combination for responsible cooperation in marital, business, friendship, and family relationships. In general, the natives respect each other and bring out the best in each other's character.

A's Jupiter Trine B's Uranus (A's ♃ △ B's ♅)

Mutual interest in scientific or occult approaches to religion and philosophy is indicated. The Uranus individual is able to inspire the Jupiter individual with unusual scientific, intuitive, and inventive insights. The Jupiter individual can help the Uranus individual to express a greater degree of creativity and expand his or her horizons within the larger social order.

The natives are likely to carry on organizational or group activities in the home. There can be interests in unusual home improvement projects and family activities. They can work together in using new methods to improve conditions in hospitals, religious institutions, schools, or other cultural institutions. There will be mutual interest in humanitarian causes or in social, political, or religious reforms. This is an excellent combination for mutual involvement in corporate business enterprises, especially if they are related to scientific research, electronics technology, travel, aircraft, law, religion, philosophy, or higher education.

A's Jupiter Trine B's Neptune (A's ♃ △ B's ♆)

This comparative trine indicates a mutual love of religious mysticism, psychic investigation, meditation, the study of reincarnation, or devotional religious practices. The natives will enjoy each other as traveling companions, especially if the travel is for educational, cultural, or religious purposes. They will confide in each other about personal extrasensory experiences and future goals and aspirations, along with past experiences.

If one of the natives is just awakening to the spiritual path, the other native will encourage that interest in spiritual unfoldment. The Jupiter native will help the Neptune individual to use his or her intuitive abilities in a way that will benefit the larger social order. The Neptune individual can help the other to be less dependent on religious orthodoxy and more aware of the spiritual guidance that comes from within.

The natives can cooperate effectively in helping those less fortunate than themselves, in connection with some kind of religious, educational, medical, or charitable institution.

A's Jupiter Trine B's Pluto (A's ♃ △ B's ♀)

This is a dynamic combination for mutual spiritual growth and unfoldment. The natives will help each other to be more dynamic and progressive in efforts to improve the status quo of the larger social order. This is an excellent comparative combination for cooperation in corporate business, scientific, cultural, occult, or religious endeavors.

The Pluto individual's dynamic will or penetrating occult insights can expand and deepen the philosophical and religious understanding of the Jupiter individual. The latter will help the Pluto individual to be more constructive and beneficial to the larger social order by using his or her will and other resourceful attributes. In general, these natives will encourage and help each other toward personal, social, and spiritual regeneration.

A's Jupiter Trine B's North Node Sextile B's South Node

See A's Jupiter Sextile B's South Node Trine B's North Node.

A's Jupiter Trine B's South Node Sextile B's North Node

See A's Jupiter Sextile B's North Node Trine B's South Node.

A's Jupiter Trine B's Ascendant Sextile B's Descendant

See A's Jupiter Sextile B's Descendant Trine B's Ascendant.

A's Jupiter Trine B's Midheaven Sextile B's Nadir

See A's Jupiter Sextile B's Nadir Trine B's Midheaven.

A's Jupiter Trine B's Descendant Sextile B's Ascendant

See A's Jupiter Sextile B's Ascendant Trine B's Descendant.

A's Jupiter Trine B's Nadir Sextile B's Midheaven

See A's Jupiter Sextile B's Midheaven Trine B's Nadir.

COMPARATIVE OPPOSITIONS

Comparative oppositions of Jupiter indicate a tendency to exaggerate events in the relationship. The natives will be inclined to make unrealistic promises and hold unrealistic expectations. This tendency can result in disappointment and tension. They can encourage each other's tendency to unrealistic optimism and overexpansion, and this can result in loss or indebtedness.

The natives can have a "let-George-do-it" attitude toward each other, resulting in a general lack of accomplishment and eventual resentment. They can encourage each other's self-indulgent, self-destructive tendencies, much as is the case with other adverse Jupiter comparative combinations. However, this can result in separation when one party has had enough. In extreme cases, lawsuits may result from the association. Also, in extreme cases, the Jupiter individual can either be gullible or can play the role of the con artist.

A's Jupiter Opposition B's Sun

See A's Sun Opposition B's Jupiter.

A's Jupiter Opposition B's Moon

See A's Moon Opposition B's Jupiter.

A's Jupiter Opposition B's Mercury

See A's Mercury Opposition B's Jupiter.

A's Jupiter Opposition B's Venus

See A's Venus Opposition B's Jupiter.

A's Jupiter Opposition B's Mars

See A's Mars Opposition B's Jupiter.

A's Jupiter Opposition B's Jupiter (A's ♃ ☍ B's ♃)

This comparative combination indicates difficulties arising out of incompatible religious, philosophical, educational, cultural, or historical viewpoints. In a marital relationship, religious or cultural differences in family background can cause problems. The natives can encourage each other's tendencies toward foolish optimism, extravagance, or self-indulgence. They can tend to promise more than they can fulfill. Often, there are differences in their approaches to family and domestic affairs.

In some cases, the natives pretend friendliness to each other merely to avoid unpleasantness or to gain some personal advantage. In general, the difficulties involved in the relationship will be similar to those in other adverse Jupiter, Venus, and Neptune comparative aspects.

A's Jupiter Opposition B's Saturn (A's ♃ ☍ B's ♄)

This is not a favorable comparative opposition for professional, family, business, marital, or educational relationships. The Saturn individual is likely to regard the Jupiter individual as too liberal, while the Jupiter individual considers the other much too conservative. Consequently, they are out of sympathy and out of phase with each other. They will question each other's moral and practical judgment, and refuse to synchronize their actions, thus losing benefits that they would otherwise enjoy. The Jupiter individual can view the Saturn individual as negative, overly conservative, and unsympathetic, and in turn be viewed as sanctimonious, hypocritical, unrealistic, and impractical.

The unsatisfactory business and professional relationships indicated by this comparative combination can result in lawsuits. The natives often conflict over professional versus family and domestic concerns and responsibilities. This is not a favorable comparative combination for mutual involvement in the affairs of hospitals or religious or educational institutions. The natives will not make good traveling companions: they will have diverse interests while traveling and tend to get in each other's way or cause each other difficulty of some kind. They are likely to have widely differing political viewpoints, and, if they are professionally involved in politics, to consider each other as rivals or enemies.

A's Jupiter Opposition B's Uranus (A's ♃ ☍ B's ♅)

Because eccentric, unstable relationships are indicated, this is not a favorable combination for cooperation in professional or corporate endeavors relating to research, electronics, education, law, travel, religion, or group or organizational activities.

The Jupiter individual is likely to regard the Uranus individual as eccentric, unreliable, revolutionary, and undependable. The Uranus individual is likely to regard the other as stodgy, sanctimonious, overly conservative, and unscientific. The natives will not agree on religious, philosophical, educational, or cultural ideas and values. They will not see eye to eye regarding group, organizational, or institutional policies and responsibilities.

In some cases, the natives' relationship will be based on ulterior motives. If they become involved in travel, they will encounter many sudden, unexpected difficulties, especially in long-distance traveling. There can be problems regarding joint finances and resources as a result of foolish extravagance and impulsive expenditures.

A's Jupiter Opposition B's Neptune (A's ♃ ☍ B's ♆)

The natives have a tendency to encourage each other's unrealistic fantasies and self-indulgent habits. They can become involved in dubious forms of religious mysticism, cults, or psychic practices.

In some cases, the Jupiter individual can regard the Neptune individual as unorthodox, deluded, psychotic, and impractical in his or her private fantasies. The Neptune individual may regard the Jupiter individual as overly orthodox, traditional, and lacking in intuitive insight and imagination.

This is not a favorable combination for cooperation in the efficient handling of practical domestic and family responsibilities. In general, the natives can feed each other's delusions of grandeur and encourage each other to avoid practical responsibility. In extreme cases, they may encourage each other to drink, use drugs, or engage in other self-destructive habits and escapist tendencies. The friendship could be based on mutual deception and ulterior motives. There can be major differences of opinion about psychological approaches to religion, philosophy, education, or mysticism.

A's Jupiter Opposition B's Pluto (A's ♃ ☍ B's ♇)

This comparative combination is not favorable for legal, business, corporate, educational, or romantic relationships. There can be disagreement on the handling of legal affairs, educational policies, religious practices, or joint finances. If the natives are involved in occult or psychic interests, there can be disagreement regarding these things as well. Lawsuits and mutual conflict can arise over inheritance, alimony, or corporate finances.

The expansive urge of the Jupiter individual, combined with the power drive of the Pluto individual, could lead to dangerous and unethical attempts to achieve power and influence in the larger social order. Their association is often based on ulterior motives; consequently, the relationship will last only as long as something is to be gained through it.

The Jupiter individual may regard the Pluto individual as ruthless, overbearing, and dictatorial and resent the Pluto individual's attempt to reorganize and remake him or her. The Pluto individual will regard the Jupiter individual as sanctimonious, stodgy, hypocritical, and, in some cases, as an idealistic, impractical dreamer.

A's Jupiter Opposition B's North Node Conjunct B's South Node

See A's Jupiter Conjunct B's South Node Opposition B's North Node.

A's Jupiter Opposition B's South Node Conjunct B's North Node

See A's Jupiter Conjunct B's North Node Opposition B's South Node.

A's Jupiter Opposition B's Ascendant Conjunct B's Descendant

See A's Jupiter Conjunct B's Descendant Opposition B's Ascendant.

A's Jupiter Opposition B's Midheaven Conjunct B's Nadir

See A's Jupiter Conjunct B's Nadir Opposition B's Midheaven.

A's Jupiter Opposition B's Descendant Conjunct B's Ascendant

See A's Jupiter Conjunct B's Ascendant Opposition B's Descendant.

A's Jupiter Opposition B's Nadir Conjunct B's Midheaven

See A's Jupiter Conjunct B's Midheaven Opposition B's Nadir.

XIII
Saturn

Comparative influences of Saturn indicate areas in which the natives have serious duties and responsibilities toward each other. In karmic relationships, Saturn's position in the comparison and in each chart indicates an area of responsibility or a debt to be paid, particularly where a task of omission or commission must be corrected through discipline, hard work, or a combination. Even in relationships that are not karmic, Saturn's influence in the comparison emphasizes the area in which the natives must strive collectively to build structure into their lives and thereby fulfill their destiny and accomplish their goals.

Saturn is exalted in the sign Libra, which rules marriage and partnership and indicates the extent to which important relationships are karmic in nature. Consequently, Saturn's placement is of great significance in determining the seriousness and intent of the natives' collaboration. Saturn is said to be the karmic teacher which sees to it that we do not bypass the consequences of our actions. Thus, an afflicted Saturn in a comparison would indicate that the natives bring out each other's problems, hardships, and heavy responsibilities, and that one or both can become a burden to the other. A favorable placement of Saturn suggests that the natives will have patience and discipline to remain together and cooperate through difficulties and uneasy times.

Relationships with strong Saturnian comparative influences often deal with business, career, and financial considerations and indicate mutual responsibility in serious group and organizational endeavors. These relationships work best if the natives have common goals and objectives. The Saturn individual is likely to make demands upon the other native in terms of discipline and work.

COMPARATIVE HOUSE PLACEMENTS

Comparative house placements of Saturn indicate mutual responsibilities with respect to the affairs ruled by Saturn's house placement. The Saturn individual will influence the house individual through discipline and organization in the affairs of the house in which Saturn falls. In whatever house Saturn falls, there will be serious relationships or serious business, financial, organizational or professional responsibilities for both individuals.

The comparative house placements of Saturn show the affairs in which the major duties and responsibilities of the relationship must be met. Patience is the key if the natives are to succeed in the demands made by Saturn. If Saturn is afflicted in its comparative house placement, the natives will have a heavy burden of responsibility, obstacles and hardships to overcome. In some cases, the Saturn individual can be selfish, burdensome, demanding, or unsympathetic.

A's Saturn in B's First House

This comparative combination indicates a serious relationship. The Saturn individual will tend to restrain and discipline the self-expression of the First House individual. Favorable comparative aspects to Saturn will help the First House individual to develop a serious, self-assured, competent, personal approach to life. Through the constructive influence of the Saturn individual, the First House individual will become more introspective and use greater forethought in planning his or her actions.

If Saturn is afflicted in the comparison, the First House individual will feel that the Saturn individual is oppressive and inhibits personal self-expression and growth. The Saturn individual will regard the First House individual as impulsive, immature, and self-centered.

If Saturn is well-aspected in the comparison, the natives can cooperate effectively in business, professional, and financial affairs. These natives can be loyal friends who will cooperate efficiently in group and organizational activities.

A's Saturn in B's Second House

Serious mutual responsibilities regarding business and financial affairs are indicated. The Saturn individual will influence the Second House individual to be prudent and thrifty in financial dealings and expenditures. The Second House individual can support the Saturn individual's professional goals financially.

The Saturn individual will work hard in mutual business endeavors and will bring practical business experience to the relationship. He or she can provide the financial security to make social activity and the enjoyment of the good things of life possible. The Saturn individual will make certain that the Second House individual is solvent and kept free of debt by restraining him or her from unnecessary expenditures.

If Saturn is afflicted in the comparison, the natives can undergo financial deprivation and hardships. The Saturn individual may be selfish or stingy. There could also be fear and lack of confidence in business activities. These negative outlooks could thwart further growth and development for both natives.

A's Saturn in B's Third House

This comparative combination indicates serious mutual intellectual pursuits. The natives can be mutually involved in business and professional activities related to writing, communications media, transportation, teaching, lecturing, or mail-order business. It can bring about a mutual sense of responsibility in community and environmental affairs.

The Saturn individual will tend to teach the Third House individual how to use his or her mental skills, such as organization in speech, writing, and study habits, and will encourage a more practical application of knowledge and ideas. The Saturn native will make the Third House individual feel responsible for brothers, sisters, and neighbors. The Third House individual can help the Saturn individual in business and professional endeavors through communicating new ideas and sharing practical knowledge. The Third House individual will communicate effectively about practical duties and responsibilities, especially if they are related to professional affairs.

If Saturn is afflicted in the comparison, the Saturn individual may have a negative, discouraging and unsympathetic attitude toward the ideas and communications of the Third House individual, and the latter will likely regard the Saturn individual as uncommunicative, negative in thinking, unresponsive to new ideas, or in extreme cases, as dull, stupid, opinionated, or prejudiced.

A's Saturn in B's Fourth House

Heavy mutual family and domestic responsibilities are indicated. There will be a need for discipline and hard work in these affairs. The Saturn individual will demand hard work from the Fourth House individual, and the Fourth House individual's domestic needs are likely to increase the work load of the Saturn individual.

If Saturn is afflicted in the comparison, there can be conflict between the professional interests of the Saturn individual and the family and domestic concerns of the Fourth House individual. The Saturn individual can be austere and emotionally unresponsive to the inner feelings, moods, and family emotional reactions of the Fourth House individual and regard him or her as a financial burden.

On the positive side, the Saturn individual can be a stabilizing influence in the home and provide domestic security through taking care of property and providing financial security through professional activities.

A's Saturn in B's Fifth House

This comparative combination is not favorable for a romantic attraction. In a romantic relationship, there can be considerable age difference. One or both parties may enter into the relationship because of material consideration or desire for status.

If Saturn is well-aspected in the comparison, this comparative combination can indicate mutual loyalty. It is an important one for parent–child relationships, especially if the parent is the Saturn individual. The Saturn individual will feel a strong responsibility toward the child and have a strong disciplinary influence. This discipline can be constructive if it is combined with wisdom and love. However, if Saturn is afflicted, there could be a lack of emotional sensitivity to the child's needs, and the child could feel unloved or harshly treated. In a teacher–student relationship, the situation is similar, particularly if the teacher is the Saturn individual. In other types of relationships, there can be a mutual interest and enjoyment of sound financial investments and business and professional affairs. This can be a good combination for serious mutual work in commercial or fine arts, including the business aspects of art and entertainment.

A's Saturn in B's Sixth House

Serious mutual responsibilities in work and service are indicated. The Saturn individual can help the Sixth House individual to be professional, better organized, and more efficient in his or her work. If Saturn is well-aspected in the comparison and the natives are mature, this is a good comparative combination for employer–employee, co-worker, and doctor–patient relationships. There will be a mutual sense of responsibility in regard to professional affairs and the services rendered. In general, if Saturn is well-aspected in the comparison, the natives will have mutual professional respect, which will result in practical worthwhile accomplishments.

If Saturn is afflicted in the comparison, the Sixth House individual may regard the Saturn individual as an unreasonable or oppressive task master and the work grind imposed by the Saturn individual as oppressive and detrimental to health. The Saturn individual may regard the Sixth House individual as inefficient, disorganized, irresponsible, and lazy in work habits.

A's Saturn in B's Seventh House

This comparative placement of Saturn imposes serious responsibilities upon the natives in marriages, business partnerships, and professional relationships.

Saturn is exalted in Libra, corresponding to the Seventh House of the natural Zodiac, and accidentally exalted in the Seventh House. Consequently, the connection of the Seventh House with partnerships and relationships makes this placement of Saturn a vital factor in determining the natives' capacity to handle mutual responsibilities amicably.

Favorable comparative aspects to Saturn will give the natives a strong sense of loyalty and a serious concern about each other's personal well-being, status, and professional success. This is a favorable indicator of a lasting marriage, with the natives fulfilling themselves through the acceptance of the responsibilities of such a relationship.

Business and professional relationships could deal in law, public relations, politics, and administrative work. The natives will acquire a strong sense of justice and fair play, and a consequent strong relationship of a personal nature will very likely develop.

Afflictions to Saturn in the comparison could cause the natives to disagree over the handling of mutual responsibilities. Each may consider the other to be selfish or emotionally unresponsive to the basic needs of the relationship. Business and professional associations can be plagued by lawsuits. In marital relationships, the Seventh House individual may feel that the Saturn native is overly concerned with status, money, or other material considerations.

A's Saturn in B's Eighth House

This placement of Saturn indicates mutual responsibilities in joint finances, corporate affairs, business dealings, and matters related to inheritances, insurance, and, in cases of divorce, alimony. It often indicates mutual involvement in the financial affairs of groups and organizations.

The Saturn individual can assist the Eighth House native to effectively organize his or her corporate financial affairs and make conscientious, wise, and conservative use of joint finances. The Eighth House individual can likewise encourage the use of joint financial resources to further the Saturn native's career and business ambitions. Thus, this is a favorable combination for business and professional alliances, particularly those involving corporate finances, insurance, tax accounting, or the handling of the affairs of the dead. It is frequently found in associations founded upon mutual desire for financial gain.

Marital relationships with this combination could falter from a lack of real love and from emotional, mental, and spiritual incompatibility. Afflictions to Saturn in the comparison can bring loss through death, conflict over inheritances, disagreement over joint finances, or discord over payments of alimony. The materialistic outlook characteristic of the negative expression of Saturn could encourage the natives' morbid tendencies and result in a deep-seated fear of death.

A's Saturn in B's Ninth House

This comparative combination indicates serious mutual interests in religion, philosophy, law, travel, and higher education in preparing for a career.

The natives will encourage each other's ambition to achieve intellectual, educational, religious, and cultural status. This is often accomplished through higher education, lecturing, travel, writing, or publishing. This comparative combination is favorable for business and professional relationships dealing with law, religion, education, travel, foreign relations, or administration of institutions. It can be a favorable combination for teacher–student relationships if Saturn is favorably aspected, especially if the Saturn individual is the teacher.

If Saturn is afflicted in the comparison, there can be differences of opinion over religious, educational, moral, philosophic, or cultural issues. The Saturn individual will often take the conservative point of view in such disagreements.

The Ninth House individual may regard the Saturn individual as materialistic, stodgy, overly conservative, negative, and concerned with preserving the status quo, and, in turn, be considered as an impractical armchair philosopher. The natives could encounter difficulties or obstacles while traveling as a result of circumstances brought about by each other's influence. When they travel together, it is usually for professional or business reasons.

When Saturn is well-aspected in the comparison, the Saturn individual can help the Ninth House individual to be more practical in the application of his educational, religious, and philosophic ideals.

A's Saturn in B's Tenth House

Business and professional interactions that are important to both natives are indicated. This comparative combination is favorable for those who work together in such fields as business administration, government, politics, law, and other professions dealing with power and status. In some cases, this comparison can indicate loyal friendship based on a long-standing professional association. This comparative combination will have serious and long-range effects for better or worse on the career and reputations of the natives. It is essential that ethical principles be strictly adhered to in all dealings and professional activities. If Saturn is well-aspected in the comparison, the natives will be allies in furthering each other's careers. If Saturn is afflicted in the comparison, however, there will be a sense of professional competition which could result in jealousy, rivalry, and a struggle for power.

The Saturn individual tends to encourage the Tenth House individual to be more cautious, prudent, and hard-working in career affairs. The natives are likely to make heavy demands on each other in terms of work load and responsibility.

If Saturn is afflicted in the comparison, selfish personal financial gain and prestige will be the primary motivating factors in the relationship, and the natives will cooperate only if they feel some personal advantage is likely to result.

A's Saturn in B's Eleventh House

This comparative combination indicates serious friendship and mutual responsibility through group and organizational affairs which are often related to the professions. It often indicates cooperation in organizations for improving professional standards in the field or fields in which the natives work. In some cases, the natives will be mutually involved in serious fraternal organizations. There can be a mutual interest in mathematics, science, engineering, and other intellectual pursuits requiring a detailed methodology and serious effort. If Saturn is well-aspected in the comparison, the natives will be loyal and steadfast friends. They will work together to realize worthwhile scientific, humanitarian, political, or professional goals and objectives. If Saturn is afflicted in the comparison, the natives may enter into the friendship for ulterior motives of financial gain.

A's Saturn in B's Twelfth House

Natives will have serious interactions involving psychic or occult pursuits, psychological investigation of the subconscious mind, or professional dealings that must be carried on in secret or behind the scenes. In some cases, the natives may be mutually involved in secret government contracts, research, investigation, hospitals, or religious or educational institutions, often in an administrative function.

The Saturn individual can help the Twelfth House individual to exercise discipline in understanding and overcoming subconscious and psychological hangups based on painful memories of the past. The Twelfth House individual can help the Saturn individual gain intuitive insight and inside information regarding matters of professional concern.

If Saturn is afflicted in the comparison, the natives can have a negative, fearful, psychologically depressing effect on each other. In extreme cases, they may even become secret enemies. The Twelfth House individual may regard the Saturn individual as oppressive, unsympathetic, and emotionally insensitive. The Saturn individual may regard the Twelfth House person as lazy, impractical, subversive, and burdensome.

There can be a karmic connection between the natives which requires sacrifice, responsibility, and discipline.

COMPARATIVE CONJUNCTIONS

Comparative conjunctions of Saturn indicate serious mutual responsibilities in the affairs of the sign and house in which they occur. There is likely to be important mutual activity in business and professional matters related to these affairs. The Saturn individual will organize and discipline the other native or natives in the affairs ruled by the planet conjuncting Saturn in the comparison.

Afflictions to these comparative conjunctions in either the comparison or in the natal horoscopes can cause the Saturn individual to be harsh, demanding, unsympathetic, or restrictive toward the other native. The other individual could, in time, become a burdensome responsibility to the Saturn native.

A's Saturn Conjunct B's Sun

See A's Sun Conjunct B's Saturn.

A's Saturn Conjunct B's Moon

See A's Moon Conjunct B's Saturn.

A's Saturn Conjunct B's Mercury

See A's Mercury Conjunct B's Saturn.

A's Saturn Conjunct B's Venus

See A's Venus Conjunct B's Saturn.

A's Saturn Conjunct B's Mars

See A's Mars Conjunct B's Saturn.

A's Saturn Conjunct B's Jupiter

See A's Jupiter Conjunct B's Saturn.

A's Saturn Conjunct B's Saturn (A's ♄ ☌ B's ♄)

This comparative conjunction indicates that the natives will have similar needs for security, stability, status, and professional advancement. They will take a similar approach to handling important responsibilities and will have similar concepts of justice and fair play. They can work together effectively in legal, professional, business and administrative affairs. They tend to bring out each other's ambitions, cautions, and conservative tendencies. If the Saturns are afflicted by natal or comparative aspects, the natives may depress each other and encourage each other's unhealthy and fearful tendencies. In some cases, their need for security can lead to competition between them for position and status.

A's Saturn Conjunct B's Uranus (A's ♄ ☌ B's ♅)

Mutual action in professional, legal, organizational, scientific, occult, or group activities is indicated. The Uranus individual will help the Saturn individual overcome fearfulness and excessive conservatism and will provide intuitive insights, new experiences, and unusual innovations which can further the Saturn individual's status, professional ambitions, goals, and objectives. The Saturn individual can, in turn, help the Uranus individual to organize and find practical application for his or her intuitive and inventive ideas and to become less precipitous and plan and organize personal affairs.

If the conjunction is afflicted, the natives will have widely differing social ideals and moral principles. The Saturn individual will consider the Uranus individual to be impractical, unstable, undependable, sensation-seeking, and much too revolutionary, while the Uranus individual will view the Saturn individual as fearful, old-fashioned, conservative, selfish, and overly concerned with materialistic values. On the positive side, the natives can be steadfast friends, and each will cooperate with the other's friends, groups, and organizational activities.

A's Saturn Conjunct B's Neptune (A's ♄ ☌ B's ♆)

This comparative conjunction indicates serious mutual interaction of a subconscious, psychological nature. If the conjunction is afflicted, at times the natives can have a depressing or oppressive influence on each other. The Saturn individual is apt to regard the Neptune individual as spaced-out and irresponsible, an impractical dreamer with psychological hangups. In turn, the Neptune individual is apt to regard the Saturn individual as emotionally, esthetically, and intuitively insensitive, oppressive, or negative.

If the conjunction is well-aspected, the natives will share an interest in serious mystical, religious, psychic, charitable, or institutional activities. There can be mutual involvement with secret professional affairs such as government research, secret investigation, administrative work that is carried on behind the scenes, or privacy related to psychological counseling.

The Saturn individual can help the Neptune to investigate, probe, structure, and discipline his or her subconscious mind and intuitive abilities through religious orders, serious meditative disciplines, psychotherapy, and so on. The Neptune individual can help the other to be more perceptive in business, career, group, or organizational affairs and less materialistic. The Saturn individual can have a stabilizing effect on the emotional state of the Neptune individual.

A's Saturn Conjunct B's Pluto (A's ♄ ☌ B's ♀)

These natives can become seriously involved in responsibilities and work related to corporate business, the affairs of the dead, or scientific or occult fields.

In cases of divorce, alimony settlements can be a major source of aggravation. If the conjunction is well-aspected, the natives can share a deep interest in mathematics, physics, or metaphysics. This is a good combination for cooperation in administrative work, engineering, research, and development. The natives may work together in such fields as recycling of industrial waste products, atomic physics, and deeper aspects of medical research, such as genetics. The natives can be mutually involved in professional activities requiring secrecy, as with some Saturn/Neptune comparative aspects.

The resourcefulness of the Pluto individual can help the Saturn individual to advance his or her political, financial, and professional ambitions. The organizing ability, experience, and prudence of the Saturn individual can help the Pluto individual to be more successful in business affairs, personal self-improvement, and efforts to regenerate existing conditions.

If the conjunction is afflicted, there can be mutual suspicion and competition for power. Ulterior motives involving money and status may be involved in the relationship. The natives could be involved together in political or business intrigues. There could be danger of lawsuits over corporate business affairs, alimony, or inheritance.

A's Saturn Conjunct B's North Node Opposition B's South Node (A's ♄ ☌ B's ☊ ☍ B's ☋)

This comparative combination indicates mutual interest in current political, professional, and business trends. The Nodes individual can help the Saturn individual gain insights into how to politically, professionally, or economically make use of prevailing popular beliefs and social trends. The Saturn individual can help the Nodes individual to organize his or her insights into a workable and practical plan for social or financial success.

If the conjunction is afflicted, there can be differences of cultural background, social ideals, or ethics. The Saturn person is likely to consider the Nodes individual as much too concerned with social trivialities. The Nodes individual may regard the Saturn individual as overly traditional and conservative.

A's Saturn Conjunct B's South Node Opposition B's North Node (A's ♄ ☌ B's ☋ ☍ B's ☊)

These natives have serious mutual concern with traditional social, professional, business, and ethical values. The natives will tend to be critical of current fads and popular beliefs regarding these things and will reinforce each other's tendency to adhere to traditional values.

A's Saturn Conjunct B's Ascendant Opposition B's Descendant (A's ♄ ☌ B's Asc. ☍ B's Desc.)

This comparative combination has basically the same meaning as "A's Saturn in B's First House." The Saturn individual will influence the Ascendant/Descendant individual to be more mature, serious, purposeful, and businesslike in personal self-expression and basic approach to life and more cautious and less impulsive in personal actions. The Ascendant/Descendant individual can help the Saturn individual to overcome fear and inertia.

If the conjunction is afflicted, the Ascendant/Descendant individual will regard the Saturn individual as a threat to freedom of self-expression in action, and the Saturn individual may regard that individual as immature, self-centered, and impulsive.

A's Saturn Conjunct B's Midheaven Opposition B's Nadir (A's ♄ ☌ B's M.C. ☍ B's Nadir)

Basically the same in significance as "A's Saturn in B's Fourth House," this comparative combination is often found in professional or business associations. The natives can work together as partners or compete with each other for positions of power and prestige. There will be mutual concern with achieving money, power, and status. This is an especially favorable combination for cooperation in law, government, business, politics, or business administration.

A's Saturn Conjunct B's Descendant Opposition B's Ascendant (A's ♄ ☌ B's Desc. ☍ B's Asc.)

This combination indicates serious mutual responsibilities through marriage, business, or professional partnerships. It has essentially the same meaning as "A's Saturn in B's Seventh House"; however, it is stronger and more immediate in effect. The dealings between these natives often involve legal contracts and binding mutual obligations. If Saturn is afflicted in the comparison, there can be lawsuits.

A's Saturn Conjunct B's Nadir Opposition B's Midheaven (A's ♄ ☌ B's Nadir ☍ B's M.C.)

This comparative combination has basically the same significance as "A's Saturn in B's Fourth House," except that it is stronger and more immediate in effect. It indicates serious mutual responsibilities through family and domestic affairs. Mutual professional or business dealings could relate to real estate, mining, farming, and ecological concerns.

COMPARATIVE SEXTILES

Comparative sextiles of Saturn indicate opportunities for the natives' mutual progress in business and professional affairs and for increased status in the world in which they move. Natives with these comparative aspects are often loyal friends and are able to cooperate in group and organizational activities. This cooperation, when applied with serious intent and discipline, can lead to accomplishments that are practical and of lasting value. The intellectual nature of the sextile aspect enables the natives to communicate about responsibilities and their practical management.

A's Saturn Sextile B's Sun

See A's Sun Sextile B's Saturn.

A's Saturn Sextile B's Moon

See A's Moon Sextile B's Saturn.

A's Saturn Sextile B's Mercury

See A's Mercury Sextile B's Saturn.

A's Saturn Sextile B's Venus

See A's Venus Sextile B's Saturn.

A's Saturn Sextile B's Mars

See A's Mars Sextile B's Saturn.

A's Saturn Sextile B's Jupiter

See A's Jupiter Sextile B's Saturn.

A's Saturn Sextile B's Saturn (A's ♄ ✶ B's ♄)

Natives have the ability to cooperate intelligently in business, professional, legal, public relations, or organizational affairs. The natives can further each other's determination and resolve to achieve political and professional goals and status through their careful and systematic planning. Intellectual pursuits of serious merit, including mathematics, economics, politics, and physical sciences, are apt to be of great interest to these natives.

A's Saturn Sextile B's Uranus (A's ♄ ✶ B's ♅)

This comparative sextile favors intelligent work and cooperation in group and organizational activities, particularly those involving administrative work in industrial research and development, corporate business, government, or large professional, scientific, and humanitarian organizations. The Uranus individual can help the Saturn native fulfill professional ambitions and responsibilities through introducing him or her to unique and inventive ideas for increasing productivity and efficiency. The Saturn individual can, in turn, assist the Uranus native to develop practical applications for creative ideas and innovations by providing official support for such activities. This is one of the finest combinations for those involved in research and development and the manufacture and distribution of new inventions and technological breakthroughs.

The natives will be steadfast friends and enjoy many worthwhile intellectual pursuits. Mathematics, science, engineering, or research and development activities may be of mutual interest. Such shared pursuits may even extend to a serious study of scientific, metaphysical, or astrological phenomena and their relationship to life on this earth.

A's Saturn Sextile B's Neptune (A's ♄ ✳ B's ♆)

If the natives are sufficiently developed, this comparative combination indicates serious cooperation and work in psychology, reincarnation, karma, and the study of mysticism. The natives can work effectively in secret or behind-the-scenes activities. This work could be related to government, research, medical, religious, educational, institutional, or occult organizations or to private, personal matters such as psychotherapy and personal emotional issues. There can be a strong mutual interest in the study of the subconscious mind. The natives can also work together in religious, occult, mystical, or charitable groups and organizations.

The Saturn individual can help the Neptune individual to develop the discipline necessary to understand and intelligently control his or her subconscious. The Neptune individual's intuitive insights can benefit the Saturn individual's career, financial, political, or status interests.

The natives can work together to gain an understanding of the subtle forces that underlie economic and political changes.

This comparative combination is helpful in developing psychological understanding of the emotional issues in marriage or partnership.

A's Saturn Sextile B's Pluto (A's ♄ ✳ B's ♇)

This comparative combination indicates profound mutual scientific and metaphysical intellectual interests in natives who are sufficiently developed. In general, the natives can cooperate effectively in work that has important, far-reaching consequences. They will share a concern with the larger issues of human survival and the political and economic fields that deal with these issues. There can be serious mutual concern with the long-range economic and ecological consequences of the handling of waste products. The natives can work together in physics, advanced scientific research development, or industrial engineering and administration. There can be mutual professional interests in tax accounting, handling the affairs of the dead, the occult, metaphysics, or programs of spiritual self-improvement.

The Saturn individual can help the Pluto individual to become more organized and self-disciplined in a practical way, so that his or her efforts at self-improvement and the regeneration of existing conditions are more effective. The Pluto individual can help the Saturn individual to gain penetrating insights into the business, professional, and political affairs that are important to him or her. The Pluto native can also awaken the Saturn individual to a more scientific and occult understanding of reality.

A's Saturn Sextile B's North Node Trine B's South Node
(A's ♄ ✳ B's ☊ △ B's ☋)

This comparative combination indicates serious mutual concern with current social, political, or economic attitudes and beliefs. The natives can use this mutual interest and understanding to economic or political advantage. The Saturn individual is likely to help the Nodes individual gain a long-range perspective on and adapt a more practical and conservative viewpoint toward prevailing social trends and popular beliefs. In turn, the Nodes individual can help the Saturn individual to be better informed about the current changes in these popular beliefs and attitudes.

A's Saturn Sextile B's South Node Trine B's North Node
(A's ♄ ✳ B's ☋ △ B's ☊)

The impact of this comparative combination is similar to that of "A's Saturn Sextile B's North Node Trine B's South Node," save that, due to the intellectual nature of this particular configuration and the conservative nature of the South Node, the natives' attitudes toward current fads and popular trends will be more critical and conservative.

A's Saturn Sextile B's Ascendant Trine B's Descendant
(A's ♄ ✳ B's Asc. △ B's Desc.)

This comparative combination indicates mutual concern and serious cooperation in marital, legal, professional, business, and organizational affairs. The natives will implement these affairs very effectively through mutual discussion and planning of their responsibilities and activities. The Ascendant/Descendant individual will be able to provide considerable energetic support for the serious goals of the Saturn native. The Saturn individual can, in turn, help the Ascendant/Descendant native build greater self-confidence, organization, maturity, and poise. The acceptance of mutual responsibility inherent in this comparative position favors enduring marriages and business and professional partnerships.

A's Saturn Sextile B's Midheaven Trine B's Nadir
(A's ♄ ✳ B's M.C. △ B's Nadir)

This is a highly favorable comparative combination for legal, professional, financial, and business cooperation. The Saturn individual will evoke in the Midheaven/Nadir native a more purposeful, practical, and responsible attitude toward achieving professional and financial status. The Midheaven/Nadir individual will, in turn, provide a home or base of operations for the efforts of the Saturn native to effect business and professional goals, and will employ his or her own power and prestige to aid their implementation.

The natives' home and family affairs will acquire stability and security and this will permit natives to devote themselves to furthering their individual careers and thus achieving professional and financial status. Effective cooperation in the fields of real estate, construction, farming, government, law, business administration, or politics is not uncommon to natives with this comparative aspect.

A's Saturn Sextile B's Descendant Trine B's Ascendant
(A's ♄ ✳ B's Desc. △ B's Asc.)

The significance of this comparative combination is much the same as that of "A's Saturn Sextile B's Ascendant Trine B's Descendant," except that these natives will concern themselves more with the intellectual than with the self-expressive aspects of their relationship.

A's Saturn Sextile B's Nadir Trine B's Midheaven
(A's ♄ ✳ B's Nadir △ B's M.C.)

This comparative combination has essentially the same significance as "A's Saturn Sextile B's Midheaven Trine B's Nadir," except that these natives' attitudes toward family and domestic matters will be much more intellectually oriented.

COMPARATIVE SQUARES

Comparative squares of Saturn indicate difficulties and obstacles in the handling of mutual business, professional, financial, and organizational responsibilities. Because of the Fourth House/Tenth House nature of the square aspect, these combinations will have a strong influence on professional, domestic, and family affairs.

The natives are apt to become aggravated with each other because of delays, obstacles, and frustrations in achieving goals and objectives that are essential to their security.

The Saturn individual is likely to make heavy demands in terms of work and discipline on the other native. One or both natives may feel that the other is a burden and oppressive responsibility. The Saturn individual may annoy, frustrate, or discourage the other native through his or her fearful, conservative, negative, or restrictive attitudes. The Saturn native may consider the other individual to be immature or irresponsible in the affairs ruled by the planet which Saturn squares in the comparison.

On the positive side, comparative squares of Saturn could indicate mutual discipline and the attempt to achieve worthwhile lasting goals through discipline and hard work.

A's Saturn Square B's Sun

See A's Sun Square B's Saturn.

A's Saturn Square B's Moon

See A's Moon Square B's Saturn.

A's Saturn Square B's Mercury

See A's Mercury Square B's Saturn.

A's Saturn Square B's Venus

See A's Venus Square B's Saturn.

A's Saturn Square B's Mars

See A's Mars Square B's Saturn.

A's Saturn Square B's Jupiter

See A's Jupiter Square B's Saturn.

A's Saturn Square B's Saturn (A's ♄ □ B's ♄)

This comparative square indicates conflicting approaches to handling professional, political, business, financial, and organizational responsibilities. There can be competition between the natives for status, power, and position. Because of this, each may represent a threat to the other's security. It is likely that the natives will add to each other's tendencies to fear, despondency, pessimism, negative thinking, or overconservatism. This comparative square does not indicate warm, friendly relationships, except in the sense that misery loves company.

On the positive side, since the square by its nature is a Saturnian aspect, the natives can further each other's discipline and resolve to overcome obstacles to their professional goals and objectives.

A's Saturn Square B's Uranus (A's ♄ □ B's ♅)

Natives may clash in their social, political, and professional ideals, goals, and objectives.

The Uranus individual will regard the Saturn individual as stodgy, fearful, negative, and overly conservative, and perhaps as materialistic, spiritually unaware, and lacking in intuition. The Saturn individual will, in turn, regard the Uranus individual as eccentric, unstable, unreliable, much too revolutionary, and inclined to unsound experimentation, or as an impractical idealist with unproven eccentric ideas.

In political affairs, the natives can be poles apart, with the Uranus individual taking a liberal stance and the Saturn individual a conservative or reactionary one. This is not a good combination for cooperation in legal, business, governmental, administrative, political, organizational, scientific, corporate, or occult matters. There can be litigation or disagreement concerning inheritances, joint finances, or alimony.

A's Saturn Square B's Neptune (A's ♄ □ B's ♆)

This comparative square indicates mutual psychological difficulties. The natives have a difficult time understanding each other, because the Saturn individual is motivated by practical business and professional concerns which conflict with the Neptune individual's orientation toward psychic, esthetic, imaginative, and subjective experiences. In professional, financial, and business relationships, there is danger of muddle and confusion caused by the Neptune individual's lack of discipline and escapist tendencies.

This comparative square creates a negative and emotionally unhealthy atmosphere for both natives. They are apt to add to each other's tendency to be emotionally depressed, anxious, and fearful. Too much time can be spent regretting the mistakes of the past and avoiding the responsibilities of the present. One of the natives may tend to physically drain the other, especially if they are associated through mental institutions and hospitals. The Neptune individual will regard the Saturn individual as materialistic and esthetically and psychologically insensitive. The Saturn individual's conservative materialistic orientation can cause emotional resentments and frustration for the Neptune individual. In turn, the subconscious psychological habits, hangups, and escapist tendencies of the Neptune individual can be extremely irritating to the Saturn individual.

This is not a good combination for cooperation or mutual interaction in hospitals, religious or educational institutions, or other professional affairs that require secrecy and behind-the-scenes work. Nor does it favor association in psychic, mystical, or occult activities. A danger of contacting unhealthy astral influences and entities arises because of the fear and anxiety this comparative combination generates.

On the positive side, the Saturn individual can be a constructive influence in awakening the Neptune individual to practical reality, even though the process may be unpleasant, and the Neptune individual could force the Saturn individual to become more aware of spiritual realities.

A's Saturn Square B's Pluto (A's ♄ □ B's ♇)

This comparative square indicates mutual distrust and intrigue in political, professional, business, or corporate affairs. This is not a favorable combination for mutual involvement in secret investigations, police matters, political intrigue, atomic physics, or secret governmental or scientific research. There can be a struggle for power and supremacy in achieving professional, financial, or political power and status. In extreme cases, the natives can be involved in dangerous subversive or underworld activities. There can be a lack of concern for long-range ecological consequences of industrial or scientific activities which were motivated by selfish desire for money, power, and status.

If the natives are involved in occult practices, there is danger of malicious or selfish use of occult powers, which will inevitably bring a karmic boomerang. There can be conflict and litigation over inheritance, insurance, taxes, corporate or business affairs.

The Saturn individual can have a negative attitude toward the Pluto individual's efforts at self-improvement, metaphysical studies, scientific work, corporate endeavors, or creative efforts at improving existing conditions. The Saturn native is likely to regard the Pluto individual as subversive, devious, anarchistic, or untrustworthy, and the Pluto individual can be a threat to his or her status quo and to the affairs and beliefs that entail his or her security. In turn, the Pluto individual will regard the Saturn individual as selfishly motivated and obstructive to necessary change.

On the positive side, the natives can increase each other's will, discipline, and determination to bring about needed professional, business, economic, and spiritual self-improvement for the sake of both survival and long-range well-being.

A's Saturn Square B's North Node Square B's South Node
(A's ♄ □ B's ☊ □ B's ☋)

The natives will have conflicting attitudes toward current social trends and popular beliefs. The Saturn individual may consider the Nodes individual to be superficial and foolish in his or her blind acceptance of currently popular beliefs and ideas. The Nodes individual may, in turn, regard the Saturn individual as old-fashioned, overly conservative, and unaware of the current social environment.

On the positive side, the Saturn individual can give the Nodes individual a deeper long-range perspective on value of current popular beliefs and fads.

This is not a good combination for cooperation in political, business, or professional affairs, especially if they relate to gaining popular acceptance for products, ideas, or political objectives.

A's Saturn Square B's South Node Square B's North Node

See A's Saturn Square B's North Node Square B's South Node.

A's Saturn Square B's Ascendant Square B's Descendant
(A's ♄ □ B's Asc. □ B's Desc.)

This comparative combination indicates conflict between the natives over professional, financial, marital, legal, domestic, and personal affairs. The Saturn individual will be a restraining, disciplining influence on the Ascendant/Descendant individual in these affairs, but the Ascendant/Descendant individual may resent this restriction and see it as a threat to freedom of action and self-expression. The Saturn individual will resent the Ascendant/Descendant individual's tendency to act impulsively without proper mutual planning. These factors can lead to coldness and emotional distance in the relationship.

A's Saturn Square B's Midheaven Square B's Nadir
(A's ♄ □ B's M.C. □ B's Nadir)

This comparative combination is not favorable for mutual harmony and understanding in professional, business, family, or personal relationships.

Because Saturn is in detriment in Cancer and the Fourth House, there can be coldness and lack of emotional understanding on the part of both natives with regard to family affairs and subjective personal feelings. There can be conflict between the domestic family interests of one native and the professional responsibilities of the other. Emotional problems at home can interfere with career interests or career responsibilities. Family affairs could be neglected when the career interest of one native becomes too all-consuming.

In employer–employee relationships or business or professional partnerships, one native may impose a heavy work load of responsibilities on the other. One or both natives may feel unjustly overworked. In some cases, there can be litigation between the natives over business or professional matters.

A's Saturn Square B's Descendant Square B's Ascendant

See A's Saturn Square B's Ascendant Square B's Descendant.

A's Saturn Square B's Nadir Square B's Midheaven

See A's Saturn Square B's Midheaven Square B's Nadir.

COMPARATIVE TRINES

These comparative trines indicate ability to cooperate harmoniously in the acceptance of mutual business, professional, and marital responsibilities.

The Saturn individual can help the other native to organize and find practical applications for creative endeavors along the lines indicated by the planet Saturn trines in the comparison. (See *The Astrologer's Handbook*, Harper & Row, pp. 407–412)

In marital relationships, the natives will show a mutual willingness to accept work and responsibility. Their capacity for practicality and patience makes for enduring unions where marital, legal, or professional affairs are involved. These combinations work best when the Saturn individual is older or in a position of leadership, such as employer or teacher. They are especially good for parent–child, teacher–student, or employer–employee relationships.

A's Saturn Trine B's Sun

See A's Sun Trine B's Saturn.

A's Saturn Trine B's Moon

See A's Moon Trine B's Saturn.

A's Saturn Trine B's Mercury

See A's Mercury Trine B's Saturn.

A's Saturn Trine B's Venus

See A's Venus Trine B's Saturn.

A's Saturn Trine B's Mars

See A's Mars Trine B's Saturn.

A's Saturn Trine B's Jupiter

See A's Jupiter Trine B's Saturn.

A's Saturn Trine B's Saturn (A's ♄ △ B's ♄)

The natives have compatible attitudes toward handling business, financial, legal, educational, and professional affairs. The natives bring out each other's qualities of patience, hard work, prudence, and forethought. In romantic and marital relationships, this comparative trine enhances the durability of the union. The natives' adherence to principle and mutual responsibility will make them steadfast and loyal friends.

This is an excellent combination for parent–child relationships: it indicates patience and constructive discipline on the part of the parent and interest in learning on the child's part. It is also good for teacher–student and employer–employee relationships, and for cooperation in politics, professional or fraternal organizations, business partnerships, public relations, or administrative affairs. It favors mutual involvement in conservative investments.

A's Saturn Trine B's Uranus (A's ♄ △ B's ♅)

This comparative trine is excellent for cooperation in the research, development, manufacture, and distribution of new technological products or inventions. Because Saturn deals with crystallized substances and Uranus with electronics, the natives can share a special interest in electronics and solid-state technology. There can be a mutual interest in improving the efficiency, cost, and ecological soundness of industrial methods. The natives can cooperate effectively in government, administration, corporate business, affairs related to professional and fraternal organizations, or in handling the goods of the dead.

The Saturn individual will help the Uranus individual to be more practical and better organized in utilizing and expressing his or her unique and inventive ideas. The Saturn native can help the Uranus individual to gain the recognition and support of well-established governmental or business institutions, or people who are in positions of power and status. The Uranus individual will in turn help the Saturn individual to make the best use of technological innovations in professional, business, industrial, and administrative affairs and will awaken him or her to a higher level of creative thought and intuitive inspiration, helping to overcome the limitations of crystallized thoughts and outmoded ways of doing things.

The natives will be loyal friends and can accomplish much that is constructive through cooperation with mutual friends, groups, and organizations. This is an excellent combination for employer–employee and teacher–student relationships involving scientific or professional areas of work or study. The natives could travel for business reasons. There could be mutual interest in life after death and mathematical or scientific approaches to life's inner mysteries. If the natives are advanced enough to be interested in occult or advanced scientific or mathematical pursuits, they will cooperate effectively in these areas. This comparative trine favors long-term compatibility in marriage and continued interest, adventure, and excitement in all relationships.

A's Saturn Trine B's Neptune (A's ♄ △ B's ♆)

These natives have a capacity for cooperation in private or secretive professional matters—these could be related to psychology, research, hospitals, institutions, or business dealings.

The intuitive insights of the Neptune individual can help the Saturn individual in strategies related to business, professional, or political affairs. The Neptune person can awaken the Saturn individual to an awareness of, and reliance on, his or her spiritual faculties and abilities. The Saturn individual can help the other to organize and find practical outlets for intuitive, imaginative, and creative abilities. The Saturn person can also help the Neptune individual to gain insight into his or her subconscious psychological problems.

This is a good comparative combination for those working together in religious, psychic, artistic, educational, or psychological fields. In romantic and marital relationships, this combination aids mutual patience and psychological understanding, thereby increasing prospects for enduring relationships. It can also be a good combination for speculative financial investments, because of the combination of Neptunian intuitive ability with Saturn business practicality. The natives may travel together for business reasons.

A's Saturn Trine B's Pluto (A's ♄ △ B's ♀)

This comparative aspect favors cooperation in scientific research—especially physics—advanced mathematics, and fields related to energy, production, recycling, or ecology. There can be effective cooperation in corporate business, affairs of the dead, insurance, tax accounting, industry, or industrial research and development. The natives could work together in secret investigations and behind-the-scenes governmental activities. If both natives are advanced enough, they can cooperate effectively in occult metaphysics.

The Pluto individual can help the Saturn individual to gain a deeper insight into the vibratory forces or occult energies that underlie the outer material level of manifestation. The Saturn individual can help the Pluto individual to use his or her insights into these matters practically and constructively through professional, business, or organizational activities.

This is a good comparative combination for parent—child and teacher—student relationships where discipline and a firm hand are needed.

This comparative trine does not produce romantic or sexual attraction; however, it can indicate greater mutual acceptance of responsibility and discipline, and it increases the prospects for a long-term, successful relationship. There will be cooperation in efforts toward self-improvement.

A's Saturn Trine B's North Node Sextile B's South Node

See A's Saturn Sextile B's South Node Trine B's North Node.

A's Saturn Trine B's South Node Sextile B's North Node

See A's Saturn Sextile B's North Node Trine B's South Node.

A's Saturn Trine B's Ascendant Sextile B's Descendant

See A's Saturn Sextile B's Descendant Trine B's Ascendant.

A's Saturn Trine B's Midheaven Sextile B's Nadir

See A's Saturn Sextile B's Nadir Trine B's Midheaven.

A's Saturn Trine B's Descendant Sextile B's Ascendant

See A's Saturn Sextile B's Ascendant Trine B's Descendant.

A's Saturn Trine B's Nadir Sextile B's Midheaven

See A's Saturn Sextile B's Midheaven Trine B's Nadir.

COMPARATIVE OPPOSITIONS

Comparative oppositions of Saturn indicate situations in which the natives must accept mutual responsibility if the relationship is to endure. These comparative aspects are of particularly strong significance because the opposition aspect is related to Libra, where Saturn is exalted. Since Libra and the opposition aspect both deal with marriage and other important partnerships, the natives must exercise justice and fair play to get along on a long-term basis. If both natives are mature, they can cooperate effectively in business, professional, political, legal, and financial affairs. If the opposition aspect is afflicted by other comparative aspects and the natives lack discipline and maturity, there can be conflict and litigation over these matters. These comparative aspects can indicate heavy responsibility and hard work in employer–employee, co-worker, and professional partnership relationships.

Relationships with comparative oppositions of Saturn are often karmic: the natives may have been involved with each other before or be brought together with someone with whom they can learn a necessary lesson of cooperation.

A's Saturn Opposition B's Sun

See A's Sun Opposition B's Saturn.

A's Saturn Opposition B's Moon

See A's Moon Opposition B's Saturn.

A's Saturn Opposition B's Mercury

See A's Mercury Opposition B's Saturn.

A's Saturn Opposition B's Venus

See A's Venus Opposition B's Saturn.

A's Saturn Opposition B's Mars

See A's Mars Opposition B's Saturn.

A's Saturn Opposition B's Jupiter

See A's Jupiter Opposition B's Saturn.

A's Saturn Opposition B's Saturn (A's ♄ ☍ B's ♄)

This comparative opposition indicates serious mutual responsibilities in marital, business, professional, political, or legal affairs. The natives may have opposing points of view toward these affairs. If they are mature, however, they will have a mutual understanding of and respect for the duties and responsibilities associated with these affairs, even though their approaches may be different. The natives are apt to make heavy demands on each other in terms of work and discipline, especially in employer–employee or professional partnership relationships. If the overall comparison is favorable, this comparative opposition can indicate a lasting relationship and a strong sense of mutual responsibility.

A's Saturn Opposition B's Uranus (A's ♄ ☍ B's ♅)

The natives' widely differing attitudes toward professional, administrative, political, or disciplinary affairs may bring about difficulties. The Saturn individual is likely to regard the Uranus individual as lacking in discipline, common sense, and good organization, or as eccentric, unpredictable, revolutionary, and a threat to traditional institutions, customs, and social ethics. The Uranus individual may, in turn, regard the other as lacking in creative ability, unintuitive, stodgy, materialistic, negative, and overconservative. The natives can stubbornly adhere to their viewpoints and personal sense of authority and be unwilling to bend or compromise.

In political and administrative affairs, the Uranus individual will be radical and the Saturn individual conservative. This is not a good combination for cooperation in industrial research or development in scientific areas because the Uranus individual will seek to make changes while the Saturn person will try to preserve the status quo.

There can be different approaches and beliefs where astrology or the occult are concerned. The natives are not likely to cooperate effectively in group or organizational activities. In some cases, this combination indicates a mutual struggle for position and status in professional, political, or organizational affairs.

A's Saturn Opposition B's Neptune (A's ♄ ☍ B's ♆)

This comparative opposition indicates a lack of mutual understanding regarding practical responsibilities and psychological interactions.

The Saturn individual is likely to regard the Neptune individual as vague, impractical, irresponsible, and lost in a dream world. The Saturn person can become annoyed with the evasive and escapist tendencies of the Neptune individual, and feel frustrated at being unable to pin the latter to definite commitments of responsibility. Even if the Saturn individual can exact such promises, the Neptune individual may not carry them out. The psychological problems of the Neptune individual can be a burden and annoyance to the Saturn individual, who may be unsympathetic to the Neptune individual's psychic perceptions and intuitive abilities.

The Saturn individual's insistence on practical accomplishment and discipline can interfere with the Neptune individual's desire for an inner spiritual search and the expression of personal inner intuitive creative abilities. The Neptune individual may regard the Saturn individual as hard, unsympathetic, unimaginative, and lacking in intuitive and psychological understanding. The natives may encourage each other's tendencies toward depression and fear.

There can be conflict between the professional and business responsibilities of the Saturn native and the psychological and family concerns of the Neptune individual. This is not a good combination for cooperation in religious, mystical, psychic, or psychological forms of work, especially if they relate to hospitals, asylums, education or religious institutions.

A's Saturn Opposition B's Pluto (A's ♄ ☍ B's ♇)

Because of mutual mistrust and conflict over corporate affairs, administrative matters, joint finances, inheritance, alimony, or occult practices, the natives can struggle with each other for control, power, status, and position. They may not see eye to eye on approaches to self-improvement and pursuing social and personal survival. In extreme cases, they may regard each other as a threat to survival. Lawsuits can arise over corporate, professional, or ecological issues.

The Saturn individual may regard the Pluto individual as a subversive influence or a threat to established institutions, as well as to his or her own position and security. The Pluto individual may regard the Saturn individual as selfish, materialistic, and unwilling to make the changes necessary for the regeneration of existing conditions.

In some industrial, administrative, or political relationships, the natives could engage in ecological abuses for the sake of personal gain. One native may attempt to stop the other's ecological abuses. This is not a good combination for mutual involvement in the occult, especially if the natives have ulterior motives.

A's Saturn Opposition B's North Node Conjunct B's South Node

See A's Saturn Conjunct B's South Node Opposition B's North Node.

A's Saturn Opposition B's South Node Conjunct B's North Node

See A's Saturn Conjunct B's North Node Opposition B's South Node.

A's Saturn Opposition B's Ascendant Conjunct B's Descendant

See A's Saturn Conjunct B's Descendant Opposition B's Ascendant.

A's Saturn Opposition B's Midheaven Conjunct B's Nadir

See A's Saturn Conjunct B's Nadir Opposition B's Midheaven.

A's Saturn Opposition B's Descendant Conjunct B's Ascendant

See A's Saturn Conjunct B's Ascendant Opposition B's Descendant.

A's Saturn Opposition B's Nadir Conjunct B's Midheaven

See A's Saturn Conjunct B's Midheaven Opposition B's Nadir.

XIV
Uranus

Comparative influences of Uranus indicate the way the natives encourage each other to embark on new and unusual experiences. These influences show how the natives can inspire each other with unique intuitive ideas and insights into the underlying spiritual realities of life. They show the ways in which the natives will be the agents for sudden change, either positive or negative, in each other's lives.

Horoscope comparisons with strong Uranus influences will often involve mutual interests in occult, scientific, technological and humanitarian activities. There could be a mutual interest in social or political reform or in altering and improving professional methods through the introduction of new ideas and the utilization of new technology.

All influences of Uranus have a liberating effect and broaden the understanding of the individuals, although this can be harsh and upsetting if the comparative influence of Uranus is adverse.

Through the comparative influences of Uranus, the natives will open up to new concepts and unbiased viewpoints. They can awaken each other to a higher level of perception and intuitive knowledge. Eventually, they will come to accept as truth only that which can be proven through direct experience. Through the Uranian experiences which the natives bring into each other's lives, they will gain a greater sense of true brotherhood and the universal values that affect all humanity.

COMPARATIVE HOUSE PLACEMENTS

These comparative house placements indicate the ways in which the unique individual self-expression of the Uranus native will influence the practical affairs of the other individual's life.

The affairs that are ruled by the house in which Uranus falls in the comparison will be subject to sudden change, unusual experiences and startling revelations. They will be influenced by intuitive ideas, modern technology, secrecy, surprises, occult interests, mutual friends and group activities. These factors give a feeling of excitement, adventure and uniqueness to the relationship.

The House individual is likely to consider the Uranus individual eccentric, revolutionary and unpredictable in the affairs ruled by the comparative house placement of Uranus. If Uranus is afflicted in the comparison, both natives will lack consistency and dependability.

A's Uranus in B's First House

This comparative combination indicates an exciting, unusual relationship. The natives encourage each other's desire for personal freedom, adventure and unique self-expression. It is important that they respect each other's free will and avoid the tendency to dominate each other.

The Uranus individual can help the First House individual to achieve personal goals and objectives, and become more aware of himself or herself as a spiritual being, rather than being dominated by cultural conditioning. This influence could take the form of mutual interest in metaphysics and such systems of self-improvement as yoga, meditations and other spiritual disciplines. The Uranus individual will be instrumental in bringing the First House individual into groups with these interests.

The First House individual can encourage the Uranus individual to be more forceful and positive in expressing unique, intuitive ideas. The First House person will initiate new ways for the Uranus individual to express personal freedom and to become involved in new, exciting experiences.

The natives bring out each other's scientific, occult, humanitarian, and social reformist tendencies. They will encourage each other to break away from tradition and boring routine.

A's Uranus in B's Second House

Unusual circumstances in the business and financial affairs of the natives are indicated. Mutual business projects could involve such things as electronic technology, scientific research, inventions, groups, organizations, corporate business affairs, and occult studies.

The Uranus individual will encourage the Second House individual to use unusual methods and modern technologies in business affairs—electronic computers, automation, or improved manufacturing techniques, among others. The Uranus native may encourage the Second House individual to invest money in new ideas and inventions, especially in electronics and technical innovations, and to be more detached and willing to take risks where money, property, and the attaining of goals are concerned. The Second House individual, in turn, can help the Uranus individual to be more practical in applying his or her unusual intuitive and inventive abilities to making money and acquiring possessions.

If Uranus is well-aspected in the comparison, the natives can acquire great wealth. If Uranus is afflicted in the comparison, there can be sudden financial loss. Even under favorable circumstances, the financial fortunes of the natives will be subject to erratic changes, which can cause an atmosphere of uncertainty and insecurity. The natives can be instrumental in bringing about important changes in each other's values. There could be mutual interest or involvement in new and unusual, or in extremely ancient, forms of art, and this, too, could relate to the use of electronics or other modern technologies.

A's Uranus in B's Third House

This comparative house placement indicates rapid and intuitive communication between the natives. There will be a strong mutual interest in new ideas, especially in such fields as science, electronics, politics, literature, occult subjects and communications media.

The natives can work together effectively in corporate enterprises and businesses related to newspapers, periodicals, writing, electronic communications and travel. There will be a special interest in innovative approaches to these things.

The Uranus individual will influence the Third House individual to be more open-minded and receptive to new ideas and will be instrumental in bringing about important changes in the latter's thinking. The Uranus native can influence the Third House individual to base ideas on direct practical experience or intuitive levels of perception. In turn, the Third House individual can help the Uranus individual acquire factual, practical information for use in creative, intuitive thinking and inventive endeavors. This is a good combination for those who are engaged in scientific research or who work together to solve technological problems. There can be sudden and unexpected travel involving mutual friends, groups, and organizations.

If Uranus is afflicted in the comparison, the natives will have unrealistic ideas and impractical, untried concepts. There can be sudden, meaningless travel or comings and goings which do not serve any useful purpose. Where brothers, sisters and neighbors are concerned, there can be disruptive circumstances, breakdowns in communication and lack of mutual understanding.

A's Uranus in B's Fourth House

The Uranus individual is responsible for the indicated unusual, possibly disruptive, events in home and family life. If the natives are married or belong to the same family, there can be many sudden changes of residence or unusual conditions in the home.

The Uranus individual will be the means of bringing about important and sometimes sudden changes in the deep-seated psychological attitudes of the Fourth House individual. These changes could be the result of sudden or unusual experiences or of occult influences. The positive aspect of this comparison is that the Uranus individual can be instrumental in liberating the Fourth House individual from subconscious emotional hangups based on childhood experiences.

In marriage relationships, the Uranus individual may choose a home that is unusual because of its location or design, and is likely to bring many unusual and gifted personal friends and groups or organizational activities, as well as unusual artifacts and gadgets, into the family life. Through this influence, the home may be used as a place to pursue scientific experimentation or occult activities.

The Fourth House individual can provide the Uranus individual with a base of operations for activities. In some cases, there could be a mutual interest in farming, building, real estate, and ecological concerns and unusual approaches to these matters.

If Uranus is afflicted in the comparison, there can be continual sudden upsets in home and family affairs. The Uranus individual will expect the Fourth House individual to accept his or her friends as family. Changes in the business or profession of the Uranus individual may necessitate changes of residence, which could be upsetting to the Fourth House individual.

A's Uranus in B's Fifth House

This comparative house placement indicates sudden romantic attraction and sexual infatuation. The natives often meet under unusual circumstances and have a powerful magnetic attraction for each other. These relationships are not enduring, however, unless other factors in the comparison promise it.

The natives will not follow traditional social codes or sexual moralities in their relationship. This is usually due to the influence of the Uranus individual. If Uranus is afflicted in the comparison, there can be abnormal sexual practices.

In corporate or business relationships, this comparative placement brings the danger of unwise and impulsive financial speculations, especially if Uranus is afflicted.

The natives may become mutually involved in businesses related to entertainment, amusements, education, children, or social or pleasurable functions. There can be an interest in unusual art forms and electronic art.

In parent–child relationships, this comparison makes for interest and excitement. If Uranus is well-aspected in the comparison, there will be sharing of scientific interests, hobbies, and unusual experiences, which make learning exciting and enjoyable. The child who is a Uranus individual will be full of surprises and unusual talents. If the parent is the Uranus individual, he or she will allow the child freedom in experimentation and will encourage expression of unique talents and abilities. However, if Uranus is afflicted in the comparison, there can be rebellion and erratic behavior if the child is the Uranus individual; and if the parent is the Uranus individual, he or she may confuse or spoil the child through inconsistency.

This combination makes interesting teacher–student relationships because of the use of exciting, unusual teaching methods.

In friendships and other relationships, the natives gain pleasure from scientific or occult activities and interests. They will be inclined to seek pleasure in the company of mutual friends or in group activities.

A's Uranus in B's Sixth House

Unusual circumstances in the natives' work, service, and health matters are indicated.

The natives may develop a mutual interest in health, diet (especially revolutionary diets), and spiritual healing. This often takes the form of meditation, use of positive thinking or yoga exercises, massage, and various other physical therapies. There will be a special awareness of the occult forces involved in such practices. In doctor–patient relationships, scientifically advanced or unusual techniques of healing will often be employed.

Mutual work activities are apt to be related to science, technology, and electronic industries. In co-worker relationships, the natives will be interested in using the latest technological developments to improve the speed and efficiency of their work. There can be a mutual interest in demanding their rights as workers, and this often results in involvement in labor unions and other professional organizations. The Uranus individual is apt to be the instigator of reform in these matters.

If Uranus is afflicted in the comparison, the Uranus individual's careless and impulsive work habits could lead to occupational hazards and accidents. His or her erratic behavior and health habits can have an adverse effect upon the nervous disposition and health of the Sixth House individual. The Uranus individual may, in turn, consider the Sixth House individual to be overly concerned with unimportant details and servitude to work for work's sake. The Uranus native could influence the Sixth House individual to adopt eccentric or unusual modes of dress.

A's Uranus in B's Seventh House

This comparative placement indicates unusual partnerships and marriages. For the relationship to be harmonious, the natives must allow each other a great deal of personal freedom. They will encourage each other to express more freedom and individuality in the pursuit of new experiences.

There can be mutual interest and involvement in scientific, humanitarian, technological, and occult activities. Business or professional partnerships are apt to involve these affairs.

In many cases, this comparative house placement indicates close friendships based on association through similar intellectual interests, mutual friends, and group or organizational activities. The natives can be attracted to each other through unusual, sudden, unexpected circumstances or events. Marriage often occurs suddenly, but its chances of durability are greater if the natives allow a reasonable time for courtship. If Uranus is afflicted in the comparison in any way, marriages with this comparative placement often end in divorce. Other effects of an afflicted Uranus in the comparison could be an unwillingness on the part of the Uranus native to sacrifice personal freedom for the sake of harmony and cooperation, or a tendency on the part of the Seventh House native to regard the Uranus individual as eccentric, unpredictable, and explosive.

A's Uranus in B's Eighth House

These natives could have strong mutual involvement in corporate business affairs, joint finances, scientific research, or occult pursuits, especially those related to scientific research, electronic industries, and the development and marketing of new inventions. Sudden, unexpected events and circumstances are apt to affect these matters.

The Uranus individual can awaken the Eighth House individual to a greater awareness of spiritual realities, life after death, and reincarnation. There could be a mutual interest in yoga, meditation, and solving problems through reliance on inner intuitive faculties.

The natives can be the agents of much drastic change in each other's lives; old conditions will be destroyed and new ones created.

If Uranus is afflicted in the comparison, joint finances, inheritance, and alimony could become sources of conflict and could cause sudden changes in the natives' lives. In cases of extreme affliction, the natives could expose each other to actual physical danger.

A's Uranus in B's Ninth House

This comparative placement indicates mutual interest in new or unusual religious, educational, and philosophic ideas and practices. The natives can become involved in sudden travel for purposes of occult investigation, corporate business, education, or love of adventure.

The Uranus individual will encourage the Ninth House individual to seek higher knowledge through experimentation and direct experience. This could include the use of clairvoyant or intuitive faculties to gain religious or philosophic insight or understanding. The individuals will encourage each other to pursue occult or mystical approaches to religion, and this can bring about mutual activity in educational, religious, mystical, or occult groups and organizations.

This comparative placement will bring out the idealistic tendencies in both natives; often they put forth strong humanitarian efforts to uplift their fellow men through the promulgation of religious ideals and philosophies.

If Uranus is afflicted in the comparison, there can be difficulty through ill-advised journeys and impractical philosophies which have not stood the test of time. If the natives are immature, they can indulge each other's tendencies to neglect studies and pursue unrealistic goals.

The Ninth House individual can help the Uranus individual to gain acceptance for new ideas and unique talents in established religious, educational, and cultural institutions. The Uranus individual can, in turn, help the Ninth House individual to advance his or her religious, educational, and cultural understanding to a higher level through scientific methods, new inventions, and intuitive perceptions.

A's Uranus in B's Tenth House

Unusual and eventful professional relationships are characteristic of this comparative placement.

The Uranus individual will influence the Tenth House individual to employ advanced scientific methods and technologies in professional affairs, and will persuade the latter to adopt more liberal and progressive attitudes in politics and in policy-making and administrative affairs. The Uranus native will also be instrumental in bringing sudden and important changes into the Tenth House individual's career and status.

The Tenth House individual can help the Uranus individual to use intuitive insights, scientific abilities and unique talents in practical and productive ways. The Tenth House person can help the Uranus individual gain official support and recognition for these talents and abilities.

If Uranus is well-aspected in the comparison, the natives can share an interest in professional and political reforms. Mutual professional business could relate to scientific research, advanced technology, electronic industries, and, in some cases, occult pursuits. This is a good combination for those mutually involved with the astrological profession.

If Uranus is afflicted in the comparison, the natives will disagree over political, administrative, and professional matters. They can tend to encourage each other in rash, impulsive acts that adversely affect their reputations and professional standing. In extreme cases, this could lead to conflict with the government or other institutions of authority.

A's Uranus in B's Eleventh House

This comparative placement indicates unusual, exciting friendships, based on similar goals and objectives, intellectual pursuits, business interests, scientific interests, or group and organizational activities.

Through mutual friends, the natives will introduce each other to many interesting, talented people and exciting experiences. There can be mutual interest in humanitarian projects and social reforms. In general, the natives will share many unusual scientific, occult, and humanitarian interests and goals. They will encourage each other's drive for freedom of self-expression and independence in thought and action.

If Uranus is afflicted in the comparison, the natives can give each other well-meaning, but impractical, advice. The Uranus individual could be unpredictable and unreliable in fulfilling commitments and mutual responsibilities. Friendships can break up suddenly and unexpectedly.

A's Uranus in B's Twelfth House

These natives are mutually involved in unusual intuitive, occult, or psychological activities. The Uranus individual can help the Twelfth House individual to release neurotic, subconscious habit patterns by introducing change and new points of view, by stirring up the subconscious mind and psychic faculties of the Twelfth House individual, and by stimulating and bringing to the surface hidden spiritual wisdom and insights. However, if Uranus is afflicted in the comparison, the Uranus individual could bring out bizarre and irrational psychological tendencies in the Twelfth House individual. If Uranus is badly afflicted, the natives should be careful to avoid psychic practices.

The natives can be mutually involved in meditation and other intuitive or psychic practices, and they are likely to be interested in reincarnation and life after death. There can also be a mutual interest in changing, updating, or reforming hospitals, asylums, or religious institutions, and involvement in the business affairs of such institutions. The natives often belong to secret religious or mystical groups and organizations. The Twelfth House individual can reinforce and encourage the intuitive faculties of the Uranus individual.

COMPARATIVE CONJUNCTIONS

Comparative conjunctions of Uranus indicate immediate, dynamic, sudden interactions. They also show the ways in which the natives will bring new interests, a higher level of awareness, and unexpected experiences into each other's lives.

The Uranus individual will influence the other native to be more scientific, intuitive, and progressive in thinking in affairs ruled by the planet Uranus conjuncts in the comparison.

The other individual is likely to regard the Uranus individual as interesting and exciting. If the conjunction is afflicted, however, the Uranus individual may be considered eccentric, unpredictable, and unreliable.

The natives could be involved together in scientific, humanitarian, reformist, and occult ideas and activities. There can be much activity involving mutual friends, groups, and organizations relating to the planet making the conjunction.

A's Uranus Conjunct B's Sun

See A's Sun Conjunct B's Uranus.

A's Uranus Conjunct B's Moon

See A's Moon Conjunct B's Uranus.

A's Uranus Conjunct B's Mercury

See A's Mercury Conjunct B's Uranus.

A's Uranus Conjunct B's Venus

See A's Venus Conjunct B's Uranus.

A's Uranus Conjunct B's Mars

See A's Mars Conjunct B's Uranus.

A's Uranus Conjunct B's Jupiter

See A's Jupiter Conjunct B's Uranus.

A's Uranus Conjunct B's Saturn

See A's Saturn Conjunct B's Uranus.

A's Uranus Conjunct B's Uranus (A's ♅ ☌ B's ♅)

This comparative conjunction occurs only with people of approximately the same age. It indicates that the natives will together experience economic, social, and political changes. Often, they experience sudden changes of fortune at the same time and in similar ways.

There will be a sense of established friendship, because the natives will share the values, goals, and objectives that are particular to their generation. Thus, they will seek their individual, creative self-expression and freedom in similar ways. They will seek out the same type of friends, groups, and organizations.

A's Uranus Conjunct B's Neptune (A's ♅ ☌ B's ♆)

These natives share a strong interest in occult, mystical experiences and pursuits. In advanced individuals, there can be natural telepathic psychic communications. There can be a mutual concern with large-scale political, scientific, economic, and sociological changes which influence the entire culture in which the natives live. These interests and concerns can lead to mutual attempts to foresee and predict the future. The natives can share an interest in advanced scientific theories and research or in the occult.

The Uranus individual can stimulate the subconscious mind and distant memories of the Neptune individual, thus encouraging the latter's imagination and clairvoyant faculties. In turn, the Neptune individual's imaginative faculties can stimulate original creative thinking in the Uranus individual.

They can also both be interested in religious reforms, humanitarian projects, and utopian ideals. Whether these reforms, projects, and ideals are practical or not depends upon the overall nature of the comparison and on how the conjunction is aspected.

A's Uranus Conjunct B's Pluto (A's ♅ ☌ B's ♇)

This comparative conjunction indicates strong mutual interests in large-scale political, economic, scientific, and sociological changes affecting the entire culture. In some cases, the natives may both be advocates of revolutionary change involving economics, politics, and ecological reform.

If the conjunction is afflicted, the natives may influence each other to rash, impulsive, dangerous actions. They could advocate the overthrow of existing social, political, religious, or economic institutions without having formulated practical replacements.

Natives with scientific ability who have this comparative conjunction can work together effectively to bring about major breakthroughs in advanced scientific research, inventions, or solutions to technical problems. There could be mutual involvement in large-scale corporate business enterprises relating to these things.

For natives who share an interest in occult or spiritual matters, this comparative conjunction indicates a strong concern with life after death, reincarnation, scientific metaphysics, and study of higher forms of energy and consciousness. This concern can take the form of a strong mutual involvement in yoga, meditation, development of clairvoyant faculties, and other methods of spiritual self-unfoldment.

In some cases, this comparative conjunction will indicate a concern with very practical matters of survival, which will help bring out the resourcefulness and strength of both individuals.

The Uranus individual will activate the Pluto individual in sudden, dramatic ways, while the Pluto individual will bring out endurance and stamina in the Uranus native.

A's Uranus Conjunct B's North Node Opposition
B's South Node (A's ♅ ☌ B's ☊ ☍ B's ☋)

These natives have a strong mutual interest in and involvement with current changes and social beliefs and popular ideas.

The natives could be mutual advocates of contemporary attitudes and beliefs and favor the overthrow of social traditions contradictory to them. If they carry this tendency too far, however, they can lose a long-range historical perspective.

The Uranus individual can influence the Nodes individual to be more independent and individualistic regarding prevailing cultural beliefs and attitudes. The Nodes individual can, in turn, help the Uranus individual to become more aware of how society sees and responds to his or her unique abilities and unusual interests.

A's Uranus Conjunct B's South Node Opposition B's North Node (A's ♅ ☌ B's ☋ ☍ B's ☊)

This comparative combination indicates many of the same attitudes and involvements as "A's Uranus Conjunct B's North Node Opposition B's South Node." These natives, however, will be more critical of prevailing popular trends and beliefs.

The Uranus individual can influence the Nodes individual to be more independent in attitudes toward such social trends and beliefs, and the Nodes individual will encourage the Uranus individual to follow personal principles, even if they are contrary to prevailing social beliefs and attitudes.

A's Uranus Conjunct B's Ascendant Opposition B's Descendant (A's ♅ ☌ B's Asc. ☍ B's Desc.)

Basically, this comparative combination has the same meaning as "A's Uranus in B's First House," except that its effects will be stronger and more immediate. The natives will encourage each other to develop their inner spiritual awareness and unique creative abilities. For the relationship to be harmonious, each person must respect the other's independence and free will.

A's Uranus Conjunct B's Midheaven Opposition B's Nadir (A's ♅ ☌ B's M.C. ☍ B's Nadir)

This comparative combination has the same basic significance as "A's Uranus in B's Tenth House," except that its effects are stronger and more immediate. The natives can be mutually involved in bringing important changes and improvements into each other's professional life.

The Uranus individual will influence the Midheaven individual to be more liberal and progressive in political, administrative, and professional methods and ideas. The Uranus native can bring about important and drastic changes which will affect status and position of the Midheaven individual. The Midheaven individual can, in turn, help the Uranus individual to gain recognition and official support for his or her unique ideas and endeavors.

A's Uranus Conjunct B's Descendant Opposition
B's Ascendant (A's ♅ ☌ B's Desc. ☍ B's Asc.)

Basically, this comparative combination has the same significance as "A's Uranus in B's Seventh House," except that its effects will be stronger and more immediate. The Uranus individual can cause important changes in the Descendant individual's attitudes toward marriage, partnership, public relations, friendship, and business dealings. The Uranus native will be instrumental in making the Descendant individual more awake and aware in these respects.

If Uranus is afflicted in the comparison, permanence in marriage or other partnerships is not favored.

The Descendant individual can introduce the Uranus individual to new acquaintances and social contacts, and can also help the latter make his or her unique ideas acceptable to others.

A's Uranus Conjunct B's Nadir Opposition
B's Midheaven (A's ♅ ☌ B's Nadir ☍ B's M.C.)

This comparative combination has basically the same significance as "A's Uranus in B's Fourth House," except that its effects will be more intense and immediate.

The Uranus individual can have a strong liberating influence on the Nadir individual's deep-seated habit patterns that are based on early childhood experiences. Sudden and drastic changes can be brought into the family and domestic affairs of the Nadir individual, often by the friends and group activities the Uranus native introduces into the domestic scene.

The business and corporate affairs of the Uranus individual can affect the Nadir individual's domestic financial affairs. The Nadir individual can provide the Uranus individual with a home or base of operations for unique creative endeavors.

COMPARATIVE SEXTILES

Comparative sextiles of Uranus are of special importance because the sextile aspect is related to Aquarius in the natural Zodiac, which Uranus rules.

The natives will share intellectual, scientific, occult, and humanitarian interests with respect to the affairs ruled by the planet making the sextile in the comparison.

These comparative sextiles are excellent for mutual association with friends and groups, and for shared organizational activities. In marital and romantic relationships, the natives share stimulating intellectual interests that keep the relationship from becoming a boring routine. They can cooperate in scientific and occult work and investigation.

These comparative sextiles are also favorable for those who work together in corporate enterprises of a scientific, industrial or technological nature. There can also be a mutual interest in social and political reforms.

A's Uranus Sextile B's Sun

See A's Sun Sextile B's Uranus.

A's Uranus Sextile B's Moon

See A's Moon Sextile B's Uranus.

A's Uranus Sextile B's Mercury

See A's Mercury Sextile B's Uranus.

A's Uranus Sextile B's Venus

See A's Venus Sextile B's Uranus.

A's Uranus Sextile B's Mars

See A's Mars Sextile B's Uranus.

A's Uranus Sextile B's Jupiter

See A's Jupiter Sextile B's Uranus.

A's Uranus Sextile B's Saturn

See A's Saturn Sextile B's Uranus.

A's Uranus Sextile B's Uranus (A's ♅ ⚹ B's ♅)

This comparative sextile indicates a relationship between individuals separated in age by approximately fourteen years. The viewpoints typical of their generations will be sufficiently similar to make possible some degree of friendly understanding in social, political, and economic outlook. The older native can help the younger native to grow in his or her unique creative self-expression through having had similar experiences. They can cooperate effectively in scientific, political, and occult work. The association can be especially helpful for younger natives, who have not reached maturity.

A's Uranus Sextile B's Neptune (A's ♅ ⚹ B's ♆)

These natives have mutual interests in religious, cultural, economic, political, and scientific evolution. These interests can lead to a desire to gain insight into historical trends and events that relate to the destiny of mankind.

If the natives are sufficiently advanced, they can cooperate effectively in religious, metaphysical, psychic and occult research. There can be a mutual interest in paraphysics, the advanced scientific fields in the borderland between science and metaphysics.

The Uranus individual will be interested in the imaginative and intuitive faculties of the Neptune individual, and the Neptune individual will, in turn, be sympathetic to the occult or scientific ideas, goals, and objectives of the Uranus individual.

There will be a sharing of humanitarian, religious, and Utopian ideas, goals, and objectives, both with each other and with mutual friends, groups, and associations. There can be mutual involvement in secret organizations. These natives can be effective in carrying on behind-the-scenes activities.

A's Uranus Sextile B's Pluto (A's ♅ ⚹ B's ♇)

This comparative sextile indicates mutual interest in deep scientific and occult activities and investigations. It has a double-Scorpio/Eighth House connotation, which could mean a special mutual interest in reincarnation and life after death. As with "A's Uranus Sextile B's Neptune," there could be a mutual involvement with paraphysics and parapsychology. There could be a mutual interest in reforming existing social, political, and economic institutions. The natives can work together effectively in groups and organizations related to the occult, science, or political, social and economic reforms. They can also work together effectively in advanced scientific research and in technological and related industries. Mutual involvement in corporate enterprises is likely to be related to these matters. There could be mutual concern with the handling of the affairs of the dead.

The Uranus individual can help the Pluto individual to be more spontaneous and decisive in action, and the Pluto individual can, in turn, help the Uranus individual develop greater long-range endurance and steadiness of purpose.

A's Uranus Sextile B's North Node Trine B's South Node
(A's ♅ ✳ B's ☊ △ B's ☋)

The natives can help each other to gain penetrating insights into prevailing trends and popular beliefs.

The Uranus individual will be in favor of modern trends and developments if they lead to greater human freedom. He or she can be critical of popular trends and attitudes that lead to conformity. However, the Uranus native will encourage the Nodes individual to follow personal convictions regardless of prevailing social beliefs. In turn, the Nodes individual can help the Uranus individual find popular acceptance for original ideas and unique endeavors.

A's Uranus Sextile B's South Node Trine B's North Node
(A's ♅ ✳ B's ☋ △ B's ☊)

The significance of this combination is essentially the same as "A's Uranus Sextile B's North Node Trine B's South Node." These natives, however, will be intellectually critical of prevailing social trends and popular beliefs and inclined to depart from these popular beliefs and trends, especially if they feel these ideas do not deserve their respect.

A's Uranus Sextile B's Ascendant Trine B's Descendant
(A's ♅ ✳ B's Asc. △ B's Desc.)

This comparative combination indicates friendly, exciting, intellectually stimulating relationships. The natives will encourage each other to express more freedom and individuality. There will be mutual interests in friends, groups, and organizational activities and common intellectual interests in scientific, sociological, and occult subjects.

In a marriage or romantic relationship, these stimulating mutual intellectual interests and activities will keep the natives from becoming bored with each other.

The Uranus individual can help the Ascendant/Descendant individual to be more aware of inner spiritual values and social relationships, and the Ascendant/Descendant individual will encourage the Uranus individual to be more open in the expression of intuitive ideas and unusual talents.

A's Uranus Sextile B's Midheaven Trine B's Nadir
(A's ♅ ✶ B's M.C. △ B's Nadir)

Unusual and interesting professional and family relationships are indicated. The Uranus individual will encourage the Midheaven/Nadir individual to employ new ideas and scientific techniques in professional affairs and domestic activities. The Uranus native will encourage the Midheaven/Nadir individual to be more friendly in professional affairs and to carry on group and organizational activities in the home. He might also introduce scientific or occult pursuits into the home life of the Midheaven/Nadir individual.

The Midheaven/Nadir individual can provide the Uranus individual with a home or a base of operations or with professional opportunities for expressing intellectual humanitarian, scientific, or occult interests and abilities.

A's Uranus Sextile B's Descendant Trine B's Ascendant
(A's ♅ ✶ B's Desc. △ B's Asc.)

This comparative combination has basically the same significance as "A's Uranus Sextile B's Ascendant Trine B's Descendant." These natives, however, will be intellectually concerned with public relations and with the psychology of their relationship.

A's Uranus Sextile B's Nadir Trine B's Midheaven
(A's ♅ ✶ B's Nadir △ B's M.C.)

The significance is basically the same as "A's Uranus Sextile B's Midheaven Trine B's Nadir," except that these natives will be more intellectually concerned with family and domestic affairs. There could be a mutual interest in ecological reforms and in new methods pertaining to farming, building and mining.

COMPARATIVE SQUARES

Comparative squares of Uranus indicate difficulties arising out of sudden, unpredictable behavior on the part of the Uranus individual. The circumstances the natives will bring into each other's lives will drastically upset their life patterns.

The Uranus individual will refuse to submit to traditional or expected ways of doing things, and this will upset or irritate the other native. The other native may not like the friends and organizational activities of the Uranus individual. He tends to see the Uranus person as radical, unpredictable, unreliable, and uncooperative. He or she may not appreciate or approve of the Uranus individual's scientific, sociological, political, or occult interests and views. In turn, the Uranus person is apt to find the other boring. These combinations are especially difficult for cooperation in professional and domestic affairs.

A's Uranus Square B's Sun

See A's Sun Square B's Uranus.

A's Uranus Square B's Moon

See A's Moon Square B's Uranus.

A's Uranus Square B's Mercury

See A's Mercury Square B's Uranus.

A's Uranus Square B's Venus

See A's Venus Square B's Uranus.

A's Uranus Square B's Mars

See A's Mars Square B's Uranus.

A's Uranus Square B's Jupiter

See A's Jupiter Square B's Uranus.

A's Uranus Square B's Saturn

See A's Saturn Square B's Uranus.

A's Uranus Square B's Uranus (A's ♅ □ B's ♅)

This comparative square can only occur among individuals with an age difference of approximately twenty-one or sixty-three years. There will be major differences in political, sociological, organizational, and scientific values because of the differing experiences of the generations.

The natives will not agree on the importance of each other's goals, friends, or group and organizational activities. They will respond to each other in an erratic and unpredictable way, and this makes it difficult to carry out plans and activities in unison. If the natives are interested in occult subjects, they will not agree as to methods and approaches.

A's Uranus Square B's Neptune (A's ♅ □ B's ♆)

These natives exhibit major differences of approach to mystical and occult subjects. The Uranus individual takes a scientific, intellectual, intuitive approach to these things, while the Neptune individual is inclined to a devotional, psychic, mystical approach. The Uranus individual is apt to be on the occult path and the Neptune individual on the mystic path to self-realization.

The Neptune individual is apt to try and retreat and hold onto the past while the Uranus individual actively supports change. The Uranus individual can become impatient with the Neptune individual's psychological self-preoccupation and introverted tendencies, while the Neptune person may regard the Uranus native as jarring, unpredictable, unsympathetic, and overly intellectual and have difficulty in understanding his or her friends and associates.

The natives will have differing attitudes toward large-scale changes in the sociological, political, economical, and scientific affairs that affect humanity as a whole.

These distinctions are only true if the natives' natal horoscopes reveal them to be strongly representative of the planets Uranus and Neptune.

A's Uranus Square B's Pluto (A's ♅ □ B's ♇)

Drastic changes in the lives of both natives can be brought about by this comparative square. These changes can be manifested as a clash of wills, or the natives may encourage each other to excessive revolutionary changes in their desire to drastically alter or overthrow existing social, economic, religious and political institutions. There could be conflict over corporate financial affairs, inheritance, alimony, affairs of the dead, or joint finances.

The natives may have different goals and objectives, or they may be rivals for power and control in economic, political, or social organizations. There could be major differences in approach to scientific, ecological, or occult methods and practices.

The Uranus individual is likely to regard the Pluto individual as power hungry and domineering, while the Pluto individual will probably see the Uranus individual as unreliable, unpredictable, eccentric and uncooperative.

A's Uranus Square B's North Node Square B's South Node (A's ♅ □ B's ☊ □ B's ☋)

This comparative combination indicates that the Uranus individual is likely to disapprove of the Nodes individual's conformity to prevailing social trends and popular beliefs. The Nodes individual will, in turn, regard the Uranus individual as nonconformist and eccentric where these trends and beliefs are concerned.

It will be difficult for the natives to cooperate in public relations, politics, and in social, group, and organizational activities.

A's Uranus Square B's South Node Square B's North Node

See A's Uranus Square B's North Node Square B's South Node.

A's Uranus Square B's Ascendant Square B's Descendant (A's ♅ □ B's Asc. □ B's Desc.)

These natives will encounter difficulties in cooperating in personal, marital, professional, domestic, and occult activities. A clash of wills is likely, and, if there is to be harmony, each native must respect the other's freedom and independence. In marital relationships, this combination does not favor an enduring relationship.

The Ascendant/Descendant individual is likely to regard the Uranus individual as inconsiderate, uncooperative, eccentric, antisocial, impractical, and much too radical. The Uranus individual may regard the Ascendant/Descendant native as self-centered, spiritually unaware, or simply nondescript.

A's Uranus Square B's Midheaven Square B's Nadir
(A's ♅ □ B's M.C. □ B's Nadir)

This is not a good comparative combination for natives in family and domestic relationships. The Uranus individual is likely to upset the professional and family routine of the Midheaven/Nadir individual, and this will be a cause of resentment. He will regard the Midheaven/Nadir individual as overly conservative, materialistic, habit-bound, and tied down to a boring routine.

The Midheaven/Nadir individual will regard the Uranus individual as out of step, uncooperative, radical, and eccentric, and may disapprove of the effect that the Uranus individual's friends and organizational activities have on that person's professional and domestic life. He or she is also likely to be unsympathtic to the scientific and occult innovations that the Uranus individual would like to bring into the Midheaven/Nadir person's professional and family life.

A's Uranus Square B's Descendant Square B's Ascendant

See A's Uranus Square B's Ascendant Square B's Descendant.

A's Uranus Square B's Nadir Square B's Midheaven

See A's Uranus Square B's Midheaven Square B's Nadir.

COMPARATIVE TRINES

Comparative trines of Uranus indicate the ways in which the natives can bring unexpected good fortune into each other's lives. This could take place through large-scale corporate business opportunities—especially in businesses related to science, technological innovations, electronics, and inventions—or through travel, romance, and new friendships.

The natives will be able to cooperate effectively in group and organizational activities related to the affairs ruled by the planet which Uranus trines in the comparison. The Uranus individual will inspire the other native with new and unique approaches to these affairs, and can awaken the other native to a broader and more comprehensive understanding of scientific, sociological, humanitarian, and occult fields of activity and investigation.

The natives will both feel exhilarated and excited by new adventures. There can be a mutual interest in applying intuitive perceptions and scientific methods to educational and creative endeavors.

These combinations favor friendships.

A's Uranus Trine B's Sun

See A's Sun Trine B's Uranus.

A's Uranus Trine B's Moon

See A's Moon Trine B's Uranus.

A's Uranus Trine B's Mercury

See A's Mercury Trine B's Uranus.

A's Uranus Trine B's Venus

See A's Venus Trine B's Uranus.

A's Uranus Trine B's Mars

See A's Mars Trine B's Uranus.

A's Uranus Trine B's Jupiter

See A's Jupiter Trine B's Uranus.

A's Uranus Trine B's Saturn

See A's Saturn Trine B's Uranus.

A's Uranus Trine B's Uranus (A's ♅ △ B's ♅)

This comparative combination can only occur among natives separated in age by twenty-eight or fifty-six years. There will be a mutual interest in progressive political, economic, scientific, and sociological changes.

The natives could be interested in scientific, sociological, and occult areas of work and investigation. They can cooperate effectively in group and organizational activities.

A's Uranus Trine B's Neptune (A's ♅ △ B's ♆)

These natives share interests in religious mysticism, occult pursuits, the concept of reincarnation, astrology, meditation, and other spiritual disciplines, though these interests will not be pronounced unless they are also indicated by the natives' natal horoscopes.

There can be mutual cooperation in group and organizational activities, psychological investigation, and sociological reforms. The natives can help each other gain a better understanding and appreciation of the large-scale political, sociological, economic, and religious changes that influence mankind's evolutionary development. They will bring out each other's Utopian idealism.

The Uranus individual can help the Neptune individual to gain a more scientific grasp of his or her own imaginative and psychic faculties. The Neptune individual will be sympathetic to and will encourage the Uranus individual's intuitive inspirations and humanitarian tendencies.

This comparative trine must be reinforced by other comparative aspects if it is to be a major determining factor in the relationship.

A's Uranus Trine B's Pluto (A's ♅ △ B's ♇)

This comparative trine indicates mutual interest and ability to cooperate in advanced scientific research, corporate business related to science and technology, political and social reform, and ecological improvements. If the natives are interested in the occult, astrology, life after death, and reincarnation, they will be able to work together effectively in these fields. They will augment each other's will power and determination in efforts at spiritual self-improvement. This can carry over into attempts to regenerate existing political, sociological, religious, educational, and economic institutions, especially where the recycling and proper handling of industrial waste products are concerned.

The Uranus individual will help the Pluto individual to be more adaptable and receptive to sudden intuitive flashes which will augment an innate capacity for penetrating insights. The Pluto individual, in turn, will help the Uranus individual to gain greater powers of concentration and steadiness of purpose, which will increase his or her capacity for deeper understanding.

A's Uranus Trine B's North Node Sextile B's South Node

See A's Uranus Sextile B's South Node Trine B's North Node.

A's Uranus Trine B's South Node Sextile B's North Node

See A's Uranus Sextile B's North Node Trine B's South Node.

A's Uranus Trine B's Ascendant Sextile B's Descendant

See A's Uranus Sextile B's Descendant Trine B's Ascendant.

A's Uranus Trine B's Midheaven Sextile B's Nadir

See A's Uranus Sextile B's Nadir Trine B's Midheaven.

A's Uranus Trine B's Descendant Sextile B's Ascendant

See A's Uranus Sextile B's Ascendant Trine B's Descendant.

A's Uranus Trine B's Nadir Sextile B's Midheaven

See A's Uranus Sextile B's Midheaven Trine B's Nadir.

COMPARATIVE OPPOSITIONS

Comparative oppositions of Uranus indicate relationship problems arising out of dependency, willfulness, or impatient and eccentric behavior.

These combinations are not favorable for marriage or other partnerships because both individuals are apt to be unwilling to sacrifice personal freedom for the sake of mutual harmony and cooperation.

The Uranus individual is apt to act in impulsive, unexpected ways, and without consulting the other native, and this is likely to arouse resentment or irritation.

The other native may not approve of the Uranus individual's friends, and is also apt to be unsympathetic to that person's scientific, sociological, political, business, inventive, organizational, or occult activities.

On the positive side, the natives will enjoy an interesting, even unpredictable, relationship. They can share exciting and unusual intellectual pursuits and experiences.

A's Uranus Opposition B's Sun

See A's Sun Opposition B's Uranus.

A's Uranus Opposition B's Moon

See A's Moon Opposition B's Uranus.

A's Uranus Opposition B's Mercury

See A's Mercury Opposition B's Uranus.

A's Uranus Opposition B's Venus

See A's Venus Opposition B's Uranus.

A's Uranus Opposition B's Mars

See A's Mars Opposition B's Uranus.

A's Uranus Opposition B's Jupiter

See A's Jupiter Opposition B's Uranus.

A's Uranus Opposition B's Saturn

See A's Saturn Opposition B's Uranus.

A's Uranus Opposition B's Uranus (A's ♅ ☍ B's ♅)

This comparative opposition can only occur among natives with forty years difference in their ages. There can be major generational differences in sociological, political, scientific, industrial, economic, ecological, and sexual beliefs and activities. The natives will also have different approaches to occult activities and interests. They will be at odds with one another's friends and group or organizational activities.

There could be disagreement or conflict over inheritance and corporate finances, with the younger native criticizing the older person's attitudes in regard to these matters.

A's Uranus Opposition B's Neptune (A's ♅ ☍ B's ♆)

Psychological and emotional difficulties in the relationship can be the result of personal insecurity caused by large-scale sociological, economic, and political change.

The Uranus individual can become annoyed and impatient with the psychological problems and subconscious escapist tendencies of the Neptune individual, regarding that person as vague and lost in a dream world, overly emotional, and intellectually unaware. The Uranus native will not appreciate the Neptune individual's emotional approach. By the same token, the Neptune individual will not appreciate the Uranus individual's intellectual approach and may regard the Uranus individual as confusing, upsetting, unpredictable, and eccentric. The Neptune individual's tendency to dwell on the past will annoy the Uranus person, while the latter can, in turn, make the Neptune native uncomfortable by a preoccupation with change and with future goals. The natives may consider each other unreasonable and difficult to understand. They will have diverse approaches to occult, mystical and psychic matters.

A's Uranus Opposition B's Pluto (A's ♅ ☍ B's ♇)

This comparative opposition can indicate relationship problems arising out of a clash of wills or a struggle for power. The Uranus individual is likely to rebel against the attempts of the Pluto individual to mold or reform him. The Pluto individual will resent the inconsistency and sudden changes in plans and commitments caused by the Uranus individual. Attempts of either native to dominate the other can cause explosive conflicts. If they are to get along harmoniously, they must respect each other's freedom and independence.

There can be major differences over political, organizational, economic, technological, ecological, and industrial methods and policies. The natives will not have the same tastes where friends, groups, and organizations are concerned. There can also be conflict over joint finances, corporate affairs, inheritances, and alimony. If the natives are concerned with occult activities, they may be at odds over methods and procedures.

A's Uranus Opposition B's North Node Conjunct B's South Node

See A's Uranus Conjunct B's South Node Opposition B's North Node.

A's Uranus Opposition B's South Node Conjunct B's North Node

See A's Uranus Conjunct B's North Node Opposition B's South Node.

A's Uranus Opposition B's Ascendant Conjunct B's Descendant

See A's Uranus Conjunct B's Descendant Opposition B's Ascendant.

A's Uranus Opposition B's Midheaven Conjunct B's Nadir

See A's Uranus Conjunct B's Nadir Opposition B's Midheaven.

A's Uranus Opposition B's Descendant Conjunct B's Ascendant

See A's Uranus Conjunct B's Ascendant Opposition B's Descendant.

A's Uranus Opposition B's Nadir Conjunct B's Midheaven

See A's Uranus Conjunct B's Midheaven Opposition B's Nadir.

XV
Neptune

Comparative influences of Neptune indicate the ways in which the psychic, intuitive abilities, the imagination, the artistic tastes, and the subconscious motivations of the natives influence each other.

Constructive comparative influences of Neptune indicate intuitive rapport and emotional empathy. In highly developed individuals, there can be definite telepathic communication. The natives will share esthetic, religious, spiritual, and psychological values.

Adverse comparative influences of Neptune indicate relationship problems caused by subconscious, psychological distortions in one or both natives. Their evasive, deceptive tendencies make it difficult for them to cooperate and for each to assume his or her responsibilities in the relationship. There could be a lack of appreciation of each other's religious and mystical perceptions, ideas, and convictions. The Neptune individual could feel misunderstood or that his or her privacy is invaded.

COMPARATIVE HOUSE PLACEMENTS

Comparative house placements of Neptune indicate the ways in which the natives will influence each other in the practical affairs of life ruled by the house in which Neptune falls in the comparison. These influences will be subconscious or psychological; often, they take the form of intuitive feelings and perceptions.

If Neptune is well-aspected in the comparison, these affairs will be improved through esthetic refinement, empathetic understanding, and psychic or intuitive insights.

If Neptune is afflicted in the comparison, the Neptune individual's subconscious, psychological hangups can have an undermining, disintegrating effect on these affairs. The Neptune individual can employ evasive, dishonest, or escapist tactics in regard to them, and they will be subject to confusion through peculiar and hard-to-define circumstances.

The affairs ruled by these comparative house placements can be benefited by secret or behind-the-scenes activities. Religious mysticism and healing spiritual influences can also have a beneficial effect.

A's Neptune in B's First House

This comparative house placement can indicate a psychic link between the natives. The intuitive perceptions and subconscious attitudes of the Neptune individual can be either constructive or a destructive influence on the self-expression and awareness of the First House individual.

If Neptune is afflicted in the comparison, the Neptune individual will have a detrimental effect on the psychology of the First House individual. The Neptune individual could encourage the First House individual in self-indulgent and destructive habits such as alcoholism, drug abuse, or negative psychic practices, or in idle and nonproductive habits. The First House individual could regard the Neptune individual as lost in a fantasy world or psychologically distorted.

If Neptune is well-aspected in the comparison, the Neptune individual will improve the First House individual's level of spiritual self-awareness. The First House individual can gain in esthetic, cultural, spiritual, and intuitive insight through the association and can, in turn, help the Neptune individual to be more positive and active in expressing and utilizing his or her imaginative, intuitive, and esthetic abilities. The natives' influence on each other in these respects will be especially strong if they are associated through family and domestic circumstances.

A's Neptune in B's Second House

Peculiar circumstances may affect the financial affairs of the natives. If Neptune is afflicted in the comparison, the Neptune individual will be a subversive influence on the solvency of the Second House individual, and as a result, the Second House individual could lose money through many peculiar and hard-to-pin-down financial leaks. Often, the Neptune individual makes financial expenditures without consulting the Second House individual, or is unaware of the extent of his or her expenditures or the limitations within which they should be confined. With a heavily afflicted Neptune, there could be fraud or dishonesty in business. Trouble can come through a lack of discipline and organization. If Neptune is afflicted, confusion could arise because of laxity in the keeping of records and financial accounts.

If Neptune is well-aspected in the comparison, however, the natives can gain through business related to art, music, psychology, photography, cinematography, or other businesses requiring insight and imagination. The Neptune individual can aid the business affairs of the Second House individual through intuitive insights into financial affairs.

A's Neptune in B's Third House

This comparative house placement indicates peculiar and, at times, confusing mental relationships. The Neptune individual operates on an intuitive, psychic, and imaginative level, while the Third House individual is concerned with logical thinking and logical, practical information. Consequently, it may be difficult for the natives to understand each other and come to a workable meeting of the minds. Much will depend on what the natal horoscopes reveal about the natives' mental characteristics. (*See* "Aspects to Neptune," *The Astrologer's Handbook*, Harper & Row.)

If Neptune is afflicted in the comparison, difficulties can arise in the relationship because of the Neptune individual's deceptiveness, vagueness, and absentmindedness. In extreme cases, communications in the relationship could become difficult because of subconscious neurotic or psychotic tendencies on the part of the Neptune individual. The Neptune individual could become a psychological burden on the Third House person. He or she could regard the Third House individual as drastically literal, overly concerned with details, and lacking in intuitive understanding.

If Neptune is well-aspected in the comparison, there can be a mutual interest in psychology, art, mysticism, religious philosophy, and religious, educational, or psychological institutions. The Neptune individual can give insight into solutions to practical problems through his or her intuitive ability and imagination. The Third House individual can help the Neptune individual to find practical applications and concrete expressions for intuitive, esthetic, and imaginative, creative abilities.

From a psychological standpoint, this can be an important comparative placement for family relationships, especially brother–sister relationships. Along with the natal horoscopes, it indicates the extent of the natives' mutual intellectual and psychological understanding. This could be a good combination for people who cooperate in writing or other communications where imagination is important. There could be a mutual interest in the use of art, music, psychology, or the psychic faculties in the communications media.

A's Neptune in B's Fourth House

These natives have strong emotional, psychic, and psychological interactions, especially in family and domestic relationships, and more pronouncedly if the people involved live under the same roof, or often, family members with this comparative combination have a karmic link. The Neptune individual will have a powerful, but subtle, influence on the emotional habit patterns of the Fourth House individual. If Neptune is well-aspected, this effect will be spiritually uplifting. However, if Neptune is afflicted in the comparison, it can be psychologically undermining. There can be a mutual interest in using the home as a quiet place for meditation and inner reflections, or for religious or charitable work. The natives will use imagination to beautify their home with works of art and beautiful music.

If Neptune is afflicted in the comparison, the natives will be subject to the possibility of a disorderly or confused domestic environment. They themselves can be disorderly and confused in the home. The Neptune individual can feel misunderstood, ignored, or rejected by the Fourth House individual. If Neptune is afflicted in the comparison, the natives tend to aggravate each other's neurotic, psychological tendencies. Religious differences could bring about family problems.

A's Neptune in B's Fifth House

Peculiar, and often karmic, romantic, parent–child, teacher–student, or artistic relationships can occur. Often these involve gambling or speculation. If Neptune is afflicted in the comparison, the pursuit of pleasure can be a detrimental factor in the relationship and bring about the self-undoing of the natives. One of the natives could be attracted to the other with no reciprocal feeling, with a one-sided relationship or unrequited love as the result. In other romantic relationships, there could be deliberate or unintentional deceit on the part of one or both parties. This is not a good comparative placement for business partnerships involving speculation or investment; unless Neptune is well-aspected, the natives could fall prey to get-rich-quick schemes. They will tend to have unrealistic expectations, while overlooking pitfalls; if one is chasing a pie-in-the-sky, the other is not apt to see the holes underfoot.

In parent–child relationships, there is danger of the extremes of parental neglect on one hand and spoiling the child on the other. If the child is the Neptune individual, he or she may deceive the parents or pretend psychological illness to avoid discipline and responsibility. This comparative placement can result in unwanted pregnancies. In a marriage, the natives may adopt a child.

The Neptune individual can help the Fifth House individual through his or her intuitive and imaginative abilities in matters related to financial investments, children and their education, artistic creativity, romance, and social affairs. The Fifth House individual can help the Neptune individual to be more expressive in utilizing intuitive, imaginative, and esthetic talents.

If Neptune is well-aspected, the natives can have a mutual interest in cinema, drama, music, and art—with a particular interest in art forms—as well as an interest in psychology and the spiritual education of children. There can be strong idealism in romantic relationships.

If Neptune is afflicted, unsuccessful romantic relationships could have a psychologically damaging effect on one or both natives, often as a result of subconscious, psychological hangups or differences in family background which affect the emotional attitudes of the Neptune individual. Another result of afflictions to Neptune can be mutual dissipation through the pursuit of pleasure in self-destructive habits such as drinking, drug abuse, overeating, or sexual excess. This comparative placement often occurs in homosexual relationships.

A's Neptune in B's Sixth House

This comparative placement indicates peculiar circumstances in work, employer–employee, co-worker, or professional partnerships. The Neptune individual can cause confusion and inefficiency in the job situation due to daydreaming, lack of attention to detail, escapist tendencies, or unwholesome habits that affect the health. He or she may feign illness in order to avoid work or responsibilities.

The Sixth House individual is likely to regard the Neptune individual as evasive, inefficient, indolent, and undisciplined where work is concerned. The Neptune individual will regard the Sixth House individual as overly concerned with details, overly critical, materialistic, psychologically insensitive, and unappreciative of spiritual values.

If Neptune is afflicted, the natives could encourage each other in drinking, drug abuse, undesirable dietary habits, or peculiar forms of dress.

If Neptune is well-aspected in the comparison, the natives can have a mutual interest in spiritual healing, diet, or service in hospitals or religious or educational institutions. There can be a strong mutual interest in psychology and mental health. The Neptune individual can have imaginative or intuitive insights into ways of making work more efficient and comfortable. There could be an interest in artistically decorating the working environment or making it more pleasant.

A's Neptune in B's Seventh House

Peculiar psychological circumstances in marriages and other partnerships are indicated. The natives will have a strong subliminal, psychological effect on each other.   If Neptune is well-aspected, there can be idealistic love and a psychological empathy between the natives, which can show itself in the sharing of spiritual, artistic, religious, psychological, intuitive, and imaginative values and perceptions.

The natives can cooperate effectively in partnerships related to art, music, or entertainment. However, this is not a good combination for most business partnerships or professional relationships because one or both natives are likely to be unreliable or ineffectual, promising more than they can deliver. The Neptune individual can be a confusing and disorienting psychic influence on the Seventh House individual.

If Neptune is afflicted in the comparison, there can be psychological separation between the natives, with one or both isolated in a private dream world. The neurotic or psychotic problems of one or both natives can distort or break down the relationship. There is also the possibility of deception and evasiveness where mutual responsibilities are concerned, especially on the part of the Neptune individual. Such conditions could undermine the relationship and lead to its termination or to divorce.

A's Neptune in B's Eighth House

Provided the natives are developed enough to be interested, this comparative placement indicates mutual interests in religious, occult, or mystical activities. These interests are apt to be specifically related to reincarnation, life after death, or spirit communication. There could be mutual involvement with corporate business affairs, taxes, insurance, inheritance, and the goods of the dead. There could be confusion, fraud, inefficiency, and deception regarding these things if Neptune is afflicted in the comparison.

If Neptune is well-aspected in the comparison, the natives could help with the financial affairs of charitable, religious, educational, psychological, or medical institutions.

The religious and mystical understanding of the Neptune individual can help the Eighth House individual to overcome a fear of death and gain a greater understanding of the spiritual life. The Eighth House individual can help the Neptune individual with the financial and business aspects of his or her religious, mystical, artistic, charitable, or imaginative pursuits.

If Neptune is well-aspected in the comparison, one or both natives could gain financially through marriage. If Neptune is afflicted in the comparison, there could be financial loss through unwise expenditures or confused financial management on the part of one or both natives.

A's Neptune in B's Ninth House

This comparative placement indicates a mutual interest in religious mysticism, foreign cultures, spiritual education, education and history related to the fine arts, travel, and religious practices of foreign cultures. In some cases, the natives will be mutually involved in travel for the purpose of spiritual adventure.

If Neptune is afflicted in the comparison, the natives can get each other involved in mystical cults of dubious value, often guru or personality cults of various types. The Ninth House individual could regard the Neptune individual as impractical, deluded, or misguided in his or her religious beliefs. The Neptune individual could consider the Ninth

House individual as much too orthodox and lacking in intuitive understanding with regard to his or her religious and philosophical beliefs. In marital relationships, difficulties could arise due to differences in religious, educational, or cultural backgrounds and beliefs. If Neptune is afflicted in the comparison of a teacher–student relationship, there will be a lack of discipline, organization, and practicality in what is being taught, as well as in methods of teaching and learning.

If Neptune is well-aspected in the comparison, the Neptune individual can help the Ninth House individual to rely on direct, intuitive experience in seeking spiritual guidance in religious precepts. The Ninth House individual can help the Neptune individual to be more expressive of inner, intuitive, spiritual insights.

A's Neptune in B's Tenth House

These natives may have peculiar, and sometimes confusing, relationships in business, professional, or political affairs. If Neptune is well-aspected, the natives could cooperate effectively in professional affairs related to photography, cinema, theater, art, music, entertainment, religion, mysticism, occult activities, and religious, educational, or charitable institutions.

If Neptune is afflicted in the comparison, there could be confusion, fraud, or deception in business or professional affairs, or eventual scandal in affairs relating to the political careers or public status of the natives. Unsavory events from the past of one or both natives could come before the public, causing embarrassment and disgrace. Psychological neuroses or family problems of one or both natives could interfere with professional responsibilities.

On the positive side, the Neptune individual can help advance the career of the Tenth House individual through his or her intuitive abilities and creative imagination. This is especially true in fields related to art, entertainment, and advertising.

A's Neptune in B's Eleventh House

This comparative placement indicates friendships based on intuitive empathy. There can be sharing of interests in religious, humanitarian, esthetic, mystical, or occult activities. The natives could be mutually involved in groups, organizations, and friendships that relate to these affairs. There can also be mutual involvement with educational, charitable, or psychological organizations or institutions.

The Neptune individual could make the Eleventh House individual more intuitively aware in relation to his or her scientific, humanitarian, organizational, or occult interests and activities. The Eleventh House individual can help the Neptune individual to utilize his intuitive and creative, imaginative abilities in group and organizational work, and to gain the interest and cooperation of friends in these endeavors.

If Neptune is afflicted in the comparison, the psychological neuroses or hangups of one or both individuals could make friendship very difficult. Where mutual responsibilities are concerned, there can be insincerity and deception that make it difficult to achieve mutual goals and objectives or to cooperate in group and organizational affairs. These difficulties could also arise out of a lack of discipline and practicality; there is a tendency to promise more than one can deliver. In some cases, the natives will only pretend to be friends in order to avoid nuisance or social unpleasantness.

A's Neptune in B's Twelfth House

These natives are involved with each other's subconscious minds and intuitive faculties. They could be associated through hospitals or charitable or religious institutions, either helping or being helped. There can be a strong mutual interest in psychology and probing the deeper levels of human consciousness. Whether Neptune is afflicted or well-aspected in the comparison, it is reasonable to suppose that the natives have a karmic link of some kind.

If Neptune is afflicted in the comparison, the natives could bring out the worst of each other's neurotic tendencies and subconscious fears, distortions, and delusions. They could be secret enemies, consciously or unconsciously, or they could bring about each other's undoing through encouraging each other in self-destructive or escapist habits.

If Neptune is well-aspected in the comparison, the natives will have a mutual interest in intuitive inspiration, art, music, mysticism, and other creative uses of the imagination.

COMPARATIVE CONJUNCTIONS

Comparative conjunctions of Neptune indicate the means by which the psychic and imaginative faculties of the Neptune individual actively influence the affairs of the other native. They favor mutual endeavors in the fields of psychology, religion, mysticism, art, music, and entertainment. Relationships or associations with these comparative aspects often come about through the natives' involvement in religious, charitable, or educational institutions.

Favorable comparative aspects to these comparative conjunctions often result in the Neptune native using intuition and creative imagination to help the other native gain insight and achieve progress in the affairs ruled by the planet conjunct Neptune in the comparison.

Afflictions to these comparative conjunctions can cause the psychological problems and subconscious hangups of the Neptune individual to be a source of confusion and aggravation to the other native. Frequently, this leads to practices of deception in the relationship

A's Neptune Conjunct B's Sun

See A's Sun Conjunct B's Neptune.

A's Neptune Conjunct B's Moon

See A's Moon Conjunct B's Neptune.

A's Neptune Conjunct B's Mercury

See A's Mercury Conjunct B's Neptune.

A's Neptune Conjunct B's Venus

See A's Venus Conjunct B's Neptune.

A's Neptune Conjunct B's Mars

See A's Mars Conjunct B's Neptune.

A's Neptune Conjunct B's Jupiter

See A's Jupiter Conjunct B's Neptune.

A's Neptune Conjunct B's Saturn

See A's Saturn Conjunct B's Neptune.

A's Neptune Conjunct B's Uranus

See A's Uranus Conjunct B's Neptune.

A's Neptune Conjunct B's Neptune (A's ♆ ☌ B's ♆)

This comparative conjunction occurs between natives of approximately the same age. It indicates common social, psychological, cultural, and esthetic values associated with the generation to which the natives belong. This comparative conjunction will not be a major distinguishing influence in the relationship unless it is heavily aspected by other planets.

Neptune's approximate fifteen-year transit through each sign has much to do with changing styles in art, music, entertainment, and sociological values. The natives will, to some extent, share a subconscious and intuitive appreciation of these cultural factors.

A's Neptune Conjunct B's Pluto (A's ♆ ☌ B's ♇)

These natives have a mutual concern with large-scale political, economic, technological, religious, and sociological changes that affect humanity as a whole. There can be mutual interest in gaining insight into the future of such trends or in reforming existing conditions. The natives can share a common destiny, shaped by large-scale forces of change within the society in which they live. In general, if they are highly evolved, there will be a sharing of interest and work in matters of profound and long-range significance and consequence.

If the natives are spiritually inclined, they can share a telepathic link and have a mutual interest in occultism, mysticism, prophecy, advanced aspects of science, or reincarnation and life after death. This combination could indicate a mutual interest in corporate affairs related to advanced technology, religious, educational, and charitable institutions, insurance, scientific research, or ecological concerns.

The Neptune individual can help the Pluto individual to greater spiritual sensitivity. The Pluto individual will help the Neptune individual gain greater will power for self-regeneration and the improvement of existing conditions.

A's Neptune Conjunct B's North Node Opposition B's South Node (A's ♆ ☌ B's ☊ ☍ B's ☋)

This comparative combination indicates a mutual interest in current popular music, art, and religious and philosophical ideas. The natives tend to be strongly influenced by the currently popular forms of entertainment. They can tend to encourage each other to blind adherence and support of these things without carefully examining their ultimate worth.

A's Neptune Conjunct B's South Node Opposition B's North Node (A's ♆ ☌ B's ☋ ☍ B's ☊)

Especially on the part of the Nodes individual, there will be a critical examination of currently popular music, entertainment, and art forms. The natives may or may not agree concerning these things—much depends on their ages, their characteristics as individuals, and the overall nature of the comparison. If this comparative combination is afflicted by other comparative aspects, the Nodes individual may consider the Neptune individual as socially deluded, unaware, incompetent, or immature. The Neptune individual may regard the Nodes individual as negative and overly conservative.

A's Neptune Conjunct B's Ascendant Opposition B's Descendant (A's ♆ ☌ B's Asc. ☍ B's Desc.)

This comparative combination has basically the same significance as "A's Neptune in B's First House," except that its effects will be stronger and more immediate. The Neptune individual will have a strong psychic influence on the Ascendant/Descendant individual which can be either spiritually uplifting or psychologically disorienting, depending on the basic character of the Neptune individual and the overall nature of the comparison. The Neptune individual can help the Ascendant/Descendant individual to become more self-aware as a spiritual being. The Ascendant/Descendant individual can help the Neptune individual to be dynamically active in expressing and utilizing intuitive insights and imaginative abilities and to overcome subconscious, psychological problems through constructive action.

A's Neptune Conjunct B's Midheaven Opposition B's Nadir (A's ♆ ☌ B's M.C. ☍ B's Nadir)

The significance of this comparative combination is basically the same as "A's Neptune in B's Tenth House." However, the effect will be stronger and more dynamic and immediate. The natives could be professionally associated through hospitals, institutions, churches, or schools. There is the possibility of mutual professional work in such fields as film, entertainment, music, art, religion, or occult endeavors.

The intuitive and imaginative ability of the Neptune individual can help the Midheaven/Nadir individual to gain more prestige and be more successful in professional and political endeavors.

If Neptune is afflicted in the comparison, there could be confusion and possibly deception in professional or political dealings. Unsavory incidents and facts regarding the life of one or both natives could come before the public and result in scandal or professional disgrace. The Neptune individual could regard the Midheaven/Nadir individual as materialistic, ambitious, and unreasonably exacting in work demands, and the Midheaven/Nadir individual could regard the Neptune individual as evasive, inefficient, and psychologically incompetent. The Neptune individual could have a subversive, undermining effect on the career of the Midheaven/Nadir.

A's Neptune Conjunct B's Descendant Opposition B's Ascendant (A's ♆ ☌ B's Desc. ☍ B's Asc.)

This comparative combination indicates a delicate psychological relationship between the natives. Its significance will be basically the same as "A's Neptune in B's Seventh House." However, it will be stronger and more immediate in its effect. The natives can be sensitive and very much attuned to each other's thoughts and feelings, especially if Neptune is well-aspected in the comparison. If Neptune is afflicted in the comparison, there is the possibility of a psychological distance between the natives caused by the Neptune individual being lost in a private dream world.

There can be a strong mutual interest in psychology, art, and in the sociological factors that affect relationships. The subconscious attitudes and conditionings of the natives will strongly influence a marital relationship; whether these influences are for good or ill depends on the overall comparison and the basic character of the individuals.

A's Neptune Conjunct B's Nadir Opposition B's Midheaven (A's ♆ ☌ B's Nadir ☍ B's M.C.)

Basically, this comparative combination has the same significance as "A's Neptune in B's Fourth House," except that it is stronger and more immediate in its effect. The Neptune individual can have a strong psychic influence on the basic consciousness of the Nadir/Midheaven individual. In marital relationships, this comparative combination can influence the degree of compatibility of the family, social, and religious backgrounds of the natives. It affects their deep-rooted psychological attitudes toward these matters.

If Neptune is well-aspected in the comparison, the natives will have a mutual interest in incorporating religious, psychological, musical, and esthetic values into the home life. If Neptune is afflicted in the comparison, the natives' neurotic and psychological problems can have a very psychologically undermining effect, detrimental to both, especially if they live under the same roof. Relatives of one or both natives could also have a confusing or undermining effect on the relationship. The proverbial in-law problem is characteristic of this combination when it is afflicted.

COMPARATIVE SEXTILES

Comparative sextiles of Neptune indicate ways in which the natives can intellectually share imaginative, intuitive, and psychological insights and ideas. These combinations could indicate mutual interest or involvement in psychological, religious, charitable, mystical, or psychic groups and organizations. They are favorable for intellectual communication and cooperation in musical and artistic endeavors, especially those related to entertainment, advertising, writing, and the communications media. These sextiles are especially good for those who work together in psychology, religion, and psychic work and the institutions related to these things.

A's Neptune Sextile B's Sun

See A's Sun Sextile B's Neptune.

A's Neptune Sextile B's Moon

See A's Moon Sextile B's Neptune.

A's Neptune Sextile B's Mercury

See A's Mercury Sextile B's Neptune.

A's Neptune Sextile B's Venus

See A's Venus Sextile B's Neptune.

A's Neptune Sextile B's Mars

See A's Mars Sextile B's Neptune.

A's Neptune Sextile B's Jupiter

See A's Jupiter Sextile B's Neptune.

A's Neptune Sextile B's Saturn

See A's Saturn Sextile B's Neptune.

A's Neptune Sextile B's Uranus

See A's Uranus Sextile B's Neptune.

A's Neptune Sextile B's Neptune (A's ♆ ⚹ B's ♆)

This comparative sextile can occur only between natives separated in age by approximately thirty years. It is helpful in teacher–student and parent–child relationships, contributing to an intuitive rapport and enabling the natives to understand the sociological and cultural forces affecting the psychological attitudes and art and entertainment forms characteristic of each other's generations. In parent–child relationships, the parent could have a psychic attunement to the child's moods, feelings, and psychological motivations. The natives could have a mutual interest in religion, mysticism, cultural history, music, or art. In general, the effects of this comparative sextile are not pronounced unless they are reinforced by other aspects.

A's Neptune Sextile B's Pluto (A's ♆ ⚹ B's ♇)

A mutual intellectual interest in large-scale political, technological, economic, sociological, or ecological issues and changes is indicated. The natives can cooperate effectively in scientific, ecological, mystical, or occult studies and pursuits. There could be mutual participation in groups and organizations related to these subjects. There can be a tele-pathic or psychic link between the natives if they are sufficiently evolved to be aware of such things. This is a good comparative combination for cooperation in corporate business enterprises related to technology or psychology, or in religious, educational, or medical institutions, or in insurance, entertainment, or popular art forms.

A's Neptune Sextile B's North Node Trine B's South Node
(A's ♆ ✶ B's ☊ △ B's ☋)

This comparative combination indicates a shared social and esthetic awareness and enjoyment of currently popular art, music, and entertainment. The intuitive and psychic abilities of the Neptune individual can help the Nodes individual to be more aware of subtle changes in the prevailing sociological, religious, educational, and cultural attitudes and beliefs. The Nodes individual can help the other individual to take advantage of these changes in his or her creative, artistic work or psychological interests and activities.

In romantic, parent–child, and teacher–student relationships, the natives can help each other achieve social, psychological, and artistically creative and expressive goals and objectives through mutual psychological understanding and rapport. They can share insights on how to gain popularity and public acceptance for these creative endeavors.

A's Neptune Sextile B's South Node Trine B's North Node
(A's ♆ ✶ B's ☋ △ B's ☊)

This comparative combination has basically the same significance as "A's Neptune Sextile B's North Node Trine B's South Node." These natives, however, will be more individualistic and intellectually critical in regard to the prevailing social trends and popular beliefs that affect art forms, sociology, and psychology.

A's Neptune Sextile B's Ascendant Trine B's Descendant
(A's ♆ ✶ B's Asc. △ B's Desc.)

These natives have an intuitive, psychological rapport. The Neptune individual can bring out spiritual, intuitive, and imaginative qualities in the Ascendant/Descendant individual and make him or her more aware of esthetic, intuitive, psychic, and psychological values. The Ascendant/Descendant individual can help the Neptune individual to be more active and expressive in utilizing intuitive, perceptive, and imaginative abilities.

The natives can help each other understand and overcome subconscious, psychological problems and hangups. This is a favorable combination in marriage, because it gives mutual patience and psychological understanding. The natives can work together effectively in art, religion, mysticism, and psychology.

A's Neptune Sextile B's Midheaven Trine B's Nadir (A's ♆ ✶ B's M.C. △ B's Nadir)

This is a favorable comparative combination for cooperation in professional, family, and domestic affairs that require intuitive understanding, esthetic sensitivity, and creative imagination. It is also good for professional cooperation in such fields as art, music, entertainment, films, advertising, psychology, religion, and occult pursuits.

In family and domestic relationships, it aids mutual psychological understanding and the incorporation of cultural, religious, spiritual, and esthetic values into the family life. In marital relationships, there will be an understanding of each other's religious, social, and psychological upbringing and conditioning.

The intuitive and imaginative abilities of the Neptune individual can aid the career and advancement of the Midheaven/Nadir individual. The Midheaven/Nadir individual can provide the Neptune individual with professional opportunities or with a home or base of operations for his or her religious and esthetic talents and abilities.

A's Neptune Sextile B's Descendant Trine B's Ascendant (A's ♆ ✶ B's Desc. △ B's Asc.)

This comparative combination has basically the same significance as "A's Neptune Sextile B's Ascendant Trine B's Descendant," except that these natives will be more intellectually concerned with the psychology of their relationship.

A's Neptune Sextile B's Nadir Trine B's Midheaven (A's ♆ ✶ B's Nadir △ B's M.C.)

This comparative combination has basically the same significance as "A's Neptune Sextile B's Midheaven Trine B's Nadir," except that these natives will be more intellectually concerned with their family affairs and domestic scene.

COMPARATIVE SQUARES

Comparative squares of Neptune indicate problems arising out of subconscious, psychological neuroses and hangups on the part of one or both natives. Efficient cooperation is hampered by confusion, disorganization, evasive tactics, escapist tendencies, and deliberate or subconscious deception on the part of one or both.

The affairs ruled by the planet making the square to Neptune in the comparison will be subject to irrational psychological distortions, confusion, and deception. These comparative squares do not favor cooperation in psychology, art, mysticism, psychic investigations, or related fields, particularly if the natives are associated through religious, medical, educational, or psychological institutions.

One or both natives could have a detrimental psychic or psychological influence on the other. In some cases, the natives could encourage each other in unwholesome, self-destructive habits, neurotic tendencies, and psychological evasion of reality and responsibility.

A's Neptune Square B's Sun

See A's Sun Square B's Neptune.

A's Neptune Square B's Moon

See A's Moon Square B's Neptune.

A's Neptune Square B's Mercury

See A's Mercury Square B's Neptune.

A's Neptune Square B's Venus

See A's Venus Square B's Neptune.

A's Neptune Square B's Mars

See A's Mars Square B's Neptune.

A's Neptune Square B's Jupiter

See A's Jupiter Square B's Neptune.

A's Neptune Square B's Saturn

See A's Saturn Square B's Neptune.

A's Neptune Square B's Uranus

See A's Uranus Square B's Neptune.

A's Neptune Square B's Neptune (A's ♆ □ B's ♆)

This comparative square can occur only between natives separated in age by approximately forty-five years. They will lack understanding of the psychology, sociological conditioning, and cultural, esthetic values of each other's generations. There will be differences in sociological, religious, and moral values and standards. This is not a favorable comparative aspect for involvement in psychic or occult activities; the natives could attract undesirable astral influences. This comparative square will not be of major importance, however, unless it is reinforced by other factors in the comparison.

A's Neptune Square B's Pluto (A's ♆ □ B's ♇)

Major differences are indicated in the natives' spiritual, economic, political, sociological, technological, and ecological goals and values. They could deceive each other about joint finances, corporate affairs, inheritance, and affairs of the dead. In some cases, the natives could involve each other in detrimental psychic or occult practices. They will have differing religious and philsophical values regarding life after death, religious practices, ecological policies, and approaches to sociological problems. They could bring difficulties into each other's lives related to large-scale changes beyond their personal control.

The Neptune individual could regard the Pluto individual as oppressive, dominating, and power hungry. The Pluto individual could regard the Neptune individual as weak, self-indulgent, indecisive, psychologically confused, and unwilling to confront reality. In some cases, the natives will encourage each other in corrupt expediency for the sake of personal gain at the expense of larger social and ecological issues. In extreme cases, the natives could drive each other to distraction and destruction through psychological, sado-masochistic forms of interaction.

A's Neptune Square B's North Node Square B's South Node
(A's ψ □ B's ☊ □ B's ☋)

This comparative combination can produce interpersonal difficulties in relation to social conduct where prevailing social standards and beliefs are concerned. The Neptune individual can appear to the Nodes individual to be oblivious and psychologically disoriented in behavior with respect to the prevailing social standards in the society in which the native functions. The Neptune individual could regard the Nodes individual as caught up in trivial social necessities and unaware of what the Neptune individual considers important esthetic and spiritual values. The natives could involve each other in a self-destructive, blind adherence to useless, trivial, or unwise beliefs and social activities popular with their peer group. This is particularly true of the fads and social conformities of adolescents and those in their early teens.

A's Neptune Square B's South Node Square B's North Node

See A's Neptune Square B's North Node Square B's South Node.

A's Neptune Square B's Ascendant Square B's Descendant
(A's ψ □ B's Asc. □ B's Desc.)

This comparative combination indicates mutual difficulties in psychological understanding due to differences in level of awareness and cultural background. The Neptune individual will seem evasive and confusing to the Ascendant/Descendant individual. The Ascendant/Descendant individual is likely to regard the Neptune individual as lost in his or her own private fantasy world, unreliable, and hard to pin down to definite mutual commitments and responsibilities. The Ascendant/Descendant individual can seem self-centered or overly aggressive to the Neptune individual, and the Neptune individual can be apprehensive of the consequences of the other's actions.

A's Neptune Square B's Midheaven Square B's Nadir
(A's ψ □ B's M.C. □ B's Nadir)

The psychological difficulties indicated between these natives can have an adverse effect on their professional and domestic affairs. In professional relationships, the Neptune individual can damage the professional reputation or career success of the Midheaven/Nadir individual through evasiveness, inefficiency, and, in some cases, deceit. In extreme cases, this could result in scandal or disgrace for one or both natives.

In marital relationships, there can be psychological difficulties caused by differences in religious or cultural upbringing or family background. The subconscious, psychological problems of one or both natives can cause a breakdown of communication in family relationships. In some cases, there could be disorderliness and confusion in household affairs. One or both natives could be physically or psychologically absent from the professional or domestic scene when they are especially needed.

A's Neptune Square B's Descendant Square B's Ascendant

See A's Neptune Square B's Ascendant Square B's Descendant.

A's Neptune Square B's Nadir Square B's Midheaven

See A's Neptune Square B's Midheaven Square B's Nadir.

COMPARATIVE TRINES

These comparative trines indicate the ways in which the natives share and enjoy social, cultural, religious, mystical, educational, and travel pursuits. They indicate a mutual intuitive rapport regarding the affairs ruled by the planet Neptune trines in the comparison. These affairs will benefit through the intuitive foresight and creative imagination of the Neptune individual. Comparative trines of Neptune are especially favorable for cooperation in artistic fields such as cinema, art, music, and entertainment. The natives can work together effectively in psychology, mysticism, or occult investigations, or with religious, charitable, educational, psychological, or medical institutions. They will both be fond of travel, especially for purposes of spiritual or educational adventure. In romantic and marital relationships, comparative trines of Neptune aid mutual sensitivity and psychological understanding. This also applies to parent–child and teacher–student relationships.

A's Neptune Trine B's Sun

See A's Sun Trine B's Neptune.

A's Neptune Trine B's Moon

See A's Moon Trine B's Neptune.

A's Neptune Trine B's Mercury

See A's Mercury Trine B's Neptune.

A's Neptune Trine B's Venus

See A's Venus Trine B's Neptune.

A's Neptune Trine B's Mars

See A's Mars Trine B's Neptune.

A's Neptune Trine B's Jupiter

See A's Jupiter Trine B's Neptune.

A's Neptune Trine B's Saturn

See A's Saturn Trine B's Neptune.

A's Neptune Trine B's Uranus

See A's Uranus Trine B's Neptune.

A's Neptune Trine B's Neptune (A's ♆ △ B's ♆)

This comparative trine can only occur between natives separated in age by approximately sixty years. Such a relationship would be characteristic of children and their grandparents or children and an older person. The older native can take an interest in the spiritual education and training of the child. He or she will be kind and sympathetic to the child's psychological needs and will gain pleasure from watching the child grow and develop. This is a favorable comparative aspect for passing on cultural values to the younger generation.

A's Neptune Trine B's Pluto (A's ♆ △ B's ♇)

A mutual interest in understanding and foreseeing the major sociological, technological, cultural, political, and economic changes which affect mankind is indicated. The natives can cooperate effectively in corporate business, religious, mystical, and institutional work. This is also a good combination for natives sufficiently evolved to be working in scientific fields that require intuitive insight and deep metaphysical understanding. It is an excellent combination for cooperation for those involved in the occult or mysticism.

The Neptune individual can help the Pluto individual gain greater inner peace, making possible a deeper level of intuitive insight. The Pluto individual can help the Neptune individual to develop the courage and determination to overcome psychological problems and to make constructive use of intuitive, visionary, and imaginative perceptions and abilities.

A's Neptune Trine B's North Node Sextile B's South Node

See A's Neptune Sextile B's South Node Trine B's North Node.

A's Neptune Trine B's South Node Sextile B's North Node

See A's Neptune Sextile B's North Node Trine B's South Node.

A's Neptune Trine B's Ascendant Sextile B's Descendant

See A's Neptune Sextile B's Descendant Trine B's Ascendant.

A's Neptune Trine B's Midheaven Sextile B's Nadir

See A's Neptune Sextile B's Nadir Trine B's Midheaven.

A's Neptune Trine B's Descendant Sextile B's Ascendant

See A's Neptune Sextile B's Ascendant Trine B's Descendant.

A's Neptune Trine B's Nadir Sextile B's Midheaven

See A's Neptune Sextile B's Midheaven Trine B's Nadir.

COMPARATIVE OPPOSITIONS

Comparative oppositions of Neptune indicate relationship difficulties arising out of neurotic and other psychological problems, unreliability, and deceptiveness on the part of one or both natives. They cause confusion and misunderstanding in regard to the affairs ruled by the planet Neptune opposes in the comparison.

In some cases, the natives' difficulties are the result of their not being tuned to the same level of consciousness. In other instances, one or both natives will exhibit self-destructive, evasive, or escapist tendencies that are damaging to the relationship. The Neptune individual may be absorbed in his or her own private fantasies, and unaware of the thoughts, feelings, and reactions of the other native.

A's Neptune Opposition B's Sun

See A's Sun Opposition B's Neptune.

A's Neptune Opposition B's Moon

See A's Moon Opposition B's Neptune.

A's Neptune Opposition B's Mercury

See A's Mercury Opposition B's Neptune.

A's Neptune Opposition B's Venus

See A's Venus Opposition B's Neptune.

A's Neptune Opposition B's Mars

See A's Mars Opposition B's Neptune.

A's Neptune Opposition B's Jupiter

See A's Jupiter Opposition B's Neptune.

A's Neptune Opposition B's Saturn

See A's Saturn Opposition B's Neptune.

A's Neptune Opposition B's Uranus

See A's Uranus Opposition B's Neptune.

A's Neptune Opposition B's Neptune (A's ♆ ☍ B's ♆)

This comparative opposition can occur only between natives separated in age by approximately ninety years. If such a relationship would occur, there would be very little interaction between the natives.

A's Neptune Opposition B's Pluto (A's ♆ ☍ B's ♇)

Relationship problems are brought about by large-scale forces in the natives' lives over which they have little or no control. Conflict could arise over joint finances, inheritances, taxes, alimony, or corporate affairs. For those involved in large business enterprises, there can be a tendency to encourage each other in expedient policies that fail to take into account the long-range ecological and sociological consequences for the society in which they live.

If the natives are interested in the occult, there could be differing viewpoints as to the proper approach to this field. This is not a favorable combination for mutual involvement in religious, educational, psychological, or medical institutions.

The Neptune individual is likely to resent attempts on the part of the Pluto individual to mold or remake his or her character or affairs. The Neptune native could regard the Pluto individual as coercive and domineering. The Pluto individual, in turn, is likely to regard the other as unreliable, evasive, devious, and confused.

A's Neptune Opposition B's North Node Conjunct B's South Node

See A's Neptune Conjunct B's South Node Opposition B's North Node.

A's Neptune Opposition B's South Node Conjunct B's North Node

See A's Neptune Conjunct B's North Node Opposition B's South Node.

A's Neptune Opposition B's Ascendant Conjunct B's Descendant

See A's Neptune Conjunct B's Descendant Opposition B's Ascendant.

A's Neptune Opposition B's Midheaven Conjunct B's Nadir

See A's Neptune Conjunct B's Nadir Opposition B's Midheaven.

A's Neptune Opposition B's Descendant Conjunct B's Ascendant

See A's Neptune Conjunct B's Ascendant Opposition B's Descendant.

A's Neptune Opposition B's Nadir Conjunct B's Midheaven

See A's Neptune Conjunct B's Midheaven Opposition B's Nadir.

XVI
Pluto

Comparative influences of Pluto indicate the ways in which the natives tend to bring important and irrevocable changes into each other's lives.

Strong comparative influences of Pluto can indicate mutual involvement in important life-and-death matters. Although these influences may not show themselves immediately, they will eventually have important and far-reaching consequences for the individuals involved.

If the natives are sufficiently developed, there can be mutual involvement in advanced scientific research and occult subjects. They can strengthen each other's will power and resolve to make necessary changes and improvements.

The natives can be mutually involved in large-scale corporate, technological, or industrial affairs.

If these comparative influences are favorable, the Pluto individual can help the other native to achieve a higher level of understanding. He can encourage the other native toward positive efforts at self-improvement and regeneration.

If Pluto is afflicted in the comparison, the natives could become involved in a struggle for power. The Pluto individual's attempts to remake the other person according to personal concepts could cause

resentment. In some cases, there could be mutual involvement in dangerous, destructive occult practices.

COMPARATIVE HOUSE PLACEMENTS

Comparative house placements of Pluto indicate the ways in which the
Pluto individual has a powerful, transforming effect on the other native,
for better or worse.

The affairs ruled by the house in one native's horoscope in which the
other's Pluto falls will be subject to deep, fundamental, and far-reaching
changes.

The Pluto individual is apt to try to transform or remake the other
individual with respect to the affairs ruled by the house in which Pluto is
placed in the comparison. If Pluto has adverse comparative aspects, the
other native is likely to resent and resist these attempts.

Corporate business, scientific research, industrial affairs, inheritances,
taxes, insurance, affairs of the dead, and, in some cases, occult activities
will influence the affairs ruled by the house in which Pluto is placed in
the comparison. If Pluto is afflicted in the comparison, these affairs can
be a source of conflict and difficulty.

A's Pluto in B's First House

This comparative house placement indicates that the Pluto individual
will have a profound effect on the basic consciousness and self-image of
the First House individual. If Pluto is well-aspected in the comparison,
the First House individual is influenced to identify with the basic principle of consciousness or attention rather than with thoughts, emotions,
and sensory perceptions, as in Uranus and Neptune comparative First
House placements. The Pluto individual can make the First House
individual more aware of herself or himself as a spiritual being, thus
helping the First House individual to develop greater self-awareness and
self-control. The latter will cooperate with the Pluto individual if Pluto
is well-aspected. However, if Pluto is afflicted in the comparison, the First
House individual will resent what will be considered coercive attempts at
restyling on the part of the Pluto individual.

If both natives are sufficiently evolved, there can be mutual interest in
occult or scientific pursuits. There can also be mutual involvement in
large-scale technological, corporate, or industrial enterprises. Natives

with this comparative placement often share a concern with important issues of survival. These could relate to large-scale political, economic, sociological, ecological, or technological changes.

A's Pluto in B's Second House

These natives have a strong mutual involvement with financial matters related to insurance, taxes, corporate affairs, scientific research, industry, and technology. The natives can profoundly affect each other's basic attitudes toward money and property, and their use.

The natives will become aware of their responsibility to the larger social order, especially where the use of collective resources is concerned. If Pluto is afflicted in the comparison, these persons could influence each other to take a short-sighted and selfish approach to these responsibilities. However, if Pluto is well-aspected in the comparison, each can help the other to be a constructive and regenerating influence in the larger economic social order.

If Pluto is afflicted in the comparison, there can be conflict over joint finances, inheritance, alimony, and corporate money. The Pluto individual is likely to try to rearrange the financial affairs of the Second House individual. If Pluto is heavily afflicted in the comparison, the natives may be tempted to use coercive tactics to acquire wealth.

If Pluto is well-aspected in the comparison, however, the natives can influence each other to be resourceful and enterprising in business affairs and the accumulation of money and possessions. The Pluto individual can teach the Second House individual to reuse and recycle resources and possessions which could otherwise be ignored or discarded, or to get rid of possessions that are no longer useful.

A's Pluto in B's Third House

Because of their mutual interest in the study of deep economic, scientific, or occult subjects, these natives will stimulate each other to investigate the fundamental causes behind everyday phenomena and experiences. They will exhibit a strong curiosity in such fields as physics, mathematics, electronics, biology, medicine, or parapsychology. There could be mutual involvement in corporate enterprises or technologies related to transportation, communication, media, and writing.

There can be many short journeys and communications in connection with some of these activities.

In some cases, the natives can experience a mutual telepathic awareness of each other's thoughts.

The Pluto individual is apt to try to alter or remake the Third House individual's relationships with brothers, sisters, and neighbors, and will influence the Third House individual toward more resourceful and penetrating thinking.

A's Pluto in B's Fourth House

This comparative house placement can have a strong and transforming effect upon the domestic and family affairs of both natives. The Pluto individual is likely to try to transform the home, family, finances, and family relationships of the Fourth House individual. If Pluto is afflicted in the comparison, the latter will react to this in an emotionally volatile way. This comparative placement can be a critical factor in family relationships or other situations where people live under the same roof. Whether it is constructive or destructive depends on how Pluto is aspected in the comparison.

If Pluto is well-aspected in the comparison, there could be a mutual love of nature, the land, the home, and a mutual concern with the ecological environment.

Mutual corporate activities could involve food, real estate, building, mining, farming, and ecological concerns. The natives can also be involved together in food co-ops, in campaigning for programs of rent control, in rent strikes, in housing projects, and in neighborhood improvement.

A's Pluto in B's Fifth House

Sexual compatibility will be a major factor in determining the success of the intense romantic relationships indicated. If Pluto is afflicted in the comparison, sexual jealousy can be a major problem in a romantic or marital relationship—one or both parties could secretly investigate each other's activities and whereabouts.

In a parent–child relationship, there can be a conflict of wills. Kindness, understanding, and consistent firm discipline on the part of the parent is needed in order to resolve the conflict, especially if the Pluto individual is the child. If Pluto is well-aspected in such a relationship, the parent can share profound scientific and spiritual truths with the child.

In teacher–student relationships, the natives can have a powerful effect in shaping each other's attitudes, beliefs, and concepts, especially if the subjects taught relate to science, politics, fine arts, or the occult.

The Pluto individual may try to reform the Fifth House individual in terms of the type of pleasures and recreational activities sought. In some cases, there can be mutual enjoyment of scientific or occult hobbies and pursuits. The natives can share an interest in unusual forms of art, especially if they make a strong impression or convey a powerful message. This is particularly true of the theater and of literature that conveys a social message.

The natives could be mutually involved in financial speculations related to corporate finance, advanced technology, and industry.

A's Pluto in B's Sixth House

This comparative placement indicates important mutual responsibilities involving work, health, and practical responsibilities. The natives' mutual work could involve advanced forms of scientific or industrial technology, or involvement in military or industrial secrecy.

If Pluto is well-aspected, the natives will influence each other to improve their health and increase their efficiency and productivity. The Pluto individual is likely to try to remake or improve the work and work habits and methods of the Sixth House individual, particularly in employer–employee or co-worker relationships. An employer who is a Pluto individual can have an autocratic attitude toward the Sixth House individual and be apt to demand a high level of performance.

In other types of relationships, the Pluto individual will try to improve the Sixth House individual's dietary, personal hygiene, and dress habits. If Pluto is afflicted in the comparison, the Sixth House individual is likely to resent this interference.

A's Pluto in B's Seventh House

This house placement indicates intense involvement in marriage partnerships or other close relationships. The natives could be involved in corporate partnerships relating to industry, science, technology, tax accounting, insurance, or handling the affairs of the dead.

If Pluto is afflicted, there could be conflict over joint finances, corporate money, inheritance, or alimony. A marriage relationship may be subject to extreme jealousy and problems of possessiveness. The Pluto individual is likely to try reform or remake the Seventh House individual in some way. Divorce or severance of the relationship could be the result of a battle of the wills or struggle for dominance and control on the part of one or both natives.

If Pluto is well-aspected in the comparison, the natives can have a dynamic, positive influence on each other's efforts at self-improvement.

A's Pluto in B's Eighth House

These natives have a strong mutual concern with the affairs of the dead, reincarnation, what occurs after death, insurance, taxes, corporate finance, advanced scientific pursuits, industry, military affairs, or occult mysteries. The Pluto individual can help the Eighth House individual gain a deeper understanding of death and the spiritual survival of the soul. The Pluto native can also help the Eighth House individual to be more effective in the handling of joint finances and more resourceful in corporate ways of making money.

If Pluto is afflicted in the comparison, both natives can suffer emotional upsets over death, and apprehension and fear of death. If the natives are sufficiently spiritually evolved, there can be mutual interest in parapsychology—advanced aspects of science dealing with energy and the occult.

A's Pluto in B's Ninth House

This comparative placement indicates strong mutual concern both with self-improvement and with regeneration of existing cultural conditions through religion, education, philosophy, travel, and cultural exchange with other parts of the world. If the natives are sufficiently evolved, they can have mutual religious convictions based on direct experience of higher states of consciousness. There can be an occult understanding of life after death and reincarnation.

If Pluto is afflicted in the comparison, there could be disagreement over philosophic, religious, educational, and cultural beliefs and attitudes. The natives sometimes work at reforming or improving religious and educational institutions. Travel could be related to corporate business affairs or affairs of the dead.

There could be a mutual interest in improving foreign relations and a mutual involvement with import or export, or the development of industry and resources in foreign countries. The natives' interest in foreign cultures could take the form of importing foreign religious beliefs and practices, and cultural art forms and customs, or they might display a missionary zeal to give the foreign natives the benefit of their own cultural and religious traditions.

A's Pluto in B's Tenth House

Mutual concern with important political, professional, and corporate business affairs is indicated by this comparative placement.

The Pluto native can have a powerful transforming influence on the career and professional standing of the Tenth House individual. Whether this influence is positive or negative, however, depends on how Pluto is aspected in the comparison. She or he will try to remake, improve, or mold the professional activities and standing of the Tenth House individual, especially if the natives are involved in a professional partnership or an employer–employee relationship.

The natives could be mutually involved in important professional issues that could have far-reaching and profound effects in the world in which they move. These issues could even relate to matters of life and death, especially if the natives are involved in scientific, political, or military affairs. Mutual professional work could relate to advanced scientific research and, in some cases, parapsychology or occult pursuits. Governmental or professional secrecy often is involved.

If Pluto is afflicted in the comparison, there could be a struggle for power or political or professional supremacy.

A's Pluto in B's Eleventh House

This comparative placement indicates important mutual involvement in the pursuit of organizational, scientific, humanitarian, or occult goals and objectives. If Pluto is well-aspected in the comparison, the natives will have a strong friendship based on mutual interest in regenerating existing conditions. This interest could relate to self-improvement, corporate business, or occult or scientific endeavors. If Pluto is afflicted in the comparison, there could be a struggle for power and dominance in organizational politics. The natives could have powerful and dynamic mutual friends who could be involved in scientific, economic, or occult activities.

There can be mutual involvement in group and organizational activities relating to business, scientific, or occult pursuits. These could be of a secretive nature. There could also be important mutual activities regarding the finances of groups and organizations or the financing of scientific research and humanitarian endeavors.

The Pluto individual is likely to try to change or reform the Eleventh House individual's goals, objectives, and friendships, often by encouraging the elimination of friends and organizational activities that do not serve a useful purpose. If Pluto is afflicted in the comparison, however, the Eleventh House individual is likely to resent this interference.

A's Pluto in B's Twelfth House

These natives' mutual involvement with the investigation and regeneration of the unconscious mind could encompass in-depth psychology, religious mysticism, parapsychology, meditation, and reincarnation. They could work together in improving conditions in hospitals, religious institutions, jails, and other places of seclusion or confinement.

The Pluto individual is likely to try to reform the subconscious neuroses of the Twelfth House individual. Possibly because of impatience with the self-indulgences or evasive and escapist tendencies of the Twelfth House individual, the Pluto native could try to force the Twelfth House individual to come out of her or his dream world and face reality. If Pluto is well-aspected in the comparison, such influences will be constructive. If Pluto is afflicted in the comparison, however, they are likely to arouse resentment and opposition. Under these circumstances, the natives could bear subconscious resentments toward each other and, in extreme cases, become secret enemies.

If Pluto is well-aspected in the comparison, each native can aid the other in uncovering intuitive wisdom and developing clairvoyant faculties.

COMPARATIVE CONJUNCTIONS

Comparative conjunctions of Pluto indicate powerful, dynamic interactions involving joint finance, corporate business, scientific, and occult pursuits. Both natives will make an effort to improve themselves and attain a higher level of consciousness.

If the conjunction is well-aspected in the comparison, the natives will bring out each other's resourceful qualities and further each other's determination and will to improve and regenerate existing conditions.

This often involves reusing or recycling things which are discarded or ignored by others.

The Pluto individual will try to regenerate or improve the affairs ruled by the planet which Pluto conjuncts in the comparison. However, if the conjunction is afflicted by other comparative aspects, there is danger of a conflict of wills; the other native is apt to resent the Pluto individual's interference.

A's Pluto Conjunct B's Sun

See A's Sun Conjunct B's Pluto.

A's Pluto Conjunct B's Moon

See A's Moon Conjunct B's Pluto.

A's Pluto Conjunct B's Mercury

See A's Mercury Conjunct B's Pluto.

A's Pluto Conjunct B's Venus

See A's Venus Conjunct B's Pluto.

A's Pluto Conjunct B's Mars

See A's Mars Conjunct B's Pluto.

A's Pluto Conjunct B's Jupiter

See A's Jupiter Conjunct B's Pluto.

A's Pluto Conjunct B's Saturn

See A's Saturn Conjunct B's Pluto.

A's Pluto Conjunct B's Uranus

See A's Uranus Conjunct B's Pluto.

A's Pluto Conjunct B's Neptune

See A's Neptune Conjunct B's Pluto.

A's Pluto Conjunct B's Pluto (A's ♀ ♂ B's ♀)

This comparative conjunction can occur only among natives of approximately the same age. There is mutual concern with scientific, economic, political, and survival issues that concern the generation to which the natives belong. Thus, the natives may share experiences involving large-scale sociological, economic, political, ecological, and military affairs which shape their destiny.

Through these common experiences the natives will develop will power and resourcefulness and the ability to survive crisis situations. These experiences could also lead to a mutual appreciation of spiritual or occult values.

A's Pluto Conjunct B's North Node Opposition
B's South Node (A's ♀ ♂ B's ☊ ☍ B's ☋)

Mutual interest in reforming or changing prevailing social trends and popular beliefs is indicated by this comparative combination.

The Pluto individual may regard the Nodes individual as superficial and lacking in insights because of his acceptance of these things, while the Nodes individual may regard the former as overly severe in social attitudes. The Pluto individual can help the Nodes individual to gain deeper prophetic insight into the history and future development of popular beliefs. There can be mutual resourcefulness in using such insights in corporate business affairs or in mutual efforts to make money.

A's Pluto Conjunct B's South Node Opposition
B's North Node (A's ♀ ♂ B's ☋ ☍ B's ☊)

Because of an individualistic and critical mutual approach to prevailing trends and popular social beliefs, these natives will encourage each other to maintain their own sense of values and the courage of their convictions, regardless of whether these values and convictions are generally accepted.

The Nodes individual could have a restraining influence on the Pluto individual, while the Pluto individual can help the Nodes person to display greater courage and determination to follow personal social beliefs and convictions.

A's Pluto Conjunct B's Ascendant Opposition B's Descendant (A's ♀ ☌ B's Asc. ☍ B's Desc.)

This comparative combination has basically the same significance as "A's Pluto in B's First House," except that its effects are stronger and more immediate. The natives encourage each other to make greater efforts toward physical and spiritual self-improvement. The Pluto individual can have a strong spiritual or occult effect on the Ascendant/Descendant individual's basic consciousness and self-awareness.

In a romantic or marital relationship, strong sexual attraction between the natives is likely.

A's Pluto Conjunct B's Midheaven Opposition B's Nadir (A's ♀ ☌ B's M.C. ☍ B's Nadir)

Basically the same as "A's Pluto in B's Tenth House," the effects of this combination, however, will be stronger and more immediate. The Pluto individual will have a strong effect in molding and changing the profession, public reputation, and practical affairs of the Midheaven/Nadir individual. If the conjunction is well-aspected, the Pluto native can help the Midheaven/Nadir individual to be more resourceful and effective professionally.

There could be mutual interest in reforming or improving existing governmental and corporate institutions. If this conjunction is afflicted by other comparative aspects, the natives could be mutually involved in political and professional intrigues, and these could adversely affect the professional reputation and standing of one or both natives. They could struggle against each other for power and position.

A's Pluto Conjunct B's Descendant Opposition B's Ascendant (A's ♀ ☌ B's Desc. ☍ B's Asc.)

This comparative combination has basically the same significance as "A's Pluto in B's Seventh House," except that its effects will be stronger and more immediate. Natives in marriage partnerships or other close relationships can be mutually involved with corporate or occult affairs.

The natives can make heavy demands on each other in terms of work and mutual cooperation. If the conjunction is afflicted by other comparative aspects, there can be sexual jealousy on the part of one or both natives.

A's Pluto Conjunct B's Nadir Opposition B's Midheaven
(A's ♀ ☌ B's Nadir ☍ B's M.C.)

The significance of this comparative combination is basically the same as that of "A's Pluto in B's Fourth House," except that the effects will be stronger and more immediate. There can be mutual interest in corporate affairs related to farming, mining, food, domestic products, or ecological concerns. The Pluto individual can have a strong subconscious effect on the deep-rooted psychological tendencies and habits of the Midheaven/Nadir individual, and will try to remake or reform the home and family affairs of the Midheaven/Nadir individual. However, if the conjunction is afflicted by other comparative aspects, the Midheaven/Nadir individual could resent this intrusion.

COMPARATIVE SEXTILES

Comparative sextiles of Pluto indicate mutual opportunities for the study of scientific, economic, and occult forces and changes. The natives have a mutual intellectual interest in pursuing goals and objectives that deal with the improvement and regeneration of economic and scientific affairs and occult endeavors and with the ecological and spiritual conditions affecting their lives and the society in which they move. This can take the form of study and development of new technological approaches in industry or the recycling of waste products. The Pluto individual can help the other native to regenerate and improve the affairs ruled by the planet which Pluto sextiles in the comparison.

A's Pluto Sextile B's Sun

See A's Sun Sextile B's Pluto.

A's Pluto Sextile B's Moon

See A's Moon Sextile B's Pluto.

A's Pluto Sextile B's Mercury

See A's Mercury Sextile B's Pluto.

A's Pluto Sextile B's Venus

See A's Venus Sextile B's Pluto.

A's Pluto Sextile B's Mars

See A's Mars Sextile B's Pluto.

A's Pluto Sextile B's Jupiter

See A's Jupiter Sextile B's Pluto.

A's Pluto Sextile B's Saturn

See A's Saturn Sextile B's Pluto.

A's Pluto Sextile B's Uranus

See A's Uranus Sextile B's Pluto.

A's Pluto Sextile B's Neptune

See A's Neptune Sextile B's Pluto.

A's Pluto Sextile B's Pluto (A's ♀ ✳ B's ♀)

Because of the extreme eccentricity of Pluto's orbit, this comparative sextile can occur only among natives separated in age by approximately thirty to sixty years.

The natives can share an intellectual interest in attempts to improve or regenerate existing economic and political institutions. Because she or he will be more sympathetic to the viewpoints and needs of the younger native's generation than are most older people, the older native can be instrumental in teaching the younger valuable scientific and spiritual concepts.

A's Pluto Sextile B's North Node Trine B's South Node
(A's ♀ ✳ B's ☊ △ B's ☋)

This comparative combination indicates mutual concern with gaining a deeper understanding of the underlying and motivating factors behind currently popular social trends and beliefs, and each native can help the other to gain a deeper level of insight. The natives can then employ these insights in joint business ventures and corporate financial affairs.

A's Pluto Sextile B's South Node Trine B's North Node
(A's ♀ ✳ B's ☋ △ B's ☊)

The significance of this comparative combination is basically the same as that of "A's Pluto Sextile B's North Node Trine B's South Node," except that these natives will be intellectually critical of popular social trends and beliefs.

A's Pluto Sextile B's Ascendant Trine B's Descendant
(A's ♀ ✳ B's Asc. △ B's Desc.)

This comparative combination indicates mutual interest in scientific, economic, and, in some cases, occult and metaphysical pursuits.

The Pluto individual can be a dynamic influence on the Ascendant/Descendant individual's efforts at self-improvement and creative self-expression, helping the latter to become more conscious and spiritually aware of superphysical forces behind the outward manifestations of life.

The natives can cooperate effectively in efforts at self-improvement and survival. They will bring out each other's qualities of resourcefulness, courage, and determination, and help each other utilize available resources more effectively.

A's Pluto Sextile B's Midheaven Trine B's Nadir
(A's ♀ ✳ B's M.C. △ B's Nadir)

These natives have mutual interest in improving and regenerating professional, family and domestic affairs that could take the form of ecological concerns, especially recycling discarded materials. There can be mutual involvement with home improvement projects and corporate business enterprises related to building, domestic products, industry, and technology. Each native will encourage the other's ambition and determination to make progress in these areas. In some cases, advanced scientific or occult activities could be brought into professional or domestic affairs.

The Pluto individual can help the Midheaven/Nadir individual to regenerate and gain a more conscious awareness of deep-rooted psychological habit patterns that result from early family conditioning. There could be a mutual interest in genealogy and mysteries related to the natives' families and political heritage or to the land itself.

A's Pluto Sextile B's Descendant Trine B's Ascendant
(A's ♀ ✶ B's Desc. △ B's Asc.)

The comparative combination has basically the same significance as "A's Pluto Sextile B's Ascendant Trine B's Descendant," except that these natives will have greater intellectual interest in the psychology of their relationship.

A's Pluto Sextile B's Nadir Trine B's Midheaven
(A's ♀ ✶ B's Nadir △ B's M.C.)

This comparative combination has basically the same significance as "A's Pluto Sextile B's Midheaven Trine B's Nadir," except that these natives will be more intellectually concerned with the improvement of family, home, and domestic affairs.

COMPARATIVE SQUARES

Comparative squares of Pluto indicate conflict in a relationship arising from struggle for control and dominance. The Pluto individual is likely to try to reform or remake the other native in the affairs ruled by the planet making the square in the comparison. The other native, who does not share the same values as the Pluto individual, usually resents this interference.

These combinations are not favorable for cooperation in corporate, financial, professional, political, family, and domestic affairs. The natives are likely to aggravate each other, and this will lead to a conflict of wills and struggle either for dominance or for independence. This can have an adverse effect on the professional status and family harmony of the natives. These comparative squares can also indicate conflict over joint finances, inheritance, corporate money, and alimony.

A's Pluto Square B's Sun

See A's Sun Square B's Pluto.

A's Pluto Square B's Moon

See A's Moon Square B's Pluto.

A's Pluto Square B's Mercury

See A's Mercury Square B's Pluto.

A's Pluto Square B's Venus

See A's Venus Square B's Pluto.

A's Pluto Square B's Mars

See A's Mars Square B's Pluto.

A's Pluto Square B's Jupiter

See A's Jupiter Square B's Pluto.

A's Pluto Square B's Saturn

See A's Saturn Square B's Pluto.

A's Pluto Square B's Uranus

See A's Uranus Square B's Pluto.

A's Pluto Square B's Neptune

See A's Neptune Square B's Pluto.

A's Pluto Square B's Pluto (A's ♀ □ B's ♀)

Due to the eccentric orbit of Pluto, this comparative square occurs only between natives separated in age by approximately forty-five to ninety years. The generations these natives belong to have different and often conflicting economic, social, political, scientific, and technological values.

The effects of this comparative square are not pronounced unless it is reinforced by other comparative aspects.

A's Pluto Square B's North Node Square B's South Node (A's ♀ □ B's ☊ □ B's ☋)

The natives will have conflicting values and attitudes in regard to prevailing social trends and popular beliefs. The Pluto individual is apt to regard the Nodes individual as superficial and frivolous for adhering to popular fads and social activities, while the Nodes individual will likely regard the Pluto individual as critical, selfish, and antisocial.

A's Pluto Square B's South Node Square B's North Node

See A's Pluto Square B's North Node Square B's South Node.

A's Pluto Square B's Ascendant Square B's Descendant (A's ♀ □ B's Asc. □ B's Desc.)

This comparative combination indicates a conflict of wills in regard to professional, family, partnership, marital, personal, and political affairs. There can be conflict over joint finances, inheritances, or alimony.

The Ascendant/Descendant individual will resent and resist the forceful attempts of the Pluto individual to remake or reform her or him, and he will regard the Pluto individual as authoritarian, self-righteous, uncooperative, and aggressive. The Pluto individual will regard the other as lazy, self-centered, and unaware of the larger political, professional, ecological, economic, or metaphysical issues of life.

A's Pluto Square B's Descendant Square B's Ascendant

See A's Pluto Square B's Ascendant Square B's Descendant.

A's Pluto Square B's Midheaven Square B's Nadir
(A's ♀ □ B's M.C. □ B's Nadir)

Conflict over political, professional, corporate business, family, or domestic affairs is indicated. Conflict over real estate or ecological issues relating to the use of the land itself is also a possibility, as is a power struggle for prominence, position or leadership in professional and political activities which affect the status of the natives.

The Pluto individual can stir up the subconscious memories and deep-rooted psychological tendencies of the Midheaven/Nadir individual. The Midheaven/Nadir individual could resent the tendency of the Pluto individual to meddle in private or personal affairs.

A's Pluto Square B's Nadir Square B's Midheaven

See A's Pluto Square B's Midheaven Square B's Nadir.

COMPARATIVE TRINES

Comparative trines of Pluto indicate mutual advancement through corporate business affairs, resourceful use of available materials, the constructive use of the will, meditation, and the application of spiritual laws.

The Pluto individual can help the other native to regenerate and improve the affairs ruled by the planet Pluto trines in the comparison. Through this influence, the other native can gain a deeper level of insight into and understanding of such affairs, and can become more resourceful and effective where they are concerned.

The natives will assist each other's efforts at spiritual self-improvement and creative self-expression, often through philosophy, religion, higher education, and travel.

In some cases, these comparative trines are positive influences in parent–child and teacher–student relationships. These trines could also indicate romantic and sexual attraction if other factors are favorable.

A's Pluto Trine B's Sun

See A's Sun Trine B's Pluto.

A's Pluto Trine B's Moon

See A's Moon Trine B's Pluto.

A's Pluto Trine B's Mercury

See A's Mercury Trine B's Pluto.

A's Pluto Trine B's Venus

See A's Venus Trine B's Pluto.

A's Pluto Trine B's Mars

See A's Mars Trine B's Pluto.

A's Pluto Trine B's Jupiter

See A's Jupiter Trine B's Pluto.

A's Pluto Trine B's Saturn

See A's Saturn Trine B's Pluto.

A's Pluto Trine B's Uranus

See A's Uranus Trine B's Pluto.

A's Pluto Trine B's Neptune

See A's Neptune Trine B's Pluto.

A's Pluto Trine B's Pluto (A's ♀ △ B's ♀)

This comparative trine rarely occurs because of the large time span separating the age of the natives—between sixty-five and one hundred and twenty years. The older native could pass on important spiritual instruction to the younger native concerning survival and the meaning of death.

A's Pluto Trine B's North Node Sextile B's South Node

See A's Pluto Sextile B's South Node Trine B's North Node.

A's Pluto Trine B's South Node Sextile B's North Node

See A's Pluto Sextile B's North Node Trine B's South Node.

A's Pluto Trine B's Ascendant Sextile B's Descendant

See A's Pluto Sextile B's Descendant Trine B's Ascendant.

A's Pluto Trine B's Midheaven Sextile B's Nadir

See A's Pluto Sextile B's Nadir Trine B's Midheaven.

A's Pluto Trine B's Descendant Sextile B's Ascendant

See A's Pluto Sextile B's Ascendant Trine B's Descendant.

A's Pluto Trine B's Nadir Sextile B's Midheaven

See A's Pluto Sextile B's Midheaven Trine B's Nadir.

COMPARATIVE OPPOSITIONS

Comparative oppositions of Pluto indicate conflict over joint finances, corporate financial affairs, inheritance, taxes, or alimony. In some cases, the natives will experience serious ego confrontations and power struggles.

The Pluto individual is likely to try to reform or remake the other native in the life areas ruled by the planet Pluto opposes in the comparison. These attempts are often met with resentment and resistance, and the other person is apt to regard the Pluto individual as dictatorial, autocratic, controlling, domineering, and meddlesome.

A's Pluto Opposition B's Sun

See A's Sun Opposition B's Pluto.

A's Pluto Opposition B's Moon

See A's Moon Opposition B's Pluto.

A's Pluto Opposition B's Mercury

See A's Mercury Opposition B's Pluto.

A's Pluto Opposition B's Venus

See A's Venus Opposition B's Pluto.

A's Pluto Opposition B's Mars

See A's Mars Opposition B's Pluto.

A's Pluto Opposition B's Jupiter

See A's Jupiter Opposition B's Pluto.

A's Pluto Opposition B's Saturn

See A's Saturn Opposition B's Pluto.

A's Pluto Opposition B's Uranus

See A's Uranus Opposition B's Pluto.

A's Pluto Opposition B's Neptune

See A's Neptune Opposition B's Pluto.

A's Pluto Opposition B's Pluto (A's ♀ ☍ B's ♀)

This comparative opposition does not occur, since the age difference between the natives is longer than a human life span.

A's Pluto Opposition B's North Node Conjunct B's South Node

See A's Pluto Conjunct B's South Node Opposition B's North Node.

A's Pluto Opposition B's South Node Conjunct B's North Node

See A's Pluto Conjunct B's North Node Opposition B's South Node.

A's Pluto Opposition B's Ascendant Conjunct B's Descendant

See A's Pluto Conjunct B's Descendant Opposition B's Ascendant.

A's Pluto Opposition B's Midheaven Conjunct B's Nadir

See A's Pluto Conjunct B's Nadir Opposition B's Midheaven.

A's Pluto Opposition B's Descendant Conjunct B's Ascendant

See A's Pluto Conjunct B's Ascendant Opposition B's Descendant.

A's Pluto Opposition B's Nadir Conjunct B's Midheaven

See A's Pluto Conjunct B's Midheaven Opposition B's Nadir.

Glossary

Ascendant   The point at which the eastern horizon intersects the ecliptic. The First House or rising sign.

Aspect   The angle formed between two imaginary lines connecting two celestial bodies or points with the Earth.

Conjunction   The occurrence of a direct or nearly direct line-up of two planets as seen from the Earth.

Cusp   The line of division between two houses. The cusps are normally named for the line between a house and the house below it. Thus, the Seventh House cusp is the line between the Seventh and Sixth houses.

Descendant   The point at which the western horizon intersects the ecliptic. It is also the cusp between the Sixth and Seventh houses.

Ecliptic   The plane of the Earth's orbit around the Sun extended into space to meet the celestial sphere. From the Earth, the ecliptic appears to be the path the Sun follows around the Earth in a year's time.

Horoscope   A map or chart of the position of the planets in the heavens at the exact time and place of one's birth. The map covers the entire sky, a full circle of 360°. Also called a *natal chart* or *map*.

House   One of twelve divisions made in the cycle of the Earth's daily rotation. Each house represents an approximate two-hour period during which one-twelfth of the Zodiac appears to pass over the horizon. The houses are named in order, beginning with the First House and continuing through to the Twelfth House. Each house presides over a different department of practical affairs and is associated with a specific sign of the Zodiac.

Meridian   A great circle on the celestial sphere passing through the north and south points of the horizon and the zenith, which is directly above the observer.

Midheaven (also written *M.C.* from the Latin *medium coeli*)   The point at which the meridian intersects the ecliptic.

Nadir   The point on the ecliptic directly opposite the Midheaven looking downward from the observer. Also called the Fourth House cusp.

Node   Each of the two points at which a planet's orbit intersects the ecliptic: once when the planet moves north across the ecliptic, and once again when it moves south. In astrology, the Nodes of the Moon are especially significant.

Opposition   An aspect representing an angular relationship of 180° between two planets. Planets in opposition generally occupy approximately the same number of degrees in two signs directly across the Zodiac from each other.

Quadruplicity   One of three fixed groups of signs, each containing four signs. The three quadruplicities relate to three characteristics—Cardinal, Fixed, and Mutable—and are concerned with basic modes of activities.

Sextile   That aspect representing an angular relationship of 60°, or one-sixth of a circle. Planets in sextile aspect are placed two signs apart and occupy approximately the same number of degrees in these signs, plus or minus 6°.

Square   That aspect representing an angular relationship of 90°. Planets in square aspect generally occupy the same number of degrees in signs which are three signs apart.

Sun signs   The twelve traditional signs of the Zodiac. They are Aries (the Ram), Taurus (the Bull), Gemini (the Twins), Cancer (the Crab), Leo (the Lion), Virgo (the Virgin), Libra (the Scales), Scorpio (the Scorpion), Sagittarius (the Archer), Capricorn (the Goat), Aquarius (the Water-bearer), and Pisces (the Fishes).

Trine   That aspect representing an angular relationship of 120° or one-third of a circle between two planets. Planets in trine aspect generally occupy the same number of degrees in signs four signs apart.

Triplicity One of four fixed groups of signs, each containing three planets. The four triplicities relate to the four elements earth, air, fire, and water. They are concerned with tendencies of the temperament.

Vernal equinox The intersection of the plane of the ecliptic with the celestial equator. This intersection occurs once a year, at the moment the Sun crosses the celestial equator moving from south to north.

Zenith That point in the celestial sphere directly above the observer.

Zodiac The band of sky 18° wide having the ecliptic as its central line. It consists of twelve parts, each 30° wide, which represent the twelve signs of the Zodiac.

Index

Mars (A's), square (s) (cont'd)
  B's Moon, see Moon (A's), square B's
  Mars
  B's Nadir square B's Midheaven, see
  Mars (A's), square B's Midheaven
  square B's Nadir
  B's Neptune, 214
  B's North Node square B's South
  Node, 215
  B's Pluto, 214–15
  B's Saturn, 213
  B's South Node square B's North
  Node, see Mars (A's), square B's
  North Node square B's South Node
  B's Sun, see Sun (A's), square B's
  Mars
  B's Uranus, 213–14
  B's Venus, see Venus (A's), square
  B's Mars
  trine (s), 216
  B's Ascendant sextile B's Descendant,
  see Mars (A's), sextile B's descen-
  dant trine Ascendant
  B's Descendant sextile B's Ascendant,
  see Mars (A's), sextile B's Ascen-
  dant trine B's Descendant
  B's Jupiter, 217
  B's Mars, 217
  B's Mercury, see Mercury (A's), trine
  B's Mars
  B's Midheaven sextile B's Nadir, see
  Mars (A's), sextile B's Nadir trine
  B's Midheaven
  B's Moon, see Moon (A's), trine B's
  Mars
  B's Nadir sextile B's Midheaven, see
  Mars (A's), sextile B's Midheaven
  trine B's Nadir
  B's Neptune, 218–19
  B's North Node sextile B's South
  Node, see Mars (A's), sextile B's
  South Node trine B's North Node
  B's Pluto, 219
  B's Saturn, 217
  B's South Node sextile B's North
  Node, see Mars (A's), sextile B's
  North Node trine B's South Node
  B's Sun, see Sun (A's), trine B's
  Mars
  B's Uranus, 218
  B's Venus, see Venus (A's), trine B's
  Mars
Mars (B's)
  A's Jupiter
  conjunct, see Mars (A's), conjunct
  B's Jupiter
  opposition, see Mars (A's), opposi-
  tion B's Jupiter
  sextile, see Mars (A's), sextile B's
  Jupiter
  square, see Mars (A's), square B's
  Jupiter
  trine, see Mars (A's), trine B's
  Jupiter

Mars (B's) (cont'd)
  A's Mars
  conjunct, 201
  opposition, 221
  sextile, 207
  square, 212
  trine, 217
  A's Mercury
  conjunct, 137
  opposition, 159
  sextile, 144
  square, 150
  trine, 155
  A's Moon
  conjunct, 101–2
  opposition, 124–25
  sextile, 108–9
  square, 114
  trine, 120
  A's Neptune
  conjunct, see Mars (A's), conjunct
  B's Neptune
  opposition, see Mars (A's), opposition B's Neptune
  sextile, see Mars (A's), sextile B's
  Neptune
  square, see Mars (A's), square B's
  Neptune
  trine, see Mars (A's), trine B's
  Neptune
  A's Pluto
  conjunct, see Mars (A's), conjunct
  B's Pluto
  opposition, see Mars (A's), opposition B's Pluto
  sextile, see Mars (A's), sextile B's
  Pluto
  square, see Mars (A's), square B's
  Pluto
  trine, see Mars (A's), trine B's Pluto
  A's Saturn
  conjunct, see Mars (A's), conjunct
  B's Saturn
  opposition, see Mars (A's), opposition B's Saturn
  sextile, see Mars (A's), sextile B's
  Saturn
  square, see Mars (A's), square B's
  Saturn
  trine, see Mars (A's), trine B's
  Saturn
  A's Sun
  conjunct, 69
  opposition, 90
  sextile, 75
  square, 80
  trine, 85–86
  A's Uranus
  conjunct, see Mars (A's), conjunct
  B's Uranus
  opposition, see Mars (A's), opposition B's Uranus
  sextile, see Mars (A's), sextile B's
  Uranus

Pluto, conjunction (s)   (cont'd)
    B's North Node opposition B's
      South Node, 348
    B's Pluto, 348
    B's Saturn, see Saturn (A's), con-
      junct B's Pluto
    B's South Node opposition B's North
      Node, 348–49
    B's Sun, see Sun (A's), conjunct B's
      Pluto
    B's Uranus, see Uranus (A's), con-
      junct B's Pluto
    B's Venus, see Venus (A's), con-
      junct B's Pluto
house (B's), placements in, 340
    First House, 340–41
    Second House, 341
    Third House, 341–42
    Fourth House, 342
    Fifth House, 342–43
    Sixth House, 343
    Seventh House, 343–44
    Eighth House, 344
    Ninth House, 344–45
    Tenth House, 345
    Eleventh House, 345–46
    Twelfth House, 346
opposition (s), 358
    B's Ascendant conjunct B's Descen-
      dant, see Pluto (A's), conjunct
      B's Descendant opposition B's
      Ascendant
    B's Descendant conjunct B's Ascen-
      dant, see Pluto (A's), conjunct
      B's Ascendant opposition B's
      Descendant
    B's Jupiter, see Jupiter (A's), op-
      position B's Pluto
    B's Mars, see Mars (A's), opposition
      B's Pluto
    B's Mercury, see Mercury (A's),
      opposition B's Pluto
    B's Midheaven conjunct B's Nadir,
      see Pluto (A's), conjunct B's
      Nadir opposition B's Midheaven
    B's Moon, see Moon (A's), op-
      position B's Pluto
    B's Nadir conjunct B's Midheaven,
      see Pluto (A's), conjunct B's Mid-
      heaven opposition B's Nadir
    B's Neptune, see Neptune (A's),
      opposition B's Pluto
    B's North Node conjunct B's South
      Node, see Pluto (A's), conjunct
      B's South Node opposition B's
      North Node
    B's Pluto, 359
    B's Saturn, see Saturn (A's), op-
      position B's Pluto
    B's South Node conjunct B's North
      Node, see Pluto (A's), conjunct
      B's North Node opposition B's
      South Node

Pluto, opposition (s)   (cont'd)
    B's Sun, see Sun (A's), opposition
      B's Pluto
    B's Uranus, see Uranus (A's), op-
      position B's Pluto
    B's Venus, see Venus (A's), opposi-
      tion B's Pluto
sextile (s), 350
    B's Ascendant trine B's Descendant,
      352
    B's Descendant trine B's Ascendant,
      353
    B's Jupiter, see Jupiter (A's), sex-
      tile B's Pluto
    B's Mars, see Mars (A's), sextile B's
      Pluto
    B's Mercury, see Mercury (A's),
      sextile B's Pluto
    B's Midheaven trine B's Nadir,
      352–53
    B's Moon, see Moon (A's), sextile
      B's Pluto
    B's Nadir trine B's Midheaven, 353
    B's Neptune, see Neptune (A's),
      sextile B's Pluto
    B's North Node trine B's South
      Node, 352
    B's Pluto, 351
    B's Saturn, see Saturn (A's), sextile
      B's Pluto
    B's South Node trine B's North
      Node, 352
    B's Sun, see Sun (A's), sextile B's
      Pluto
    B's Uranus, see Uranus (A's), sextile
      B's Pluto
    B's Venus, see Venus (A's), sextile
      B's Pluto
square (s), 353–54
    B's Ascendant square B's Descen-
      dant, 355
    B's Descendant square B's Ascendant,
      see Pluto (A's), square B's Ascen-
      dant square B's Descendant
    B's Jupiter, see Jupiter (A's), square
      B's Pluto
    B's Mars, see Mars (A's), square
      B's Pluto
    B's Mercury, see Mercury (A's),
      square B's Pluto
    B's Midheaven square B's Nadir,
      356
    B's Moon, see Moon (A's), square
      B's Pluto
    B's Nadir square B's Midheaven,
      see Pluto (A's), square B's Mid-
      heaven square B's Nadir
    B's Neptune, see Neptune (A's),
      square B's Pluto
    B's North Node square B's South
      Node, 355
    B's Pluto, 355
    B's Saturn, see Saturn (A's), square
      B's Pluto

ACA, Inc., Box 395, Weston, Massachusetts 02193

Please send me the comparative horoscopes offered in *The Astrology of Human Relationships*. I am enclosing $9.50 (check or money order—do not send cash).

Mail to

Name_____

Address_____

City_____State_____Zip code_____

Birth Information for subject A

Name_____

Date of birth: Month_____Day_____Year_____

Time of birth: (exact local time if known) _____A.M. ( ) P.M. ( )

Time of birth unknown ( ). Local noon will be used in this case.

Place of birth:
   City_____State_____Country_____

Birth Information for subject B

Name_____

Date of birth: Month_____Day_____Year_____

Time of birth: (exact local time if known) _____A.M. ( ) P.M. ( )

Time of birth unknown ( ). Local noon will be used in this case.

Place of birth:
   City_____State_____Country_____

IF YOU DO NOT WISH TO REMOVE THIS PAGE, INFORMATION MAY BE SUPPLIED ON A PLAIN SHEET OF PAPER. DO NOT FORGET TO PROVIDE ALL INFORMATION.

Note: The price of $9.50 for the two natal charts and comparison may change after publication. Readers may wish to confirm the price with ACA.

ACA, Inc., Box 395, Weston, Massachusetts 02193

Please send me the comparative horoscopes offered in *The Astrology of Human Relationships*. I am enclosing $9.50 (check or money order— do not send cash).

Mail to

Name_____

Address_____

City_____State_____Zip code_____

Birth Information for subject A

Name_____

Date of birth: Month_____Day_____Year_____

Time of birth: (exact local time if known) _____A.M. ( )   P.M. ( )

Time of birth unknown ( ). Local noon will be used in this case.

Place of birth:
   City_____State_____Country_____

Birth Information for subject B

Name_____

Date of birth: Month_____Day_____Year_____

Time of birth: (exact local time if known) _____A.M. ( )   P.M. ( )

Time of birth unknown ( ). Local noon will be used in this case.

Place of birth:
   City_____State_____Country_____

IF YOU DO NOT WISH TO REMOVE THIS PAGE, INFORMATION MAY BE SUPPLIED ON A PLAIN SHEET OF PAPER. DO NOT FORGET TO PROVIDE ALL INFORMATION.

Note: The price of $9.50 for the two natal charts and comparison may change after publication. Readers may wish to confirm the price with ACA.

ACA, Inc., Box 395, Weston, Massachusetts 02193

Please send me the comparative horoscopes offered in *The Astrology of Human Relationships*. I am enclosing $9.50 (check or money order—do not send cash).

Mail to

Name_____

Address_____

City_____State_____Zip code_____

Birth Information for subject A

Name_____

Date of birth: Month_____Day_____Year_____

Time of birth: (exact local time if known) _____A.M. ( ) P.M. ( )

Time of birth unknown ( ). Local noon will be used in this case.

Place of birth:

City_____State_____Country_____

Birth Information for subject B

Name_____

Date of birth: Month_____Day_____Year_____

Time of birth: (exact local time if known) _____A.M. ( ) P.M. ( )

Time of birth unknown ( ). Local noon will be used in this case.

Place of birth:

City_____State_____Country_____

IF YOU DO NOT WISH TO REMOVE THIS PAGE, INFORMATION MAY BE SUPPLIED ON A PLAIN SHEET OF PAPER. DO NOT FORGET TO PROVIDE ALL INFORMATION.

Note: The price of $9.50 for the two natal charts and comparison may change after publication. Readers may wish to confirm the price with ACA.

ACA, Inc., Box 395, Weston, Massachusetts 02193

Please send me the comparative horoscopes offered in *The Astrology of Human Relationships*. I am enclosing $9.50 (check or money order—do not send cash).

Mail to

Name_____

Address_____

City_____State_____Zip code_____

Birth Information for subject A

Name_____

Date of birth: Month_____Day_____Year_____

Time of birth: (exact local time if known) _____A.M. ( )   P.M. ( )

Time of birth unknown ( ). Local noon will be used in this case.

Place of birth:
   City_____State_____Country_____

Birth Information for subject B

Name_____

Date of birth: Month_____Day_____Year_____

Time of birth: (exact local time if known) _____A.M. ( )   P.M. ( )

Time of birth unknown ( ). Local noon will be used in this case.

Place of birth:
   City_____State_____Country_____

IF YOU DO NOT WISH TO REMOVE THIS PAGE, INFORMATION MAY BE SUPPLIED ON A PLAIN SHEET OF PAPER. DO NOT FORGET TO PROVIDE ALL INFORMATION.

Note: The price of $9.50 for the two natal charts and comparison may change after publication. Readers may wish to confirm the price with ACA.